To Mom,
Merry Christmas!
lots of love,
Margaret & Walt

THE DOLLS' DRESSMAKER

THE DOLLS' DRESSMAKER

The Complete Pattern Book

VENUS A. DODGE

A David & Charles Craft Book

Plate 1
The doll in the centre of the picture is GP Ceramic's 20in (51cm) reproduction AM 1894. She wears a rust-coloured cotton dress with short puffed sleeves and a gathered skirt, and a pinafore dress with pockets and a matching triangular scarf in a co-ordinating green and rust cotton print. Both fabrics are from Village Fabrics. Her straw hat and black cotton stockings are both from Hello Dolly. The hat is trimmed with a green ribbon band and an artificial flower.

The 19in (48.5cm) antique doll on the right wears a smock dress in rust-coloured printed needlecord with a Peter Pan collar and long full sleeves. The dress is trimmed with narrow rust-coloured velvet ribbon. The doll wears a rust felt beret and carries schoolbooks from GP Ceramics.

The 14in (35.5cm) doll (author's collection) on the left wears a rust-coloured needlecord pinafore dress with a square neckline and gathered skirt trimmed with tiny buttons from GP Ceramics. Her shirt is made in checked Viyella, her beret in brown felt and her shoulder-bag in brown leather. The ribbed cotton socks are from Recollect.

The 14in (35.5cm) antique doll wears a short round-yoke dress in cream printed cotton with a Peter Pan collar and short puffed sleeves trimmed with lace, over matching knickers. Her hat is made in hessian from the picture-hat pattern, with the brim rolled back and trimmed with artificial flowers.

British Library Cataloguing in Publication Data

Dodge, Venus
    The dolls dressmaker over 120 designs with actual-size patterns
    1. Doll clothes
    I. Title
    745.592'2   TT175.7

    ISBN 0-7453-8780-4 (hbk)
          0-7153-9289 1 (pbk)

Colour photographs by Jonathon Bosley
Drawings by Martin Dodge

Text and drawings © Venus A. Dodge 1987
Colour photographs © Venus A. Dodge and David & Charles 1987

First published 1987
Second impression 1987
Third impression 1988
Paperback edition 1988

Typeset by Typesetters (Birmingham) Ltd, Smethwick, West Midlands
and printed in Hong Kong
for David & Charles Publishers plc
Brunel House   Newton Abbot   Devon

Distribution in the
United States by
Sterling Publishing Co. Inc.
2 Park Avenue, New York, NY 10016

CONTENTS

INTRODUCTION

Dolls' dressmaking is a craft with many aspects. If you are an antique doll collector, it is a necessary adjunct to your hobby, providing suitable costumes for the dolls in your collection in styles and fabrics appropriate to the period. For the doll artist, producing reproduction or original dolls, it is an essential part of the creative process, and to the harassed 'mum' whose daughter has a doll with insatiable sartorial demands, it is an economical way of satisfying those demands.

As a creative hobby, dolls' dressmaking is enormously satisfying. Dolls are small enough to dress, in even the most elaborate clothes, in a fraction of the time it would take to make them in life-size, and at a fraction of the cost. The artistic side in all of us finds an outlet in choosing styles and fabrics, colours and trimmings and the end result can give great pleasure to collector and child alike.

Frustrated romantics will find, in dolls' clothes, a place for the silks, velvets and laces which modern life makes impossible to wear, and somewhere to display a small piece of exquisite old embroidery or lace – too small to 'do anything with' but too lovely to throw away!

Needleworkers, embroiderers and lacemakers may find dolls' clothes an excellent way to display their work and the tailor, milliner or leatherworker might enjoy working in miniature. Dressing dolls always was, and still is, a splendid way of introducing children to the pleasures of making things for yourself.

I have always felt that the best dolls' clothes are those which look like 'real' clothes – antique or modern – so that if they were scaled-up in size they might be worn by a real person. I have often dressed dolls in versions of my own clothes and most ladies would be delighted with a doll dressed in a miniature of their own wedding dress or favourite outfit. A doll 'bridesmaid' would also make a charming gift to a little girl as a memento of her own role.

With 'real' clothes in mind, I have designed this book as a collection of more than 120 designs for dolls' clothes with patterns to make them in five sizes for dolls between 11in (28cm) and 25in (63.5cm) tall. The patterns cover a wide range of styles, suitable for baby dolls, boys, girls and ladies – antique and modern – with full making-up instructions for every garment. A collection of simple knitting and crochet patterns for a variety of garments has been included, and patterns and instructions for hats, shoes and accessories are also given. I have tried to include something for everyone, from a baby's bib to a 'diamond' tiara.

Most of the patterns and methods are very simple, and beginners, following the instructions, should have no difficulty in making the clothes, but I hope that experienced dolls' dressmakers will also find the book useful, as it offers styles and ideas they may not have tried.

Plate 2
The 20in (51cm) reproduction Kestner from Recollect in the centre of the picture wears a green and white checked lawn dress with a tucked bodice, long full sleeves and a gathered skirt. The neckline and sleeve ends are bound with white, and the sash ties at the back. The cameo pendant is life-size jewellery.

The 18in (45.5cm) doll on the right is a reproduction KR 117 from Reflect Reproduction Dolls. She wears a lilac cotton A-line dress with a pintucked front bodice, shaped waistband and long plain sleeves. Appliqué flower motifs trim the dress at the bound neckline and waistband.

Reflect's 14in (35.5cm) reproduction 'French girl' on the left wears a Wedgwood-blue cotton A-line dress with box pleats at front and back, long straight sleeves and a band collar. The dress is trimmed with white lace and has a ribbon sash slotted through the trimming at hip level. Her doll is a 4in (11cm) fully dressed miniature from Sunday Dolls, complete with its own minute doll, and her brooch is a broken earring.

The seated baby doll is 12in (30.5cm) 'William', made from a kit from Ridings Craft. He wears pale-blue cotton rompers with a smock yoke and puffed sleeves trimmed with an embroidered flower motif and white lace.

The 10in (25.5cm) girl doll (author's collection) wears a simple waisted dress with puffed sleeves and a gathered skirt in pale-pink embroidered lawn with a pink satin-ribbon sash.

Chapter 1 explains how to use the patterns and how to choose what to make for your doll. It covers tools and equipment and discusses suitable fabrics and trimmings. Chapters 2–7 are instructions for making up the garments shown in the drawings and photographs throughout the book – from underwear to jackets and coats. Chapter 8 contains all the knitting and crochet patterns. Chapter 9 gives patterns and instructions for making hats and bonnets, and Chapter 10 gives patterns and instructions for shoemaking. A wide range of accessories from bustles to bags and jewellery will be found in Chapter 11.

The clothes are modelled in the colour plates by a variety of dolls, antique, reproduction and modern, in a range of materials, porcelain, composition, cloth and vinyl – illustrating some of the styles which may be made from the patterns. Most of the dolls are commercially available and the names of the suppliers have all been given in the captions, so that any reader who 'falls in love' with one of my models will know where to find a similar doll. I have also named sources of supply of fabrics, trimmings and dolls' accessories, and a full list of tried-and-tested stockists can be found at the end of the book.

I hope that you will find the full-size trace-off patterns easy to use, the making-up instructions clear and concise, and the designs appealing – but if something does go wrong, you will find a few notes on pages 188–9 on how to put it right. Even the most experienced dolls dressmaker can make mistakes!

1 BEFORE YOU BEGIN

Choosing the style

Through the book, in drawings and colour photographs, there are more than 120 original designs for dolls' clothes, from knickers to coats, suitable for girl, boy, baby and lady dolls. The style you choose will depend on your own taste and skills and on the type of doll you are dressing. Some styles are designed for lady dolls, and would look quite wrong on babies or toddlers, other styles will suit a variety of dolls. The designs are shown on figures with proportions which suit the style and notes are given with each drawing where a style will suit other proportions. Fig 1 shows how different the same style will look on dolls of different proportions. Whether you are dressing an antique or reproduction doll or a modern one will also affect your choice. The notes accompanying the drawings give details of the styles which are suitable for antique dolls, and the dates at which they were fashionable. For example the French dress shown in Fig 33 is particularly suitable for French bébés of the 1880s. I have included something suitable for each period from 1850 onwards, so whether your doll is a hundred years old or 'bought yesterday' there should be something here to suit her.

When choosing the clothes you will make, consider the type of doll you are dressing. A child's play doll will need simple clothes with easy fastenings in washable fabrics. Antique or collectors' dolls will require something more elaborate. Save your best fabrics and pieces of old lace for dolls which will show them to advantage.

To choose the style, assess your doll's proportions and shape. Is it a lady doll, a child or a toddler? This is the most important consideration, as the proportions are the main factor in the success or otherwise of the costume. For example, a wedding gown, however well-made or elaborate, will not look attractive on a doll with chubby, child-like proportions. Consider also whether your doll needs modern or period clothes, what sort of underwear she will need, and whether a hat or shoes should be made to match the dress. Consider how much time you want to spend on the costume; a simple dress is quickly made, but an elaborately trimmed French dress, jacket and bonnet do take time, and require more expensive fabrics.

For all antique and collectors' dolls, I recommend putting them on a doll stand (Fig 2) to dress. This gives the doll safe support, and makes the dressmaking much easier. The stands (see 'Stockists') should be fitted over the doll's drawers and under the petticoat, and the clothes are cut and fitted to the doll on the stand. A good costume is displayed to advantage on a standing doll which prevents the clothes from creasing.

Some dolls benefit from a little padding to their figures, to make the costume fit properly. For example, a lady doll might look better with a fuller bosom, or a porcelain shoulder head on a cloth body might need a little padding over the shoulders to give them better shape. I recommend Terylene wadding, cut to size. On cloth bodies, this can be pinned or tacked to the body, on plastic or composition dolls, use a piece of surgical tape. See also the bustle pads and bust improver in Chapter 11, 'Accessories'.

Fig 1 One dress style shown on dolls of different proportions

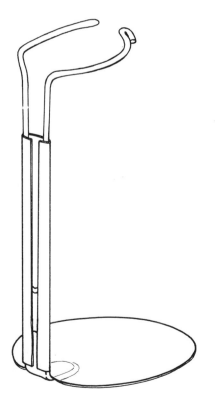

Fig 2 Doll stand

How to use the patterns

All the patterns in the book are drawn full size and include a ½in (1.2cm) seam allowance on all pieces. Used with the instructions given, they will make every garment illustrated in the book in line drawings and colour photographs. The patterns are grouped in sections throughout the book according to size, ie patterns for 11in (28cm) and 14–15in (35.5–38cm) dolls are on pages 19 to 32, patterns for 16–18in (40.5–45.5cm) dolls are on pages 43 to 55 etc. Each pattern piece is identified by a 'code' letter, which is the same for that piece in all sizes, eg pattern piece O – Peter Pan collar; pattern piece I – straight sleeve.

A full list of pattern pieces with their identifying code letters is given on page 18. The text accompanying the line drawings gives full details of the pattern pieces required for each garment so to make any of the clothes shown in the drawings you simply select the pieces required in the appropriate size and trace them. For example, to make the waisted, back-opening dress with puffed sleeves and Peter Pan collar shown in Fig 16 view b for a 16–18in (40.5–45.5cm) doll, you will need pieces Di bodice front, Dii bodice back, J full sleeve and O collar from the section of patterns for 16–18in (40.5–45.5cm) dolls in pages 43 to 55.

Most of the pattern pieces are given in each size, but in the case of a few pieces, eg the A-line dress, the pieces are given in only the smaller sizes, larger sizes being too big to fit onto the page. In these cases, larger sizes may be simply adapted from other patterns (see Fig 35) or enlarged from the patterns given.

Sizing

The patterns are sized to dolls by height, but as dolls, obviously, do not conform to standard sizes any more than people, the sizes given should be regarded only as a guide. For example, baby dolls usually have fairly chubby bodies and short limbs, so a 14in (35.5cm) baby doll may need patterns from the 18–20in (45.5–51cm) size or a slim 18in (45.5cm) lady doll may need patterns from the 14–16in (35.5–40.5cm) size.

To decide the pattern size your doll needs, first measure the height, then measure the chest across the front from armpit to armpit (plus seam allowance) and check this against the bodice front pattern *Di* in the pattern given for that height. For example, for an 18in girl doll, front chest measurement 6in without a seam allowance, pattern *Di* in 16–18in size would be too small as the pattern measures 6½in (with seam allowances) across the chest – the 18–20in size will fit however as it measures 7in across the chest. Or an 11in baby doll, chest measurement 4½in will fit pattern *Di* for 14–15in dolls (5½in).

As pattern toiles are made to fit the individual doll, the book patterns need only be approximately the right size, but choosing the best fit at this stage saves time and effort later. If the doll falls between two sizes, use the larger size patterns.

Cutting patterns

Having selected the pattern pieces required, and the appropriate size, cut the pattern toile in paper kitchen-towels, if you plan to use it only once, or in lightweight Vilene if you will use it again. This is most easily done by slipping the paper towel (or Vilene) under the page with a piece of carbon paper between them and drawing around the pattern piece with an empty ballpoint pen or something similar. Transfer pattern markings, ie code, grain line etc, to the pattern toile and cut out the piece. The drawn line is the cutting line, as a ½in (1.2cm) seam allowance is included on the pattern.

When you have cut pattern toiles for all the pieces needed for the garment you are making, pin or tack them together and fit them on the doll. Make any adjustments and trim the toile pieces if necessary; then unpin them and use these patterns to cut the garment. Fitting instructions are given with the basic making-up instructions for each pattern. All garments should be tried on the doll several times during making up, dresses over underwear, coats over dresses etc.

Tools and equipment

Dolls' dressmaking does not require any special equipment – it can be done simply with a needle and thread, a pair of scissors, a tape measure and a ruler and pencil – but there are several items which make things easier, and extend the range of trimmings and effects possible.

Whether you sew by hand or machine is a matter of individual preference. I recommend using a sewing machine for seams, gathering etc, but hemming and finishing by hand. It is easier to make small neat stitches with small needles (I recommend 10 sharps). Thread should complement the dress fabric, ie cotton for cotton, silk for silk, polyester for polyester, etc, and the colour should match the fabric as closely as possible. If a perfect match is not available use a lighter shade on light-coloured fabrics, a darker shade on dark fabrics. Seams should be neatened by French seaming (on fine fabrics), machine edging or zigzag. Buttonhole or blanket stitch might be used at waist seams or around armholes; or on larger garments, these seams might be bound with bias binding. 'Fray Check' is a colourless fluid (available from haberdashery departments or Sunday Dolls) which can be painted on to prevent fabric fraying and is particularly useful for small garments and trimmings. Small, sharp scissors are best for cutting dolls' clothes, and a 'Fadeaway' marker pen (available from haberdashery departments or Sunday Dolls) is useful for marking button positions etc as the lines disappear after a day or two. (Tailor's chalk is an alternative.) Use a ruler to mark straight lines for skirts or pleats, and clean sharp pins (I recommend the glass-headed type – so much easier to find when you drop them on the floor!) that will not spoil the fabric.

Other items you might find useful include millinery wire (for hat making – available from haberdashery departments or Ridings Craft); surgical tape (from chemists) for binding wire ends; cotton buds for tiny turning-through; a knitting needle for turning-through; a selection of felt pens for colouring trimmings; a stitch-ripper for unpicking mistakes; a bodkin for threading ribbon or elastic; shirring elastic in several colours and hat elastic. A glue gun (Sunday Dolls) is very useful for putting tiny blobs of glue where you want them.

Fabrics

The materials you choose will depend on your own taste and the doll you are dressing. Suggestions for colours and fabrics are given with each of the drawings, but these are just suggestions. As a general rule, natural fabrics, eg cotton, wool and silk, make more successful clothes than man-made fibres as they gather and hang well. Modern non-crease fabrics tend to look bunchy and clumsy but there are of course, exceptions. The polyester silks are usually very good and polyester cotton looks well on modern dolls. But whatever you choose make sure that it is relatively lightweight, especially for small dolls, and that any pattern on the material is small in scale. For pure cotton fabrics in plain colours and tiny prints I recommend those from Village Fabrics (see 'Stockists'). If you are dressing antique dolls it is nice to use old fabrics of the same period as the doll – if they suit the doll and the proposed costume – but careful choice will provide good new fabric equivalents if old fabrics are hard to find. Jumble sales are an excellent source of material. Look for baby gowns, evening dresses etc (the black satin and sequin gown on the doll in the plate on page 187 was made from a jumble-sale evening dress). Needlecord, velveteen, Viyella, taffeta, denim, cotton, lawn, dotted swiss, soft satin, organdy, silk, fine wool and brocade can all be used for dolls' dressmaking. Scraps left from life-size dressmaking can sometimes be used, but usually it is better to choose new fabrics, which really suit the doll and the costume you are making. Half a yard (45.5cm) of 36in (91cm) wide fabric will dress most dolls up to 16in (40.5cm), a yard (91cm) for dolls up to 22in (56cm) and 1½ yards (1.37m) for large dolls (depending on the length and fullness of the skirt). Look also at handkerchiefs, scarves, table linen, lightweight furnishing fabrics and wide lace or broderie anglaise trimmings. Check that the fabric pattern is small enough by looking at a small piece rather than the full width and drape it around the doll to see if it suits her colouring etc. Clothes for antique dolls should be 'right' in fabric as well as style. Notes on styles suitable for antique dolls are given with the drawings, with fabric suggestions; for further information consult *Making Old Fashioned Dolls* (see Bibliography) or a good costume reference book.

Colour

When choosing the fabrics for dolls' dressmaking, consider the colours carefully – as you would for life-size dressmaking. Not only must the colour be appropriate for the costume you are making, but it must also suit the doll's own colouring.

In the notes with the style drawings, I have described colours in four main groups – pastel, strong, subtle and bright. The first group, pastel colours, are those pale shades of colour which have white in them, eg pale pink, pale blue, primrose yellow, pale green and pale mauve. These colours look well trimmed with white lace and ribbons in a darker shade of the same colour, eg pale pink trimmed with white lace and rose-pink ribbons. Pastel colours suit most dolls except some pale bisque (porcelain) antique or reproduction dolls who look a bit 'washed-out' in pastels. Included in the pastel group are the soft whites, ivory and cream shades, though these colours often suit pale dolls very well, especially when trimmed with a strong contrast, eg an ivory dress with gold or green trimming, or a cream dress with brown trimmings. Off-white, ivory and cream look better trimmed with matching lace rather than white.

The second group, strong colours, are deep shades of colours other than primary colours. Included in the group are crimson, emerald or dark green, midnight blue, brown, gold and deep purple. These colours can look very striking, but tend to be more appropriate for period dolls (especially ladies or French bébés) than for modern dolls. They look well trimmed with black, or a toning shade of the same colour in a different fabric, eg a crimson velvet dress trimmed with crimson satin, or a gold silk dress trimmed with black velvet. Consider black or coffee lace trimming with these colours. Strong colours look beautiful on dolls with pale complexions, but do not suit dolls with rosy cheeks – they tend to heighten the doll's colouring.

Subtle colours are those shades which have a hint of grey in them, and include lavender, cinnamon, smoky blues, dusty pink, lemon yellow, eau-de-Nil, and grey itself. Also included in this group are colours like rust, lilac, beige and navy. Most dolls can wear subtle colours, if the colour suits the eye and hair colouring, and they look well on both antique and modern dolls. Trimmings in toning strong colours look attractive, eg purple trimming on grey, or dark green on eau-de-Nil. They also look well with strong contrasts, eg black with rust or cinnamon, white with smoky blue or lemon yellow, and rose pink on beige.

A warning here about greens, which can be tricky to match. Greens are either blue-greens or yellow-greens. The blue-greens look good with blue shades, eg pale blue and pine green, and the yellow-greens look good with yellow shades, eg moss green and golden yellow.

Turquoise, which is a mixture of blue and green, follows the same rules: if the shade is more blue than green, use it with blue shades; if it is more green than blue use it with green shades. All shades of turquoise look good with white.

The last group of colours, the bright colours, are the primary colours, ie red, blue and yellow, and bright shades of the secondary colours, eg green and purple – think of rainbows. These colours are good for simple, modern dolls' clothes but look quite wrong on antique or reproduction dolls. They usually look best with other bright colours, eg poster red with royal blue or yellow, or with white.

To decide if the colour suits the doll, drape the fabric around her – does it go well with her complexion, eyes and hair colouring? If you have set your heart on a colour which doesn't really suit the doll, consider changing her wig (if this is possible). This will change her colouring, often quite dramatically. For example, if your auburn-haired doll looks unattractive in pale pink, try a brunette wig. There are no hard-and-fast rules – your own taste must be the deciding factor here.

When choosing colours which are appropriate to the period of the doll and the style of costume, things are easier. Different colours and groups of colours were fashionable at different times. Any good costume reference book (see Bibliography) will be a guide, and, especially when dressing antique dolls, some research is advisable. Turquoise, orange and peach are modern colours and look wrong on old dolls; lemon

Fig 3 Stitches

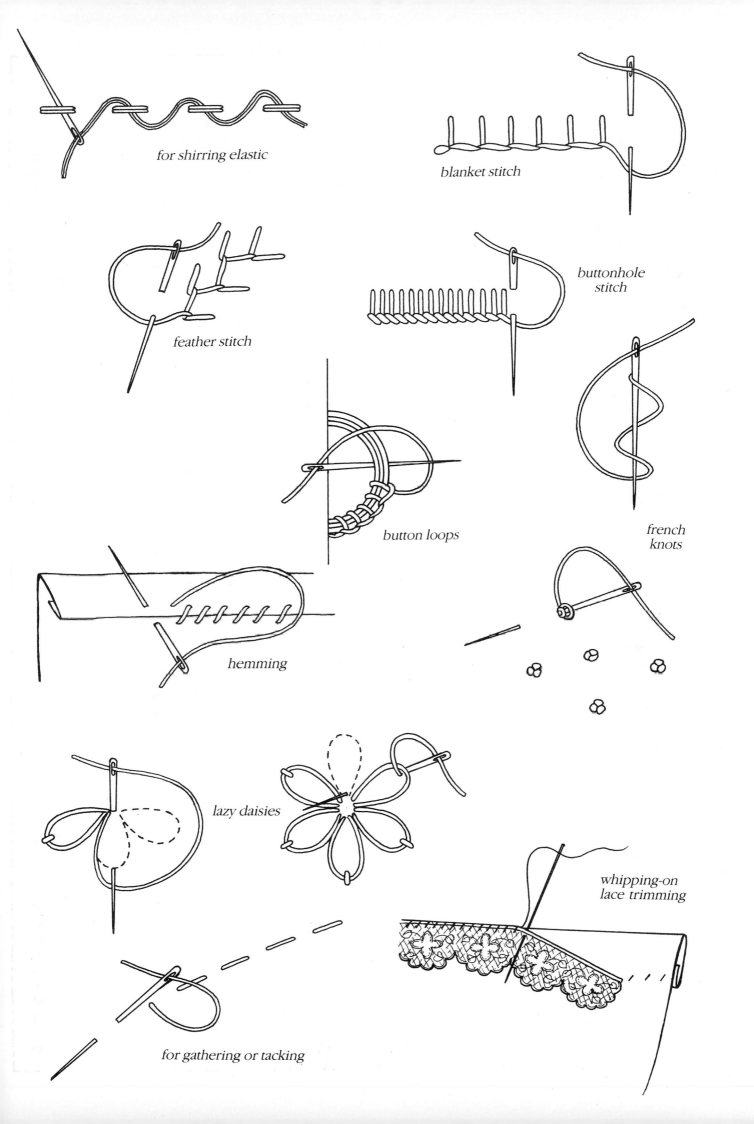

for shirring elastic

blanket stitch

feather stitch

buttonhole
stitch

button loops

french
knots

hemming

lazy daisies

whipping-on
lace trimming

for gathering or tacking

yellow was a 'new' colour in the 1890s – fashionable then, but inappropriate for dolls earlier than that date. An evening spent with the costume reference book will prevent mistakes of this sort, and will provide tips for trimmings and accessories.

When planning colours for the dress and trimmings, plan also for the hat, shoes and coat (if the doll is to have them). Perhaps, if you are making an all-white outfit for an antique German girl doll, she may have red shoes, or a golden-yellow sash. Often, just one touch of colour like this on an all-white outfit will 'lift' it out of the ordinary and make it look special. Equally, one touch of a contrasting colour used with an outfit can make the other colours look richer or more dramatic – see the crimson rose on the AT doll dressed in black and cream in the colour plate on page 187.

Trimmings

The clothes in the book show a wide variety of trimmings, and demonstrate how they can be used to make an enormous range of styles from a basic pattern. Lace is one of the most versatile trimmings. Wide lace may be used over lightweight fabrics, for the whole dress or as a yoke or an overskirt. Lace frills may be used at necklines, sleeve ends or skirt hems and lace edging will emphasise a collar, cuff or pintucked bodice. Insertion lace may be let into a sheer fabric, or used over coloured ribbon as decoration. For antique or reproduction dolls, the lace should be cotton or silk; reserve nylon lace for modern dolls. When used as an edging, eg on a petticoat hem, lace is prettier if it is very slightly gathered or fluted. (To flute lace, iron it in a curve, gently stretching the lower edge as you iron.) White lace may be dyed beige in weak tea or coffee. Look out for pieces of old lace to use for old dolls.

Ribbons are used in a variety of ways, from bands of narrow velvet ribbon used as trimming on skirts or jacket cuffs, to wide satin ribbon used as sashes. Narrow silk ribbon may be used in casings at the neckline or knees of underwear, tied in tiny bows or made into roses for dress trimmings. Sunday Dolls, as well as supplying an enormous range of doll-size trimmings including fine cotton laces, narrow silk ribbons and tiny braids, also sell ingenious little gadgets to make perfect tiny ribbon bows, roses and rosettes (see 'Stockists'). Embroidered ribbons make lovely trimmings on plain fabrics, and plain ribbons look well on toning patterned fabrics. (GP Ceramics also have a good range of pleated lace and ribbon trimmings.) To prevent ribbon ends from fraying, seal them with Fray Check.

Bias binding in satin or printed cotton is a useful trimming for necklines, cuffs, collars or jacket edges and may be bought ready-made or made from bias-cut strips of dress fabric.

Braids can be used to trim dresses, coats or jackets

Plate 3
A group of Sasha dolls, 16in (40.5cm) boy and girls and 11in (28cm) baby. The brunette girl wears a cream cotton dress with a pintucked bodice, long full sleeves and a frilled, gathered skirt. The dress is trimmed with cream lace edging and tiny pearl bead 'buttons'.

The blonde girl in the centre of the picture wears a gold cotton dress with a Peter Pan collar, short puffed sleeves and gathered skirt and a pinafore in a co-ordinating brown and gold print cotton with pockets. Both fabrics are from a range of print and plain co-ordinating cottons from Village Fabrics. The white lawn handkerchief is trimmed with narrow white lace.

The boy wears a cream cotton shirt with long sleeves and olive-green needlecord dungarees, the straps fastened with buttons and buttonholes.

The blonde girl on the right wears a crimson velveteen dress with long plain sleeves and a full-length gathered skirt. The heavy cream lace collar and cuffs are made from old table mats. Her brooch is a life-size earring.

The baby doll wears a bunnysuit with a hood made in pink fleece fabric with a zip fastening.

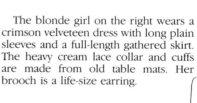

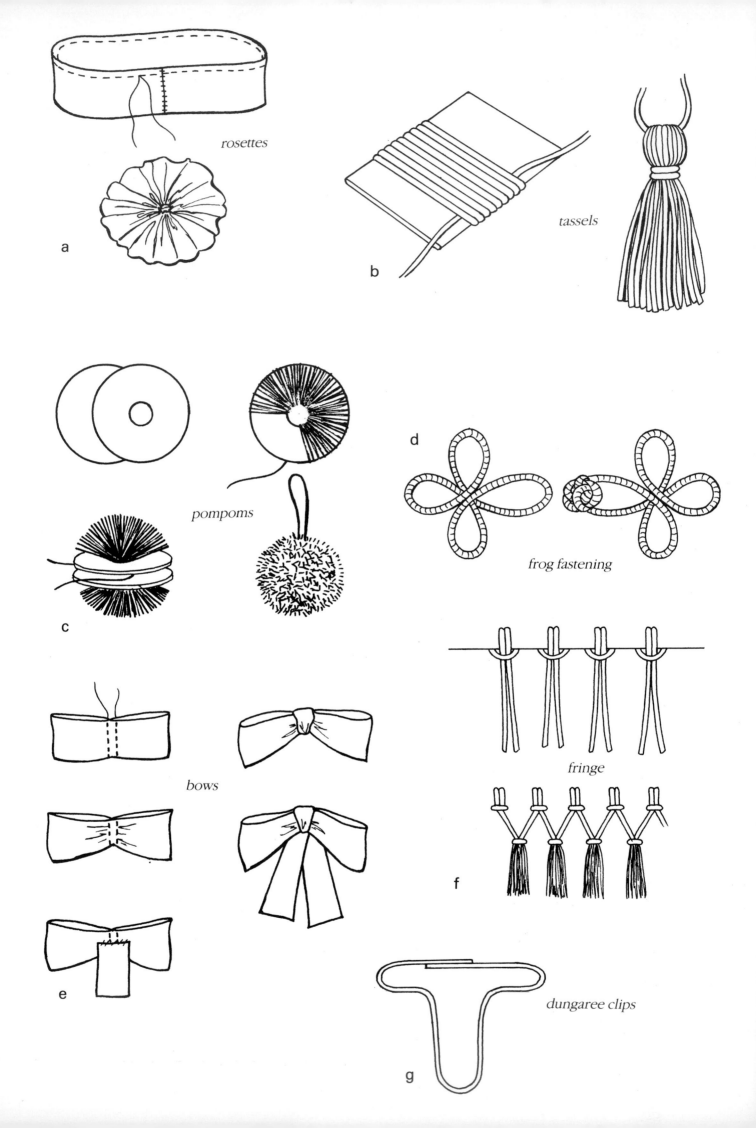

rosettes

tassels

pompoms

frog fastening

bows

fringe

dungaree clips

a

b

c

d

e

f

g

and range from the silky kind used for lampshades to pretty flower motifs in ribbon or silk floss. The tassels from lampshade braid also make effective trimmings on period dolls' clothes.

Embroidered motifs (from haberdashery departments) are invaluable for those of us who cannot embroider; and for those who can, many dolls' clothes benefit from the addition of a little feather stitching or a few lazy daisies (see Fig 3). Most antique dolls' outfits include some feather-stitched underwear.

Artificial flowers may be used to decorate dolls' hats and clothes as well – perhaps a posy tucked in the sash, or a buttonhole. Tiny flowers can be found in the millinery department of most large stores or in shops which sell items for decorating cakes. Consider small dried flowers as an alternative to fabric ones – or make your own from silk ribbons. Fabric flowers and narrow ribbons may be coloured with felt-tipped pens to match a garment.

Making trimmings

Rosettes (Fig 4a) Rosettes may be made in any size from odd lengths of ribbon or lace. Cut the length about 6 times the width, eg 1½in (3.7cm) of ¼in (6mm) ribbon – 3in (7.5cm) of ½in (1.2cm) ribbon etc. Blanket-stitch the short edges together on the wrong side. With small stitches, gather along one edge, pull up tightly and fasten off. A rosette of lace, over a rosette of wider ribbon, with a tiny ribbon bow in the centre, is very pretty, or a ribbon and/or lace rosette may be trimmed with a bead or flower motif in the centre. Use the rosettes to trim dresses, at either side of a baby's bonnet, or, in small sizes, on the fronts of shoes.

Tassels (Fig 4b) The tassels from silky lampshade trimmings are useful, but the range of colours is limited. To make simple tassels using embroidery silk or floss, cut a piece of stiff cardboard a little larger than you want the tassel. Wind the silk or floss around the cardboard, evenly, and as thick as required. Slip a length of silk through the wound strands and tie a firm knot. Cut the strands; pull them down over the knot and tie another strand around two or three times and tie another firm knot. Trim all the ends evenly to the required length.

Pompoms (Fig 4c) Ready-made pompoms can be bought in craft shops or cut from bobble-edged lampshade trimming. To make pompoms, cut two circles of stiff cardboard, the size of the pompom required. Cut small circles from the centres of both pieces. Wind yarn around and around the circles evenly, through the hole in the centre, until this is filled. With small sharp scissors, snip through the yarn between the two card circles and ease them slightly apart. Tie a length of yarn tightly around the centre of

Fig 4 Making trimmings

the pompom and knot firmly. Remove the card circles and trim the pompom. The pompoms may be used to trim berets or pull-on hats, the sides of bonnets or (if small) the fronts of shoes.

Frog fastenings (Fig 4d) The frog fastenings available in haberdashery departments are usually too large for dolls and the colour range is very limited. To make frog fastenings, use fine cord or Russian braid. Work on a piece of cork or cardboard which you can push pins into. Form the braid into three loops of equal size and a slightly larger loop, holding them in place with pins and a tiny dab of glue where the loops cross. When the glue (UHU or similar) is dry, stitch the loops together where they cross and oversew the cut ends on the underside to neaten. One of the pair has a small button (made of coiled, glued and stitched cord if you wish) stitched to the longer loop. Frog fastenings look very attractive on coats and jackets which fasten edge-to-edge and they may also be used purely as decoration, perhaps on a jacket cuff.

Bows (Fig 4e) A bow of ribbon may, of course, just be tied; but a tied fabric bow would be too bulky, so the bow is made up in pieces and then stitched in place. Make up a good length of fabric. This might be single thickness, hemmed or sealed with Fray Check – or double thickness, sewn into a tube, turned through and pressed. Cut a length of this fabric, twice as long as the width of the finished bow. Fold the cut ends to the centre and sew gathering stitches through both sides; pull up and fasten off. Cut a short length of fabric to wrap around the centre of the bow; secure the end to the back of the bow; wrap the other end around the front and secure it on the back. Gather along the lower (and upper if you wish) edge of the centre and pull up slightly. Cut two lengths to make ribbon 'ends' and stitch to the back of the bow. (On double-thickness fabric, turn in the lower edges and slipstitch closed.) Large bows made this way can be used to trim hats and bonnets, dresses and jackets, and may be stitched in place or pinned on with safety pins.

Fringes (Fig 4f) To make fringes for knitted shawls etc, wind strands of yarn around a piece of card as wide as the length of the required fringe. Cut through the strands so that they are all the same length. Use the strands singly or in small groups. Fold the length in half and pull the folded end through the edge of the shawl (a crochet hook is useful for this). Pull the cut ends through the loop. Trim the ends. If the fringed ends are long, they may be knotted together to make a more decorative fringe.

Fastenings

The fastenings you choose will depend on the garment you are making. Bodices which overlap may be fastened with small press-studs or buttons and buttonholes. Garments which fasten edge-to-edge may have worked thread loops (see Fig 3) and buttons, or hooks and eyes. Sometimes a garment will fasten with press-studs and have mock buttons on the outside. Waist-bands on underwear may have hooks, buttons or tape ties. A wrapover bodice may fasten with buttons or a sash, and a bunnysuit or babygro may have a small zip down the centre front.

Tiny buttons are available from several of the specialist suppliers (see 'Stockists'), from mother-of-pearl buttons from Hello Dolly to plastic in a wide range of colours from GP Ceramics. Check also in jumble sales and junk shops and raid friends' button boxes. Tiny buckles for belts can be found at Sunday Dolls and occasionally in haberdashery departments or taken from watch straps or old shoes. On coats or jackets, cord loops and buttons or frog fastenings can look very attractive but be sure they are not too big. Small beads make effective buttons, either glass, wood or pearl varieties (plastic can be used for dolls dressed in modern clothes). Stud fastenings may be used on modern jackets, dungarees or coats. The dungaree clips in Fig 4g are made from large wire paper-clips, bent with pliers and wide enough to allow the strap through. On clothes for antique dolls, tape strings or hooks and eyes are most authentic; buttons and buttonholes and press-studs are more commonly found in the twentieth century.

	PATTERN PIECES AND CODES			SIZES			
Code	Pattern piece	11in (28cm)	14–15in (35.5–38cm)	16–18in (40.5–45.5cm)	18–20in (45.5–51cm)	20–22in (51–56cm)	23–25in (58.5–63.5cm)
A	Knickers	−	/	/	/	/	/
B	Drawers	−	/	/	/	/	/
C	Combinations	−	/	/	/	/	−
Di	Back-opening bodice front	−	/	/	/	/	/
Dii	Back-opening bodice back	−	/	/	/	/	/
Ei	Front-opening bodice front	−	/	/	/	/	/
Eii	Front-opening bodice back	−	/	/	/	/	/
F	Wrapover bodice front	−	/	/	/	/	/
Gi	Smock-yoke front	−	/	/	/	/	/
Gii	Smock-yoke back	−	/	/	/	/	/
Hi	Round-yoke front	−	/	/	/	/	/
Hii	Round-yoke back	−	/	/	/	/	/
Hiii	Round-yoke sleeve	−	/	/	/	/	/
I	Straight sleeve	−	/	/	/	/	/
J	Full sleeve	−	/	/	/	/	/
Ki	Shirt/blouse front	−	/	/	/	/	/
Kii	Shirt/blouse back	−	/	/	/	/	/
Kiii	Shirt/blouse sleeve	−	/	/	/	/	/
Kiv	Shirt/blouse collar	−	/	/	/	/	/
Li	Jacket front	−	/	/	/	/	/
Lii	Jacket back	−	/	/	/	/	/
M	Trousers	−	/	/	/	/	/
Ni	French dress front	−	/	/	/	/	/
Nii	French dress back	−	/	/	/	/	/
Niii	French dress plastron	−	/	/	/	/	/
O	Peter Pan collar	−	/	/	/	/	/
P	Round collar	−	/	/	/	/	/
Q	Square collar	−	/	/	/	/	/
R	Sailor collar	−	/	/	/	/	/
S	Shawl collar	−	/	/	/	/	/
T	Pockets	−	/	/	/	/	/
U	Cuff	−	/	/	/	/	/
Vi	A-line dress front	−	/	/	−	−	−
Vii	A-line dress back	−	/	/	−	−	−
W	Dungarees	−	/	/	−	−	−
X	Bunnysuit	/	/	−	−	−	−
Y	Picture hat (3 pieces)	small	medium	large			
Z	Poke bonnet (3 pieces)	small	medium	large			
AA	Bibbed skirt	−	/	−	−	−	−
BB	Baby bib	small	medium				
CC	Buttoned nappy	small	medium			/ Pattern available	
DD	Bag	small	−	large		− Pattern not available	

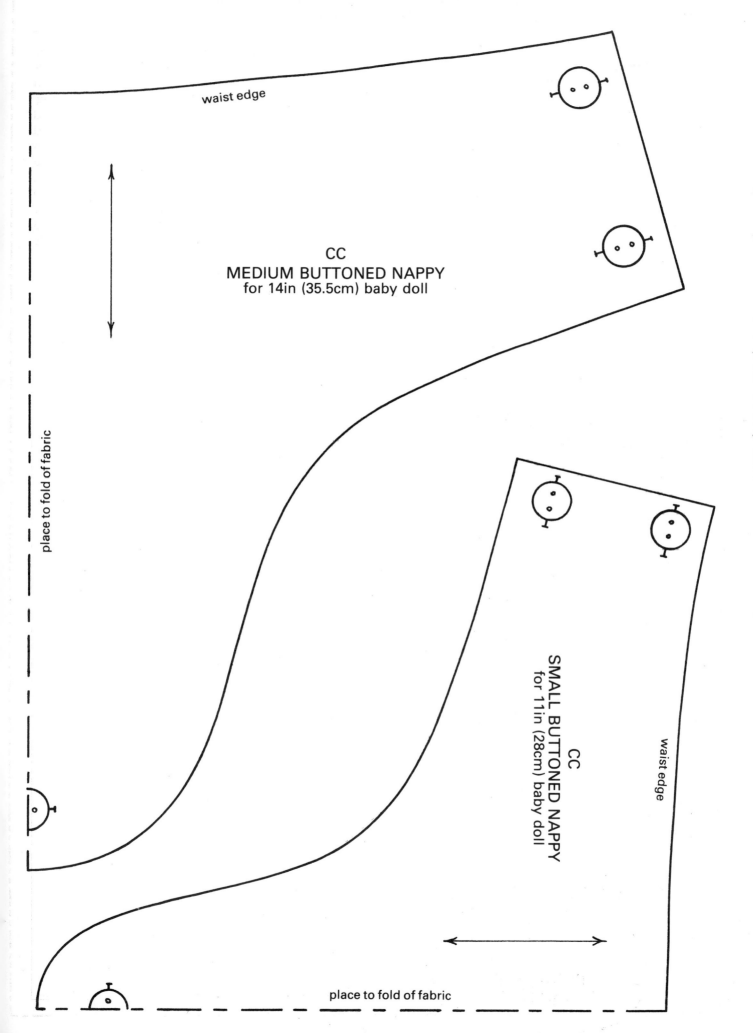

waist edge

CC
MEDIUM BUTTONED NAPPY
for 14in (35.5cm) baby doll

place to fold of fabric

CC
SMALL BUTTONED NAPPY
for 11in (28cm) baby doll

waist edge

place to fold of fabric

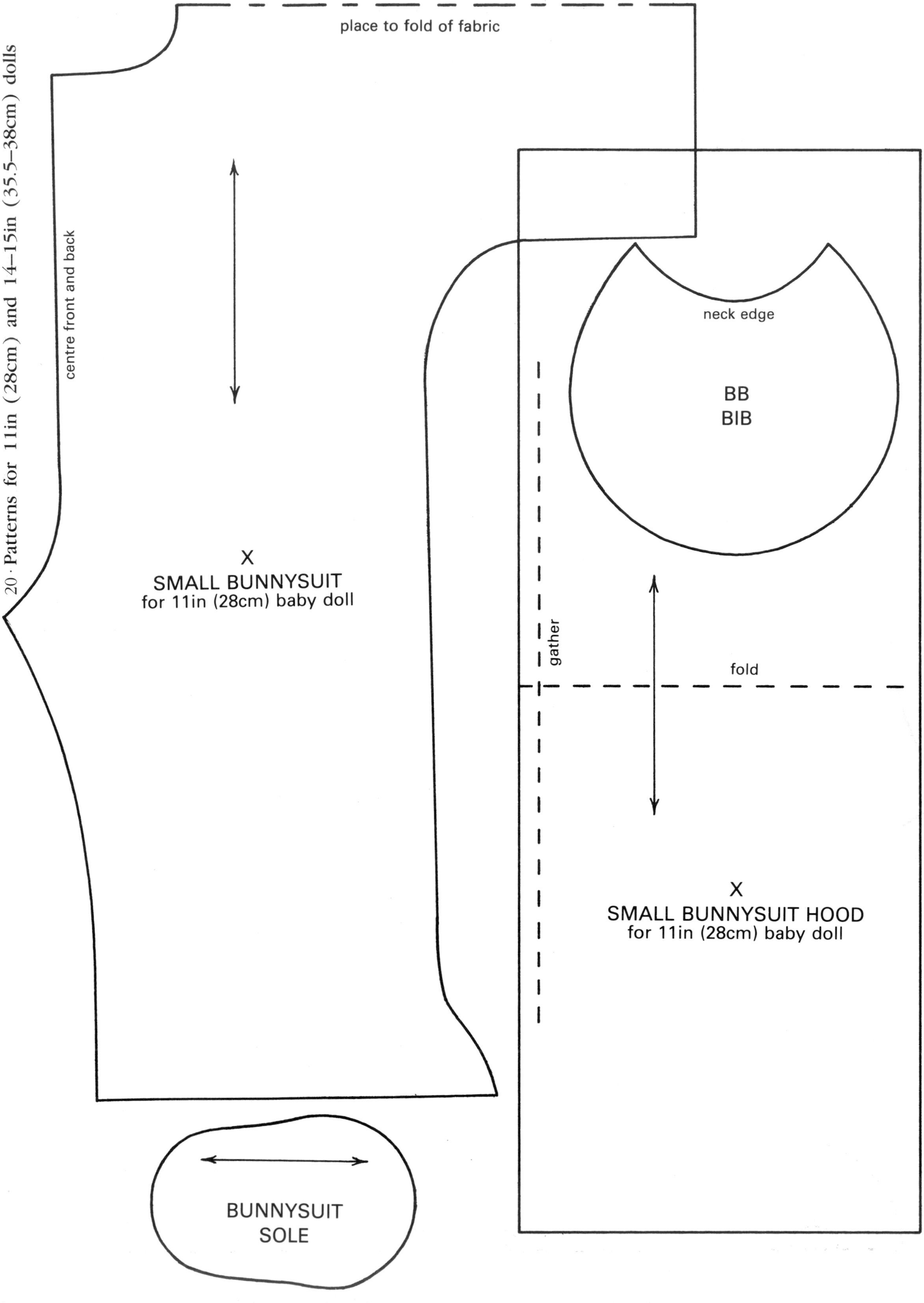

place to fold of fabric

centre front and back

neck edge

BB
BIB

X
SMALL BUNNYSUIT
for 11in (28cm) baby doll

gather

fold

X
SMALL BUNNYSUIT HOOD
for 11in (28cm) baby doll

BUNNYSUIT
SOLE

place to fold of fabric

lengthen as required

X
MEDIUM BUNNYSUIT
for 14–15in (35.5–38cm) baby doll

centre front and back

neck edge

BB
BIB

X
BUNNYSUIT
SOLE

22 · Patterns for 14–15in (35.5–38cm) dolls

place to fold of fabric

M
TROUSERS

centre front and back

C
COMBINATIONS

place to fold of fabric

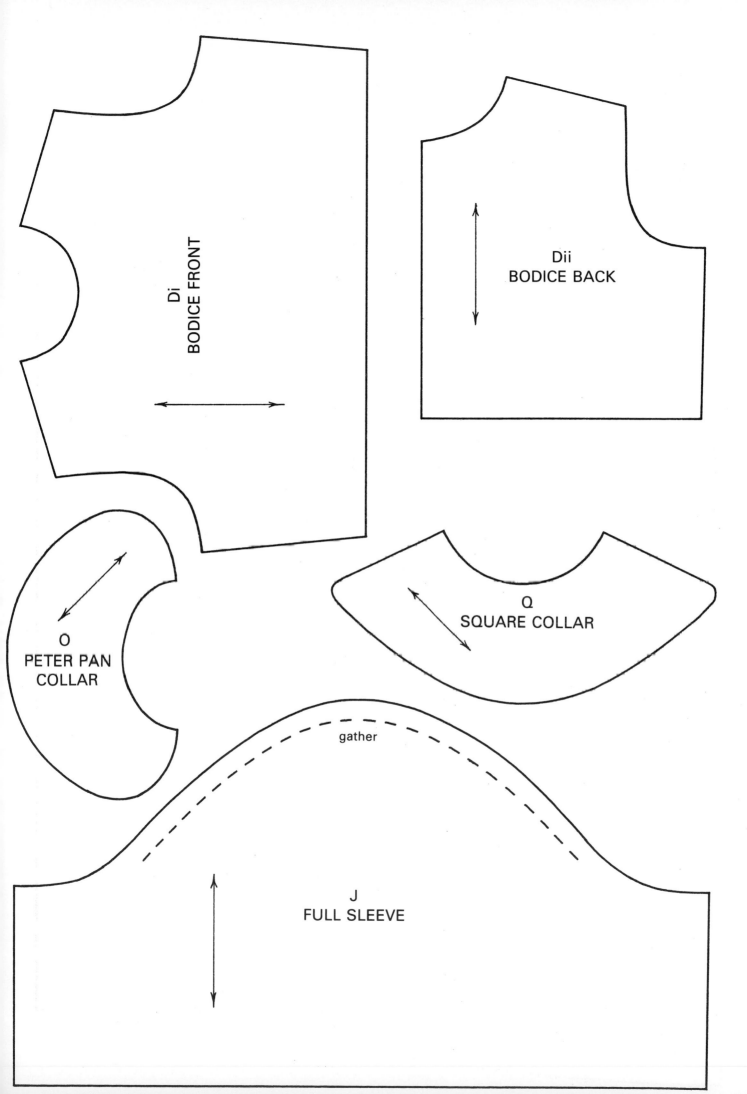

Di
BODICE FRONT

Dii
BODICE BACK

O
PETER PAN
COLLAR

Q
SQUARE COLLAR

gather

J
FULL SLEEVE

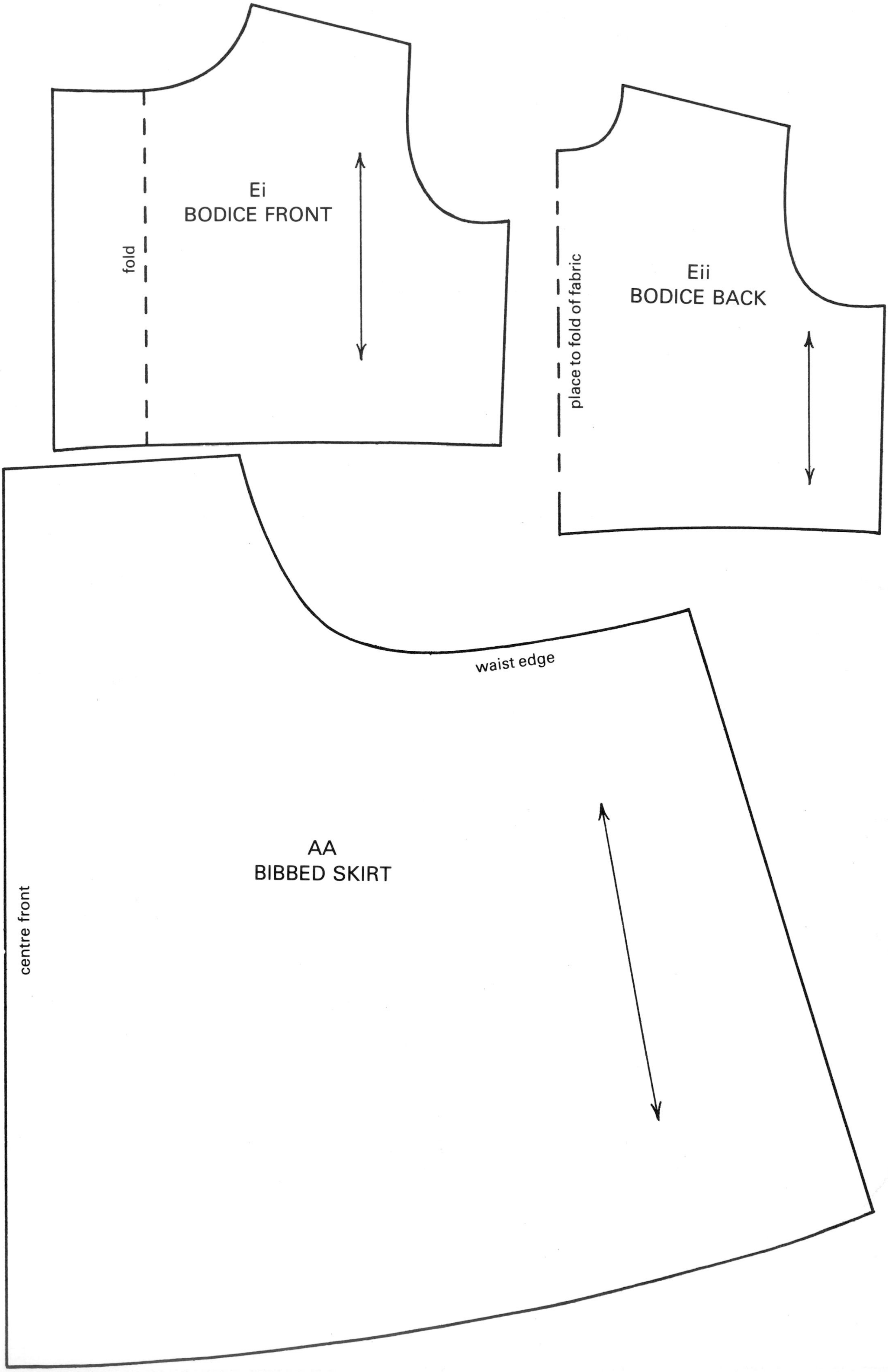

Ei
BODICE FRONT

fold

Eii
BODICE BACK

place to fold of fabric

waist edge

AA
BIBBED SKIRT

centre front

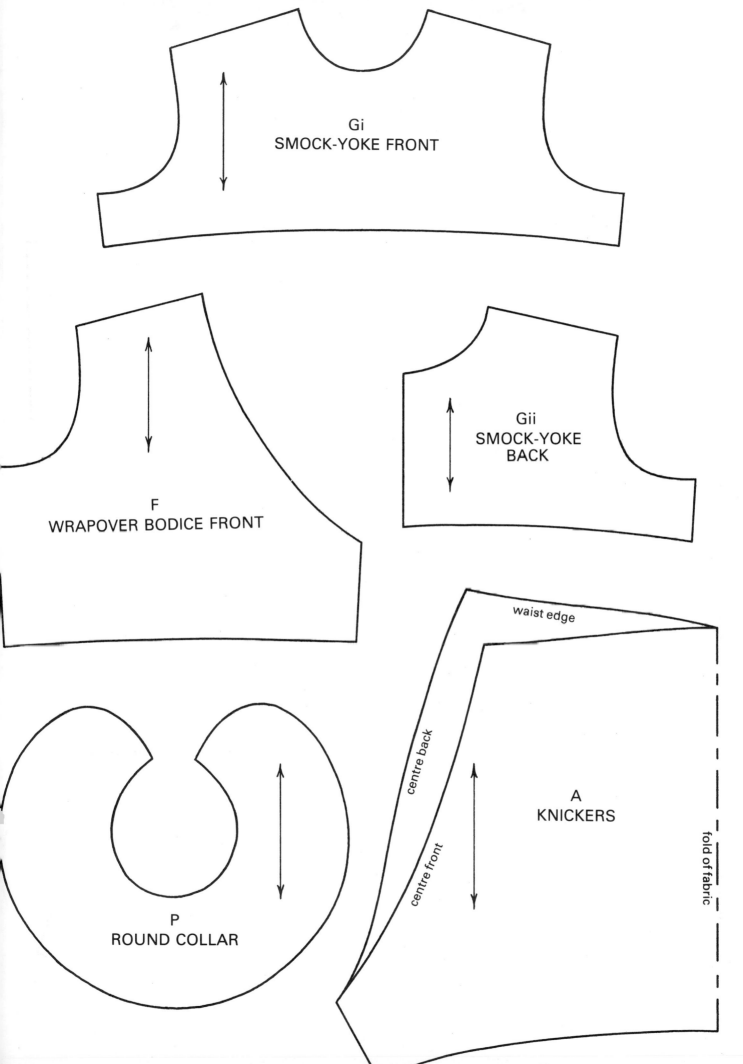

Gi
SMOCK-YOKE FRONT

Gii
SMOCK-YOKE
BACK

F
WRAPOVER BODICE FRONT

P
ROUND COLLAR

waist edge

centre back

centre front

A
KNICKERS

fold of fabric

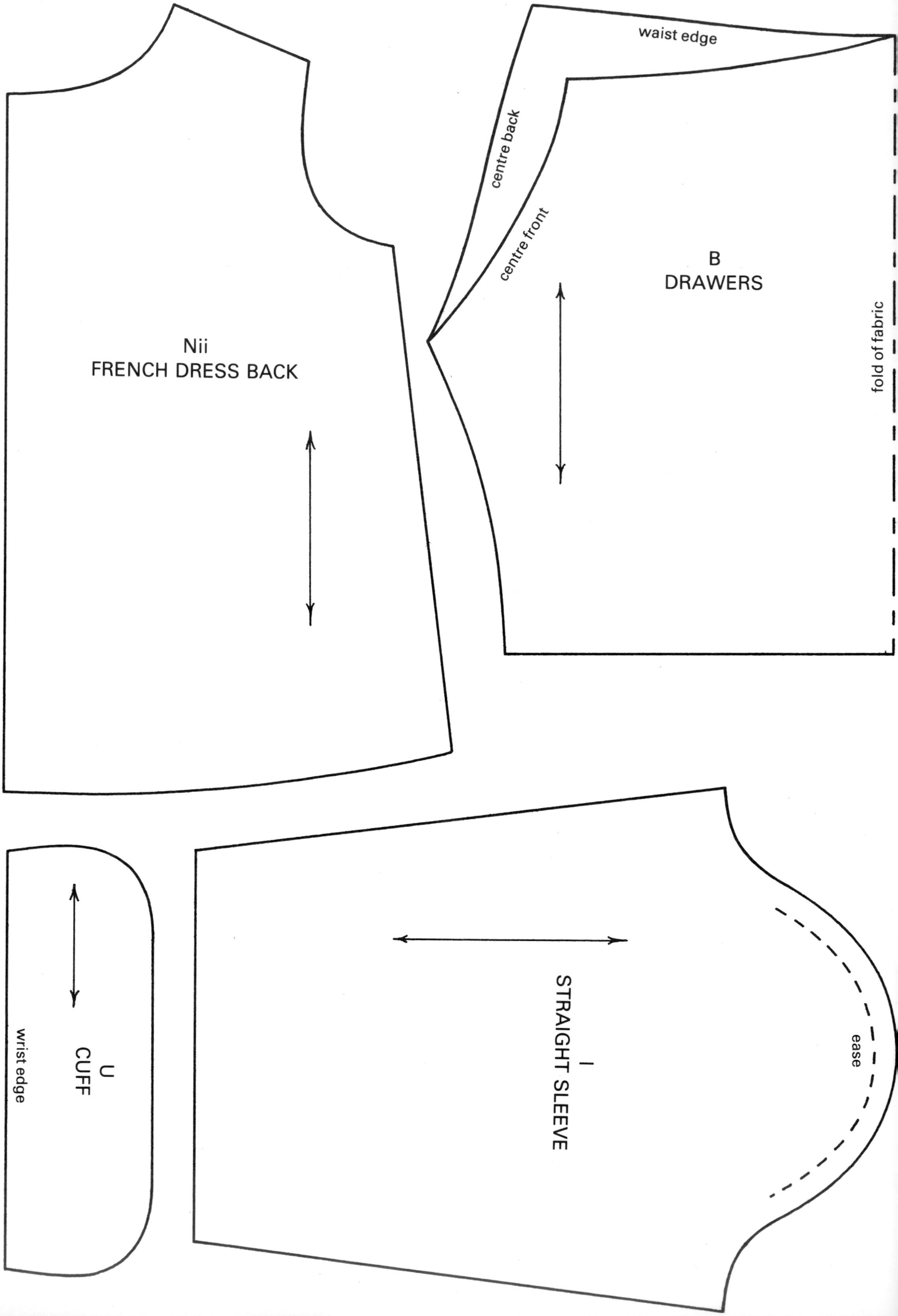

Nii
FRENCH DRESS BACK

waist edge

centre back

centre front

B
DRAWERS

fold of fabric

U
CUFF

wrist edge

STRAIGHT SLEEVE

ease

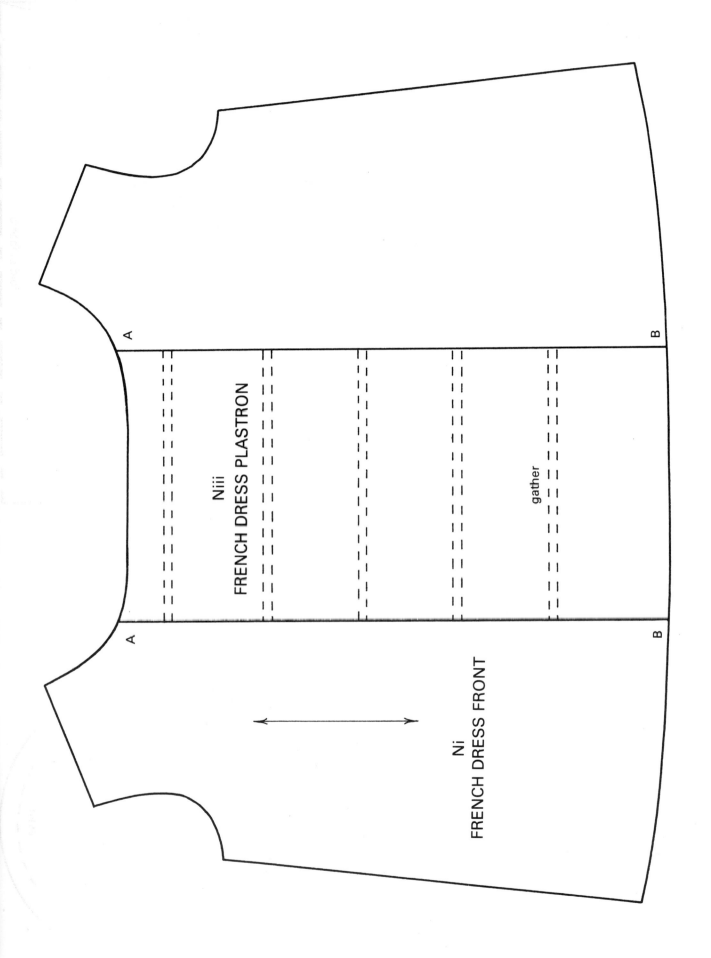

Niii
FRENCH DRESS PLASTRON

gather

A

B

A

B

Ni
FRENCH DRESS FRONT

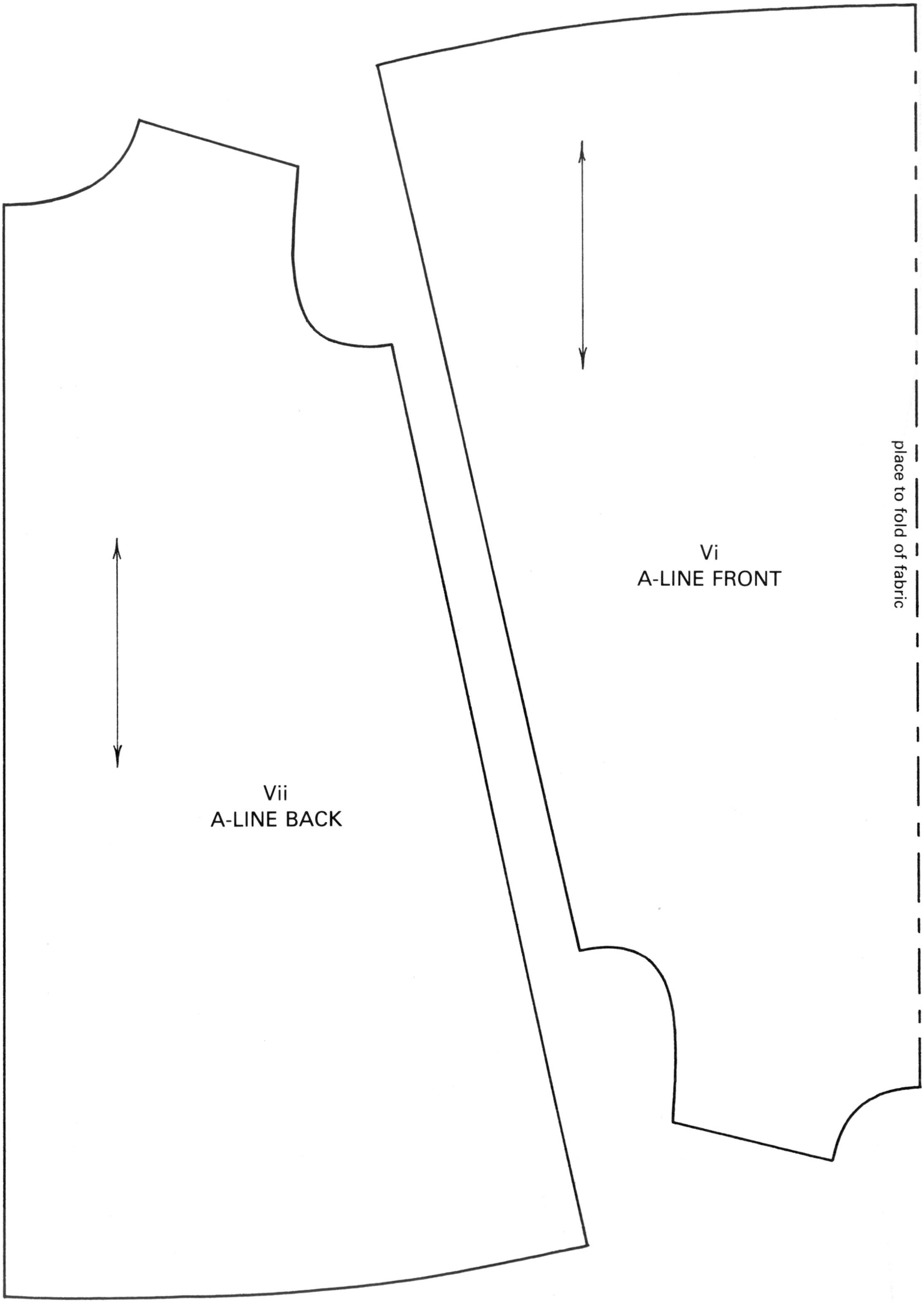

Vi
A-LINE FRONT

Vii
A-LINE BACK

place to fold of fabric

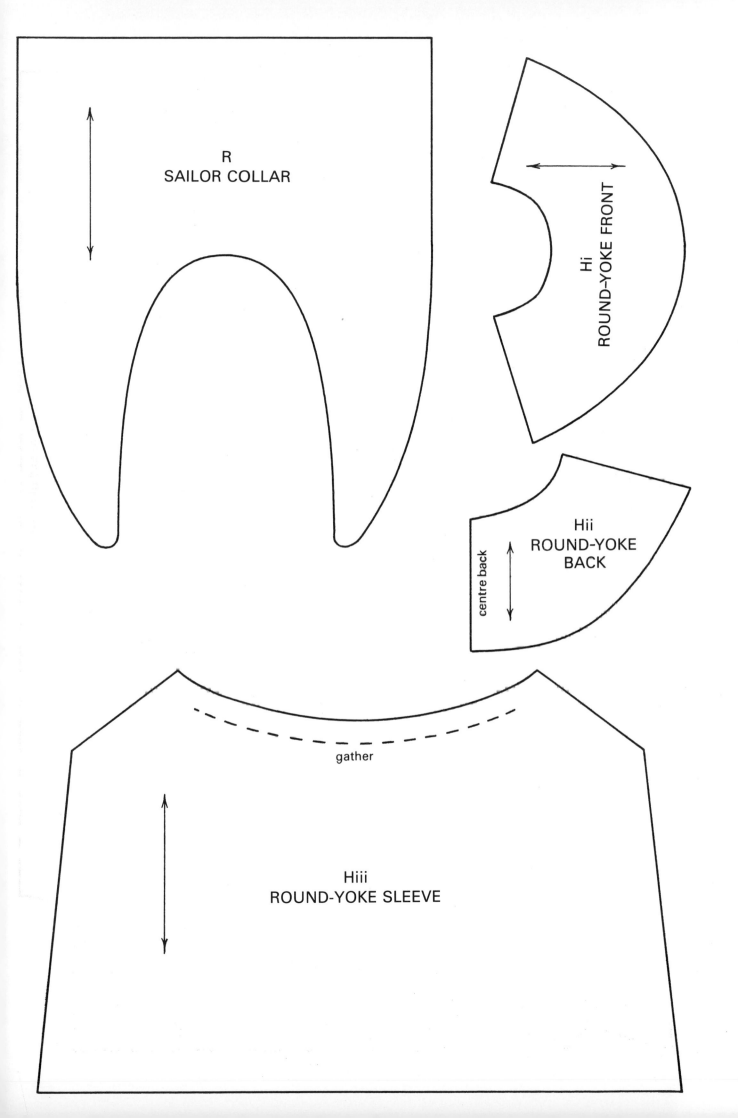

R
SAILOR COLLAR

Hi
ROUND-YOKE FRONT

Hii
ROUND-YOKE
BACK

centre back

gather

Hiii
ROUND-YOKE SLEEVE

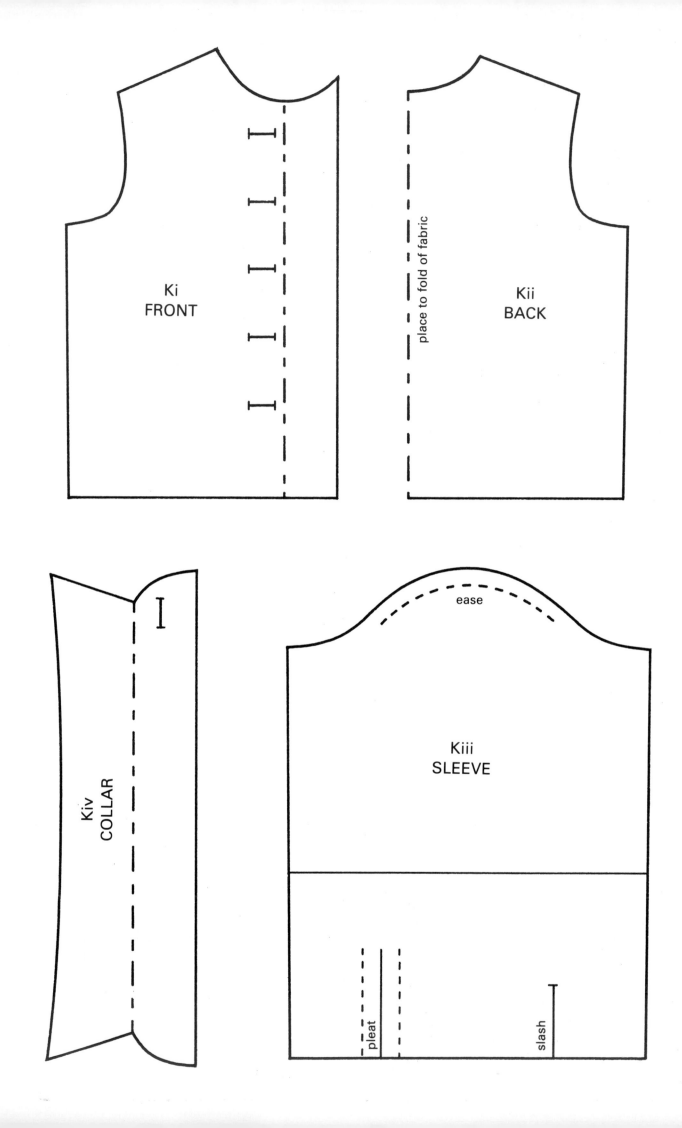

Ki
FRONT

place to fold of fabric

Kii
BACK

Kiv
COLLAR

ease

Kiii
SLEEVE

pleat

slash

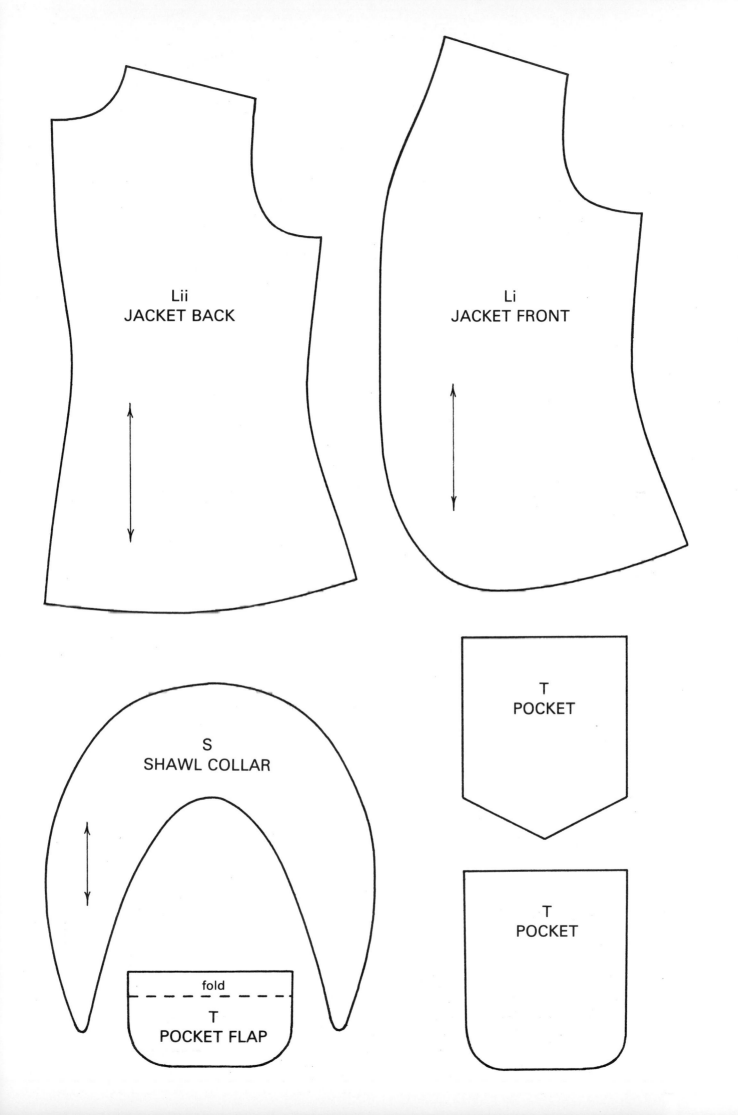

Lii
JACKET BACK

Li
JACKET FRONT

S
SHAWL COLLAR

T
POCKET

T
POCKET

fold

T
POCKET FLAP

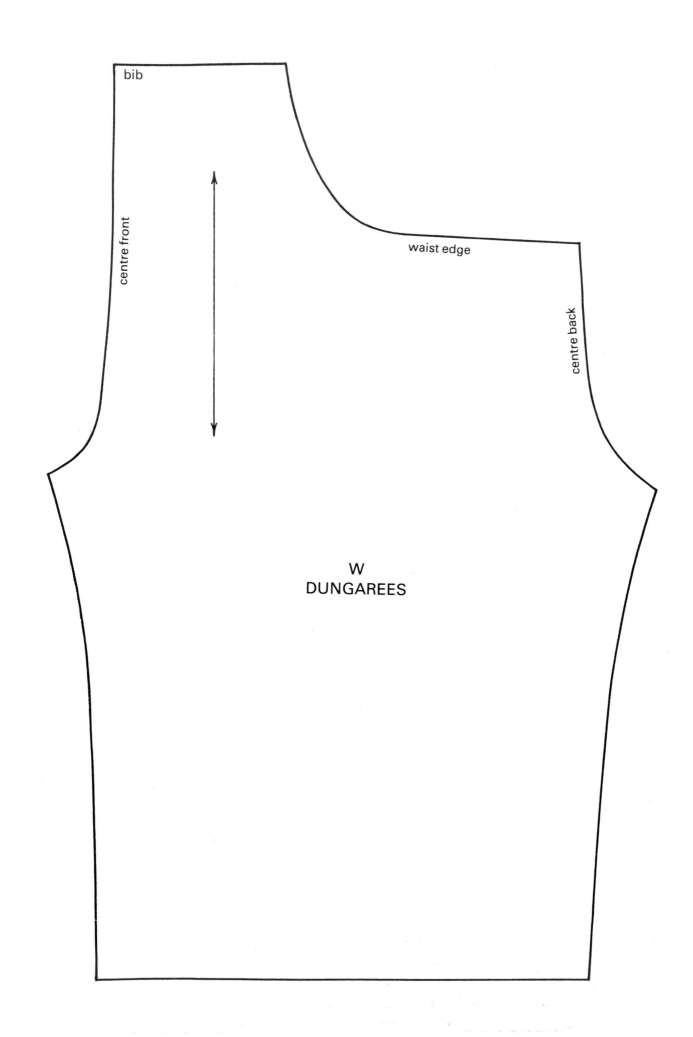

bib

centre front

waist edge

centre back

W
DUNGAREES

2 UNDERWEAR

Socks, stockings and tights

Several of the specialist stockists supply dolls' socks in a range of sizes in cotton or nylon, from the lacy cotton socks from Recollect, perfect for antique or reproduction dolls, to the simple nylon socks from Hello Dolly suitable for modern dolls. Hello Dolly also sell long cotton stockings in black or white, and Ridings Craft sell tubular-knitted nylon stocking material which is simply seamed across the foot to fit any size. This tubular material can also be used to make tights, or ready-made tights are available from Hello Dolly.

If you prefer to make your own, life-size socks provide the material. These may be white, coloured or patterned, and plain, ribbed or lacy, in cotton, nylon or wool. Choose material which complements the doll's clothes. For example, if the doll is wearing a sailor suit in navy blue wool, then navy blue wool socks will look good, of if the doll is wearing a pastel-coloured silk dress then lace stockings would look attractive.

To make socks or stockings, make use of the top edge for the doll-size version, and simply cut pieces large enough to fit the doll's leg, and stitch the centre-back seam and under the foot (see Fig 5a). Because of the stretchiness of the fabric, these simple 'bags' will mould themselves to the shape of the doll's leg. Consider also using children's vests and T-shirts in stretch-cotton in stripes or patterns. Narrow horizontal stripes in blue and white or red and white look very good on Victorian dolls.

Tights are made by cutting two legs – long enough to reach the waist – seaming the legs, then stitching the two legs together from back to front around the crotch (see Fig 5c). Make a casing at the top edge and thread elastic to fit the doll's waist. Coloured nylon 'pop socks' designed for adults make excellent tights for

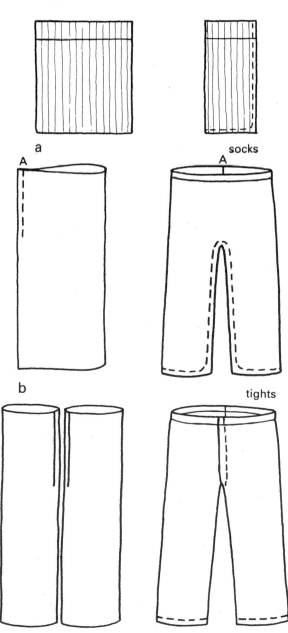

Fig 5 Socks and tights

dolls and are available in an enormous range of colours. For most dolls, one sock is wide enough to make tights; simply cut the material in two pieces for the legs and seam around them (see Fig 5b).

Socks may be dyed to match an outfit – for a small amount of 'dye' sufficient for socks, the colour tube from a felt-tipped pen dissolved in a cup of water works well and felt-tipped pens offer a wide range of colours. The socks might also be trimmed with coloured lace around the top edge.

If your doll needs suspenders to hold her stockings up, the petticoat-strap clips sold in haberdashery departments work well; or you could make elastic garters.

If you have an antique doll with skinny legs, two pairs of stockings will fatten them and make them look more attractive.

Knickers
(pattern piece A)

Knickers (Fig 6a) may be made in fabric to match the dress, particularly for toddler dolls, or in white cotton. The legs may be trimmed with lace or broderie anglaise. For Edwardian dolls, navy blue knickers are appropriate, especially with sailor suits.

To make the knickers, cut two pieces (reversing the pattern for the second piece). Hem the legs to make casings and add trimming if required. Thread elastic through the casings to fit the doll's legs and secure both ends. Stitch the leg seams, then seam the two legs together from front to back through the crotch. Turn a casing at the waist edge and thread elastic to fit the doll's waist.

Fitting notes Check that the pattern is large enough – knickers look better if they are full. Check that the back waist-to-crotch seam is long enough, especially if your doll has a big bottom.

Drawers
(pattern piece B)

The pattern is designed to be made with a waistband, cut to fit the doll's waist – if you prefer an elastic casing, lengthen the top edge to allow for it. The drawers may be made in any cotton fabric, but for antique or reproduction dolls, white cotton lawn is recommended. Make use of the fabric selvedge (if there is one) for the leg ends, and if you want pintucks, make them before cutting the drawers (see Fig 15). Leg ends may be trimmed with lace or broderie anglaise or ribbon through insertion, or may be made with casings for elastic or ribbon, or bands, with or without frills (see Fig 6). The opening may be made at centre back, simply by leaving the top inch or two of the back seam open, or at the side (or both sides) by slashing and hemming an opening as required.

To make the drawers, cut a waistband to fit the doll's

Plate 4
The 20in (51cm) doll on the left of the picture is a reproduction A. Marque from GP Ceramics. She wears a dropped-waist petticoat in white lawn trimmed with pintucks and cotton lace over matching drawers. Next to her is a 24in (61cm) reproduction AT11, also from GP Ceramics, wearing simple combinations in white lawn, trimmed with cotton lace and pink silk ribbons. Both dolls wear lacy cotton socks from Recollect.

The 25in (63.5cm) antique doll in the centre wears a buttoned liberty bodice in winceyette, trimmed with cotton tape, and drawers with pintucks and broderie anglaise frills and a pocket. Her stockings are made from tubular stocking material from Ridings Craft. The blonde doll on the right is a 20in (51cm) reproduction Bru from Recollect. She wears simple combinations trimmed with cotton lace edging and pink silk ribbons, and a waist petticoat with one tuck and lace edging to match the combinations. Her white lace stockings are made from a life-size stocking.

The small doll is a 14in (35.5cm) reproduction 'French girl' from Reflect Reproduction Dolls. Her A-line petticoat, trimmed with lace edging and a flower motif, is worn over matching drawers. Her white socks are made from a life-size sock. The baby doll is 14in (35.5cm) tall and was made from a kit from Hello Dolly. He wears a nappy, booties and an A-line petticoat trimmed with cotton lace and a silk ribbon bow.

a

b

c

d

e

f

waist. Cut two pieces (reversing the pattern for the second piece). Trim or make casings at the leg ends as required. Slash and hem a side-opening if required. Stitch the leg seams; then stitch the legs together from front to back through the crotch (leaving a back-opening if required). Gather the top edge, concentrating the fullness at the back, and stitch to the waistband. Fasten the waistband with a button and buttonhole or tape ties. Finish the leg ends as required.

Fitting notes Check that the waist-to-crotch seam is long enough at back and front, and that the inside leg is long enough (allow for trimmings). If the doll has a large waist, use the next size pattern and shorten if necessary.

Buttoned nappy
(*pattern piece CC*)

The nappy, designed for baby dolls, is given in small and medium sizes (enlarge as required). Make in towelling or winceyette – lined, hemmed or bound as you prefer. Towelling may be bound with bias binding, or lined with lawn; winceyette may be lined with lawn or hemmed.

To make the nappy, cut one piece (and one piece in the lining material if required). Hem or bind all the way around (or, with right sides facing, stitch to the lining, leaving a small gap – turn through, close the gap and press). Make two buttonholes on one side and one on the curved lower edge, as shown on the pattern. Stitch two buttons to the other side. Wrap around the doll; button the sides together; bring the lower edge up through the legs and button to the upper or lower button (Fig 7).

Fitting notes Check the waist measurement. Check the

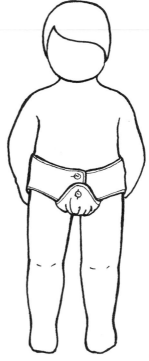

Fig 7 Buttoned nappy

length of the back waist through the crotch to the front.

Liberty bodice
(*pattern pieces front Ei and back Eii*)

Adapt front-opening bodice patterns by scooping out the neckline (see Fig 17). The liberty bodice is made in white or cream winceyette or flannelette, lined with lawn, bound with bias binding and buttoned at the front (see Fig 6c).

Fig 6 Underwear

View a Vest and knickers. The simple vest is made in stretch fabric adapting pattern pieces front *Di* and back *Eii*. The knickers are made from pattern piece *A* in light-weight cotton fabric. The waist and legs are elasticated, and the legs have narrow lace trimming.

View b Camisole and French knickers. The camisole is a band of fabric cut to fit loosely around the doll's body with a loop and button fastening at the centre back and ribbon shoulder straps. The French knickers are cut from the drawers pattern piece *B*, with the top lengthened to make a casing for elastic and the legs shortened. The camisole and French knickers are suitable for fine white or pastel-coloured fabrics, eg lawn or silk, trimmed with lace and tiny ribbon bows.

View c Liberty bodice and drawers. The

liberty bodice is cut from pattern pieces front *Ei* and back *Eii* with the neckline scooped out. Made in winceyette, lined with lawn, it buttons at the centre front. The drawers, cut from pattern piece *B*, have pintucks and broderie anglaise frills at the leg ends; the legs are stitched to a waistband opening at the centre back. The drawers are in white cotton lawn. Suitable for antique dolls circa 1900–20. (Shown in colour on page 35.)

View d Bloomers. Cut from the drawers pattern piece *B*, the bloomers have a slashed opening at one side and are stitched to a buttoned waistband. The legs are edged with broderie anglaise frills and elasticated. Suitable for white cotton lawn, or, omitting the frills, for navy blue winceyette. Suitable for antique dolls circa 1890–1920.

View e Chemise and drawers. The chemise is cut from pattern pieces front *Di* and

back *Eii* adapted to buttoned shoulder fastenings (see Fig 35) and A-line. It is cut to hip length, and the neckline, armholes and hem are edged with narrow lace. It fastens on the shoulders with tiny buttons and buttonholes. The drawers are cut from pattern piece *B* with slashed openings on both sides, gathered to a waistband which buttons at both sides. The leg ends are gathered to bands at the knee and have lace frills. Both chemise and drawers are in white cotton lawn. Suitable for antique dolls circa 1870–1900.

View f Combinations. Cut from pattern piece *C*, these simple combinations have a button front closure, narrow lace trimming at the neckline and armholes and (optional) pintucks and lace trimming at the leg ends. Made without trimming, in white or cream Viyella or winceyette, these combinations are suitable for boy or girl dolls – in white lawn they are suitable for girl or lady dolls – circa 1870–1910.

To make the liberty bodice cut one back and two fronts in winceyette and in lining. Stitch the shoulder and side seams. With right sides facing, stitch the fabric to the lining down the front edges and around the neckline; clip, turn through and press. Bind the armholes, and face the lower edge with bias binding. Make buttonholes and stitch buttons to the front edges. If required the liberty bodice may have white cotton tape bands stitched to the bodice front, over the shoulders and to the bodice back, and 'suspenders' stitched to the lower edges back and front.

Fitting notes Check the chest and waist measurements – the bodice should fit closely. Check the length.

Chemise
(pattern pieces front Di and back Eii)

Adapt both pattern pieces for buttoned shoulders and slight A-line, and cut as long as required. The chemise should be hip to mid-thigh length, made in white cotton lawn and trimmed with narrow lace (Fig 6e).

To make the chemise, stitch both side seams and hem the lower edge. Roll fine hems around the armholes, shoulders and neckline and whip on fine lace trimming. Make small buttonholes on the shoulder fronts and sew small buttons to the shoulder backs. Whip narrow lace trimming to the hem if required.

Fitting notes Check the chest measurement. Check that the garment will slip easily over the doll's head and shoulders (or up the body).

Combinations
Simple combinations *(pattern piece C)*

Combinations may be made in cotton fabrics, in winceyette or flannelette or in stretch-cotton T-shirt fabric in white or cream. Untrimmed they are suitable for boy dolls, trimmed with fine lace edging for girl or lady dolls. White cotton lawn is recommended for antique dolls. (Make pintucks before cutting out.)

To make the simple combinations (Fig 6f), cut two pieces (reversing the pattern for the second piece). Stitch the centre-back seam from neck to crotch. Stitch the centre-front seam from crotch to below the doll's stomach, turn back and hem the remainder of the front edges to form facings. Stitch the inside leg seam, from the leg end, through the crotch to the other leg end. Hem the leg ends, and add trimming if required. Roll fine hems around the armholes and neckline and add trimming if required (or face with bias binding). Work buttonholes and sew buttons to the front edges. If required, thread narrow silk ribbon through the neckline hem, pull up to fit and tie a bow.

Fitting notes Check the chest measurement. Check that the length from shoulder to crotch is sufficient at the back, especially if your doll has a big bottom. If necessary, lengthen the pattern by cutting at the

waistline and inserting the required amount.

To make more authentic combinations, use pattern pieces bodice front *Ei* and back *Eii* and drawers *B* with a waistband cut to fit the doll's waist (see Fig 8), in fabrics and trimmings as above.

To make the combinations, cut two waistbands to fit the doll's waist. Cut one back and two front bodice pieces and two drawers pieces. Stitch the centre-back seam in the drawers. Stitch the centre-front seam to a little below the doll's stomach, turn under the remainder and hem as facings. Stitch the inside leg seam – from leg end, through the crotch to the other leg end. Gather the top edge and stitch to one waistband. Stitch the bodice shoulder and side seams. Hem the front edges as facings. Stitch the bodice to the waistband. Hem the other waistband to the inside to

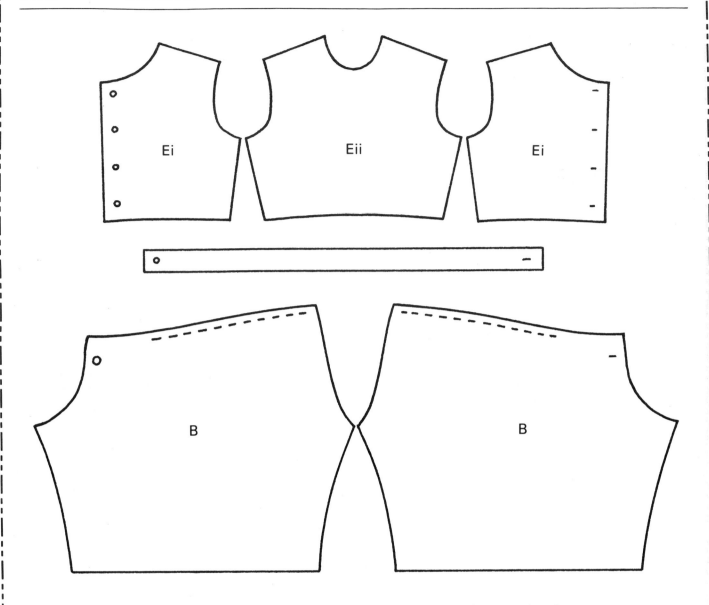

Fig 8 To make more authentic combinations, use patterns for bodice and drawers, in the relevant size

Fig 9 Petticoats

View a Simple waist petticoat with broderie anglaise at the hem and an elasticated waist casing. Made in a white cotton fabric trimmed with a tiny coloured ribbon bow.

View b Waist petticoat with a side (or back) buttoned waistband and a gathered skirt with a gathered frill at the hem. Made in cotton lawn in white or pastel colours, the petticoat can have a narrow lace trimming on the frill hem. Suitable (in white lawn) for antique dolls circa 1870–1920.

View c A-line petticoat with a back fastening (pattern pieces front *Vi* and back *Vii*) or buttoned shoulders (pattern pieces front *Di* and back *Eii*, adapted to A-line – see Fig 35). The neckline, armholes and hem are edged with narrow lace. Made in white cotton lawn. Shortened, this pattern makes a chemise. Suitable for antique dolls circa 1870–1920.

View d This full-length petticoat with a bodice cut from pattern pieces front *Di* and back *Dii* has a gathered skirt with pintucks and lace edging at the hem. Made in white cotton lawn. Suitable for antique dolls circa 1870–1920.

View e This A-line petticoat with a pintucked front, cut from pattern pieces front *Vi* and back *Vii*, has a back fastening and a lace trim at the hem. Made in white cotton lawn. Shortened, this pattern makes a chemise. Suitable for antique dolls circa 1870–1920.

View f This dropped-waist petticoat has a back-fastening bodice cut from pattern pieces front *Di* and back *Dii* adapted to A-line (see Fig 35) with lace trimming at the neckline and armholes. The gathered skirt has lace trimming at the hem. Made in white cotton lawn. Suitable for antique dolls circa 1880–1910.

a

b

c

d

e

f

cover the raw edges. Finish as for the simple combinations above. *Fitting notes* as above.

Petticoats (Fig 9)

Petticoats may be made in fabrics and trimmings to match the drawers, or in white cotton fabrics trimmed with broderie anglaise, lace or ribbon through insertion. White cotton lawn is recommended for antique dolls; other possibilities include white or cream Viyella or winceyette. Pintucks should be made before cutting out.

Waist Petticoat

To make a simple waist petticoat with elasticated waist (Fig 9a), measure the doll's waist and cut fabric 2–3 times this width and to the length required plus hem allowance (allow for any trimming at the hem). Stitch the centre-back seam, make a casing at the top edge and thread elastic to fit the doll's waist. Hem and trim the lower edge.

To make a petticoat with a waistband (Fig 9b), cut the waistband to fit the doll's waist. Cut the skirt 2–3 times as wide as the waistband and to the length required plus hem allowance (allow for any trimming). Stitch the centre-back seam to 2in (5cm) below the waist and turn back the remainder as facings. Gather the top edge evenly and stitch to the waistband. Hem and trim the lower edge and fasten the waistband with a button and buttonhole or loop and button. *Fitting notes* Check the finished length and the fullness (the petticoat should be slightly less full than the dress).

Full-length petticoat

For a petticoat with a bodice, use pattern pieces front *Di* and back *Dii*, with the neckline scooped out as required (see Fig 17). Fabrics and trimmings are as above. Make up the skirt as described above, omitting the waistband. Stitch the bodice backs to the front at the shoulder and side seams. Roll fine hems around the neckline and armholes (or face with bias binding) and trim with whipped-on lace if required. Gather the skirt to fit the bodice, and stitch. Turn under and hem the back edges as facings on the bodice and upper part of the skirt. Fasten the back bodice with buttons and buttonholes or loops or press-studs.

For a dropped-waist petticoat, use the pattern and instructions as above; simply adapt the bodice pattern to a slight A-line (see Fig 35), and lengthen as required. *Fitting notes* Check the chest measurement, the finished back length and the fullness of the skirt (the petticoat skirt should be slightly less full than the dress).

A-line petticoat

An A-line petticoat with buttoned shoulders may be made in exactly the same way as the chemise (above) – simply cut longer.

For a petticoat with a back opening use pattern pieces front *Di* and back *Dii* – adapted to A-line (see Fig 35). The front may be pintucked before cutting out to give added fullness. Fabrics and trimmings are as above.

To make the A-line petticoat with a back opening, cut one front and two back pieces. Stitch the shoulder and side seams. Roll fine hems around the armholes and neckline (or face with bias binding) and trim if required. Stitch the centre-back seam up to just above the doll's waist, turn back the remainder of the back edges and hem as facings. Hem and trim the lower edge. Fasten the back with loops and buttons.
Fitting notes Check the chest measurement, the finished length and the fullness of the skirt (the petticoat should be slightly less full than the dress).

Frills

For petticoat frills in self fabric, allow 1¼–1½ times the width of the skirt. For broderie anglaise or lace frills, allow 1¼ times the width of the skirt. When measuring/checking the finished length, allow for the frills. To gather frills – in fabric, broderie anglaise or lace – use two threads ½in (1.2cm) apart; pull up, spreading the gathers evenly and stitch to the skirt between the gathering threads. Remove the threads. Neaten by machine stitching the seam several times and trimming; or by zigzag or blanket stitching or binding with bias binding.

Lace frills may be whipped on by hand, or machine stitched, by placing the frill – right sides facing – upside down, above the hemline, and stitching in place. The hem is then turned up behind the frill.

Consider trimming underwear with tiny ribbon bows or flower motifs (see 'Trimmings' above).

Padded petticoat

If the doll is to wear a full-length crinoline-style skirt, eg on a ball gown, the petticoat may be made with a padded hem which will support the skirt. Cut the petticoat long enough to make a very deep hem (2–4in/5–10cm) and cut a strip of Terylene wadding the same width as the hem and long enough to go around the bottom edge of the petticoat. Turn up, pin and press the hem. Slip the strip of wadding inside the hem; then stitch the hem in place. This padded petticoat will make an effective crinoline, supporting the skirt in a bell shape, without extra weight or bulk at the waist. (Terylene wadding – sold for lining tea cosies – can be bought in haberdashery departments.) See also 'Bustle pad and bust improver' in Chapter 11.

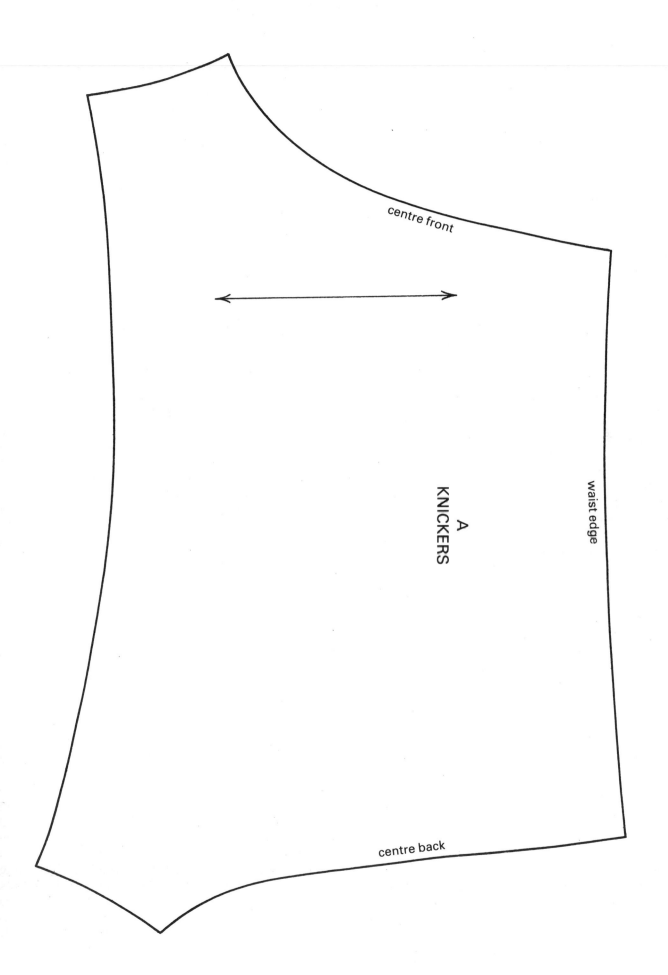

centre front

waist edge

A
KNICKERS

centre back

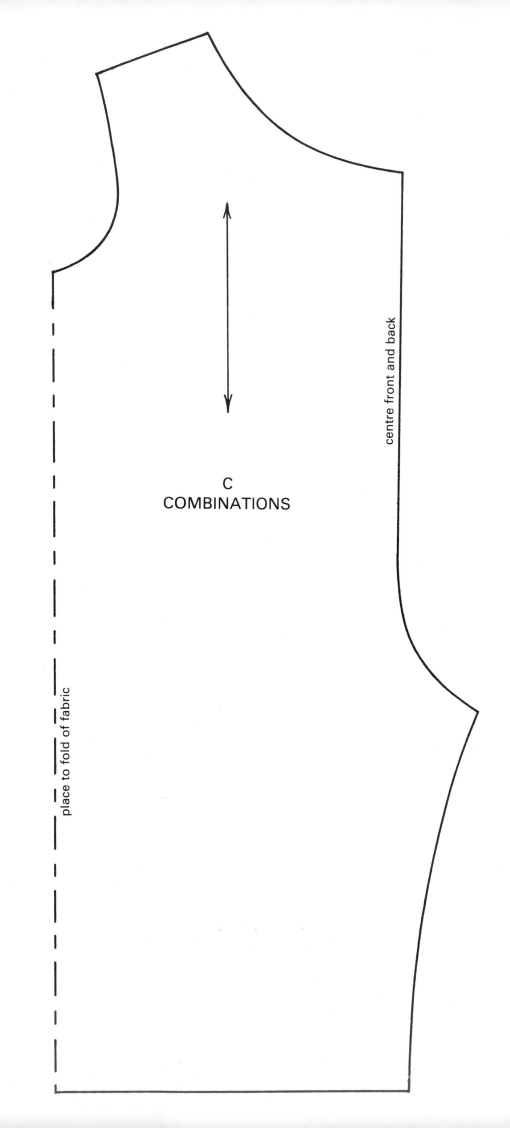

C
COMBINATIONS

centre front and back

place to fold of fabric

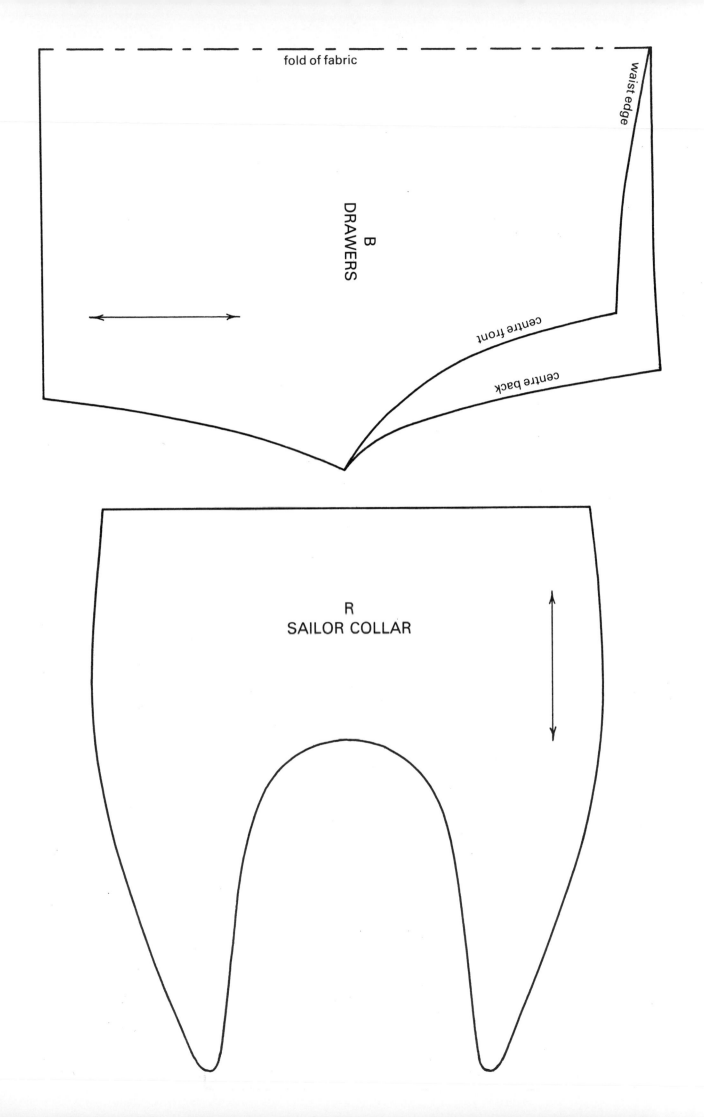

fold of fabric

waist edge

B
DRAWERS

centre front

centre back

R
SAILOR COLLAR

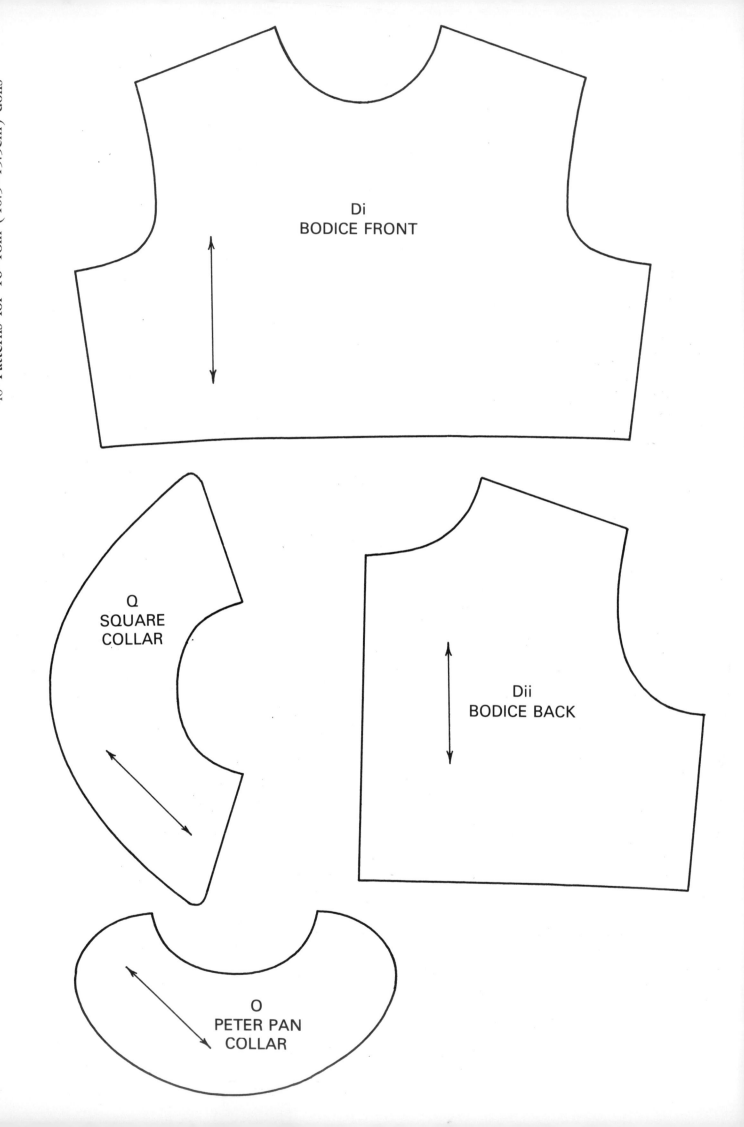

Di
BODICE FRONT

Q
SQUARE
COLLAR

Dii
BODICE BACK

O
PETER PAN
COLLAR

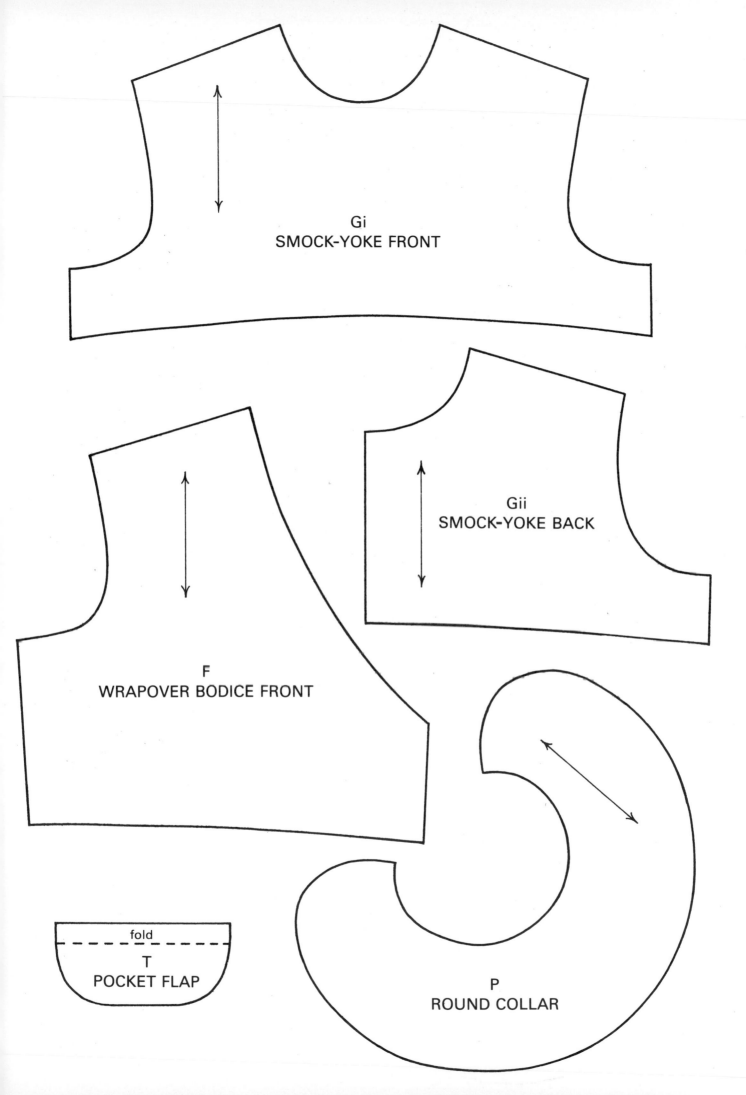

Gi
SMOCK-YOKE FRONT

Gii
SMOCK-YOKE BACK

F
WRAPOVER BODICE FRONT

fold

T
POCKET FLAP

P
ROUND COLLAR

I
STRAIGHT SLEEVE

ease

U
CUFF

wrist edge

gather

J
FULL SLEEVE

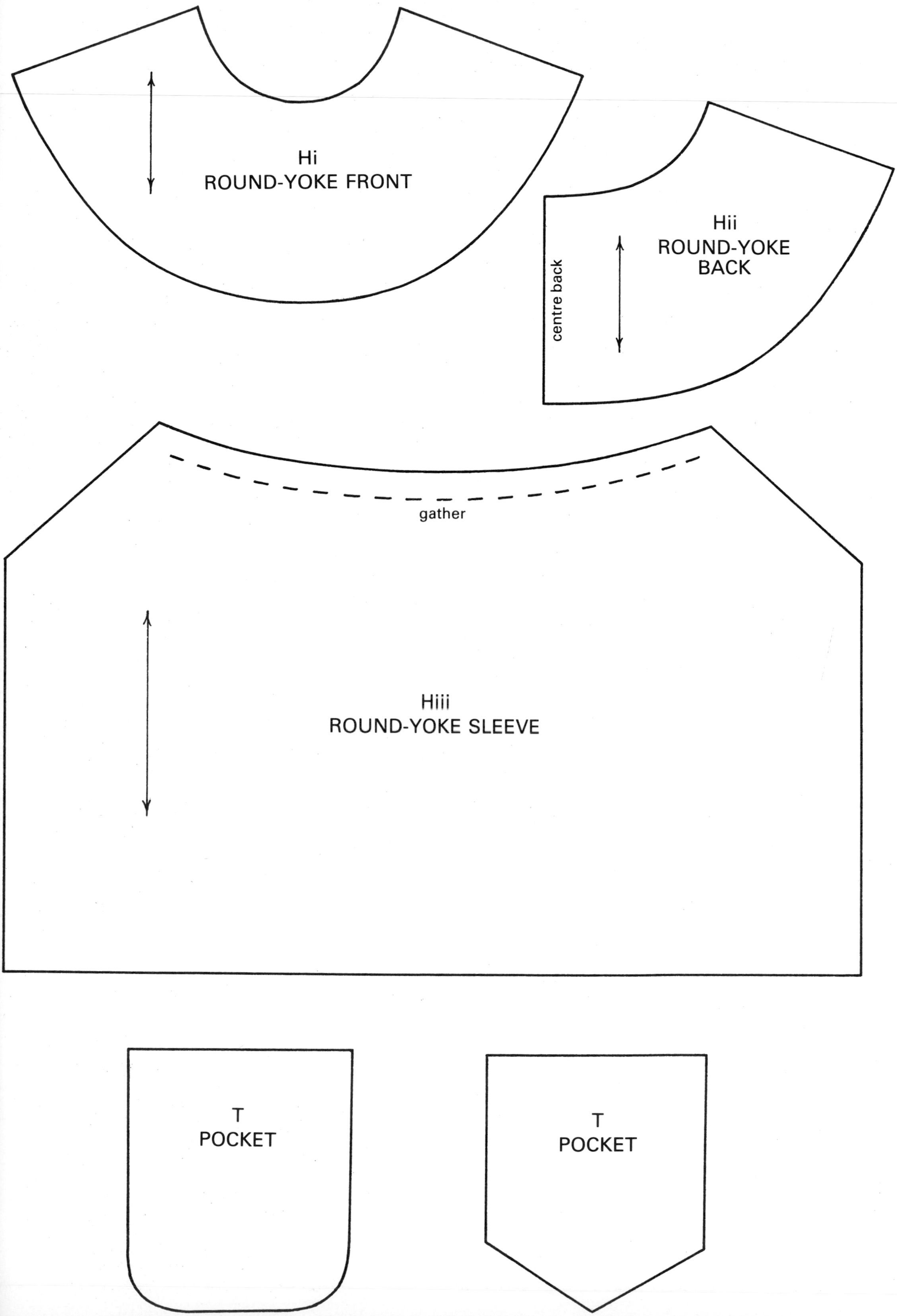

Hi
ROUND-YOKE FRONT

Hii
ROUND-YOKE
BACK

centre back

gather

Hiii
ROUND-YOKE SLEEVE

T
POCKET

T
POCKET

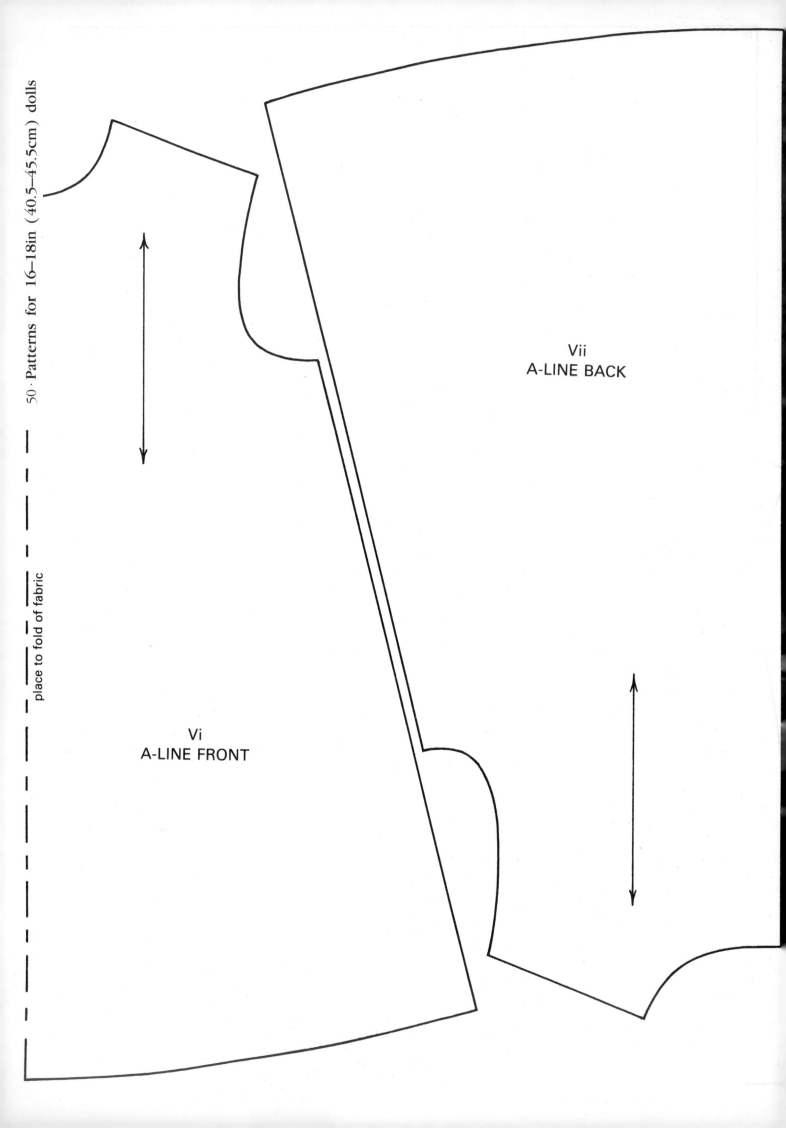

place to fold of fabric

Vi
A-LINE FRONT

Vii
A-LINE BACK

51 · Patterns for 16–18in (40.5–45.5cm) dolls

A
A
gather
Niii
FRENCH DRESS PLASTRON
gather
B
B
B
Ni
FRENCH DRESS
FRONT
A
Nii
FRENCH DRESS BACK

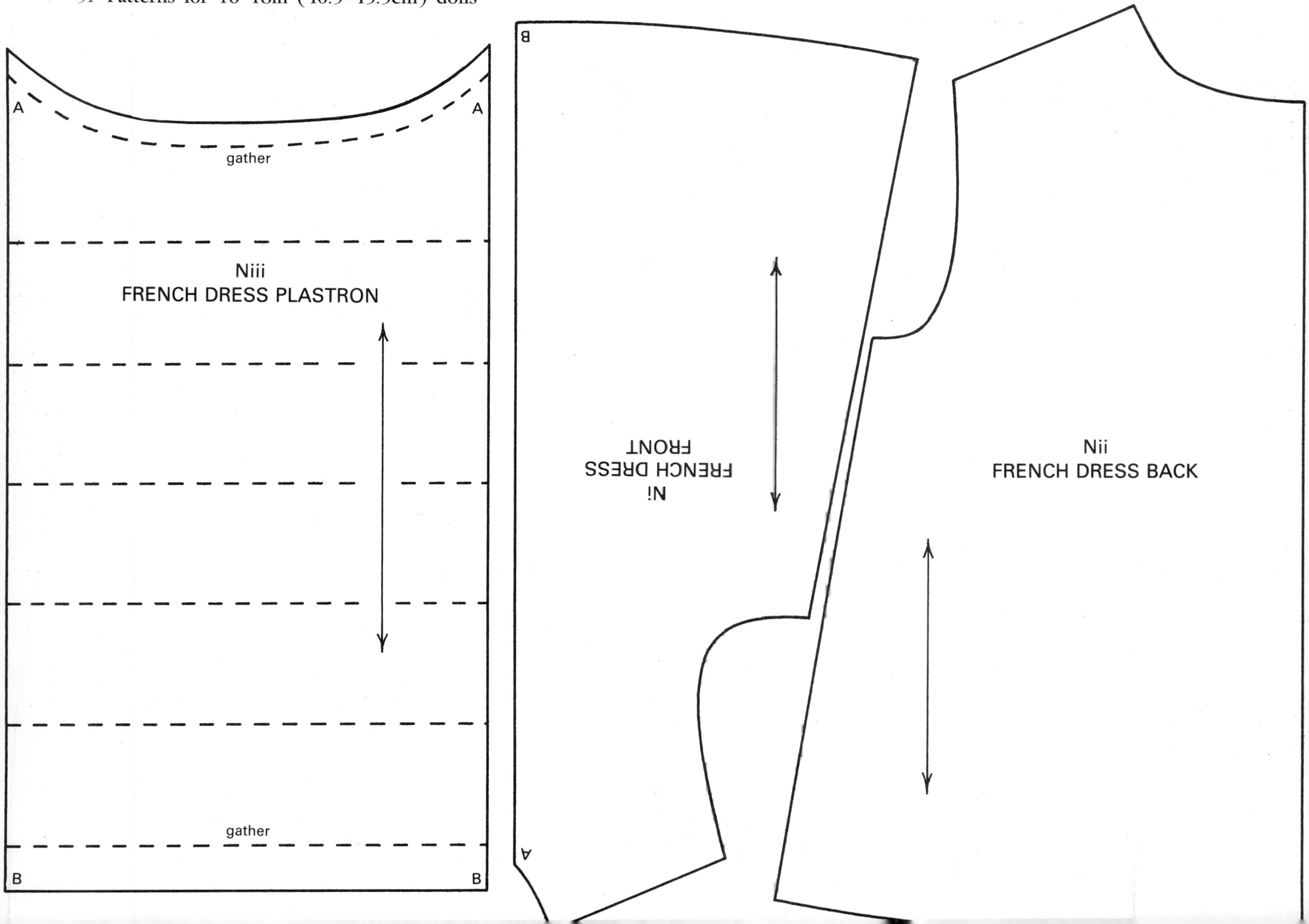

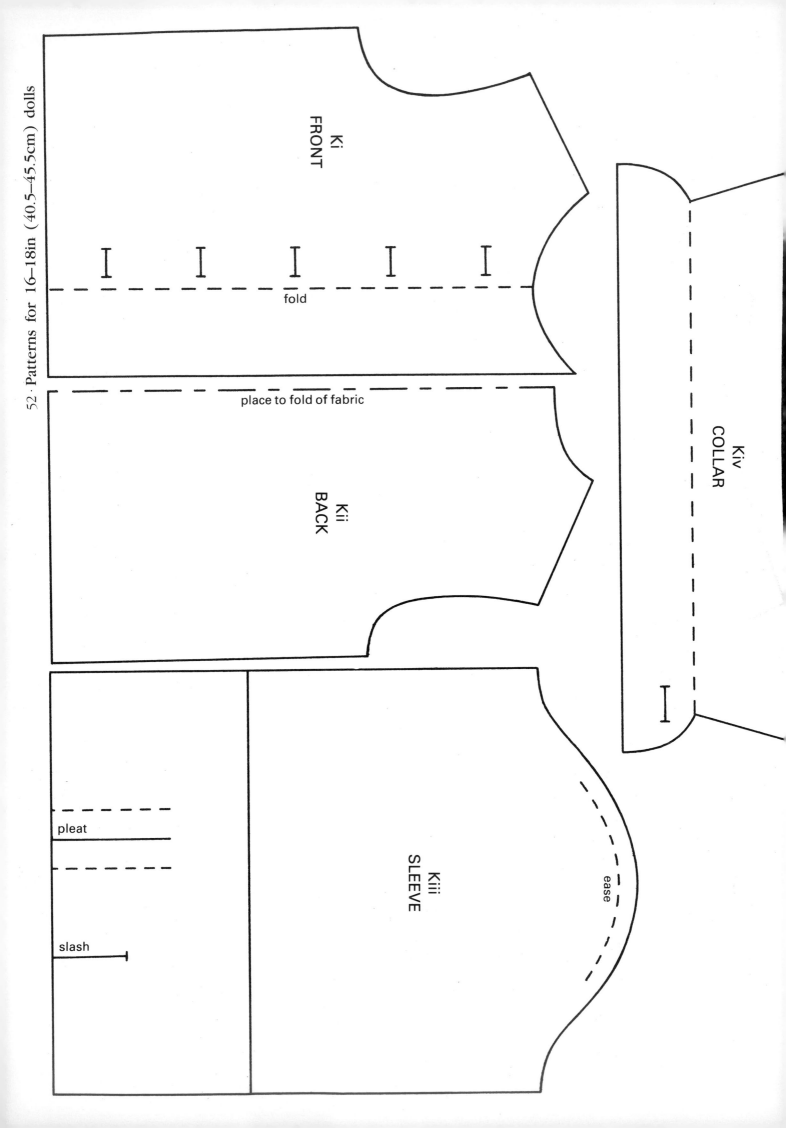

Ki
FRONT

fold

place to fold of fabric

Kii
BACK

Kiv
COLLAR

pleat

Kiii
SLEEVE

ease

slash

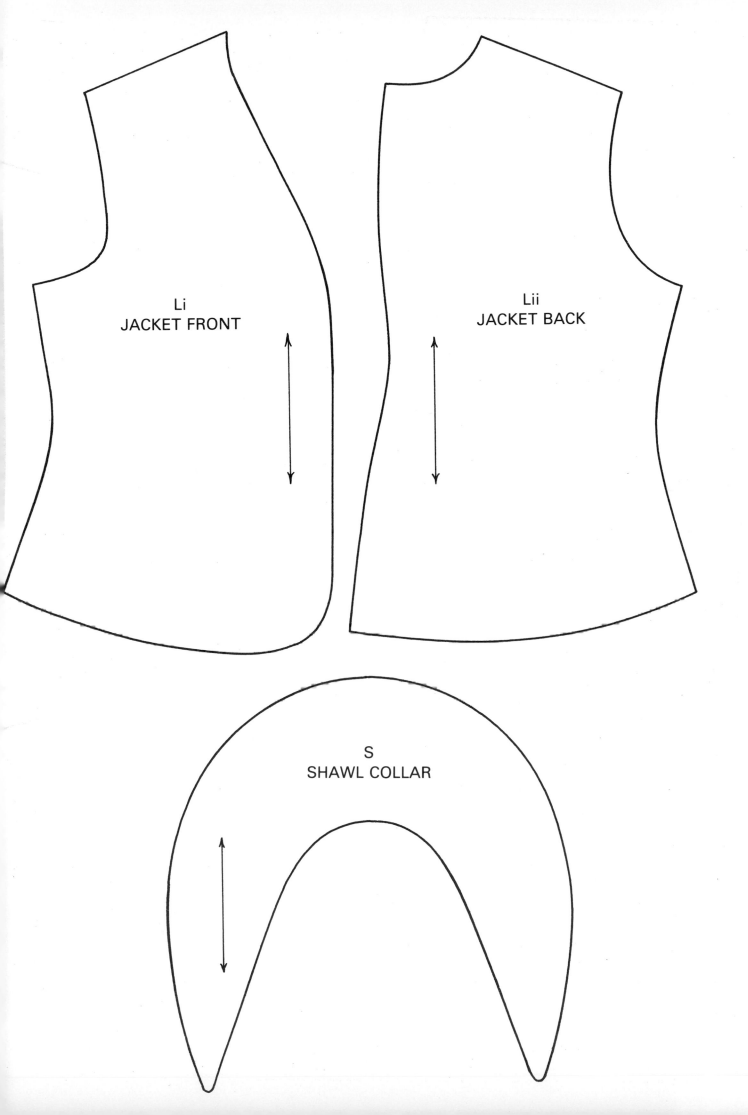

Li
JACKET FRONT

Lii
JACKET BACK

S
SHAWL COLLAR

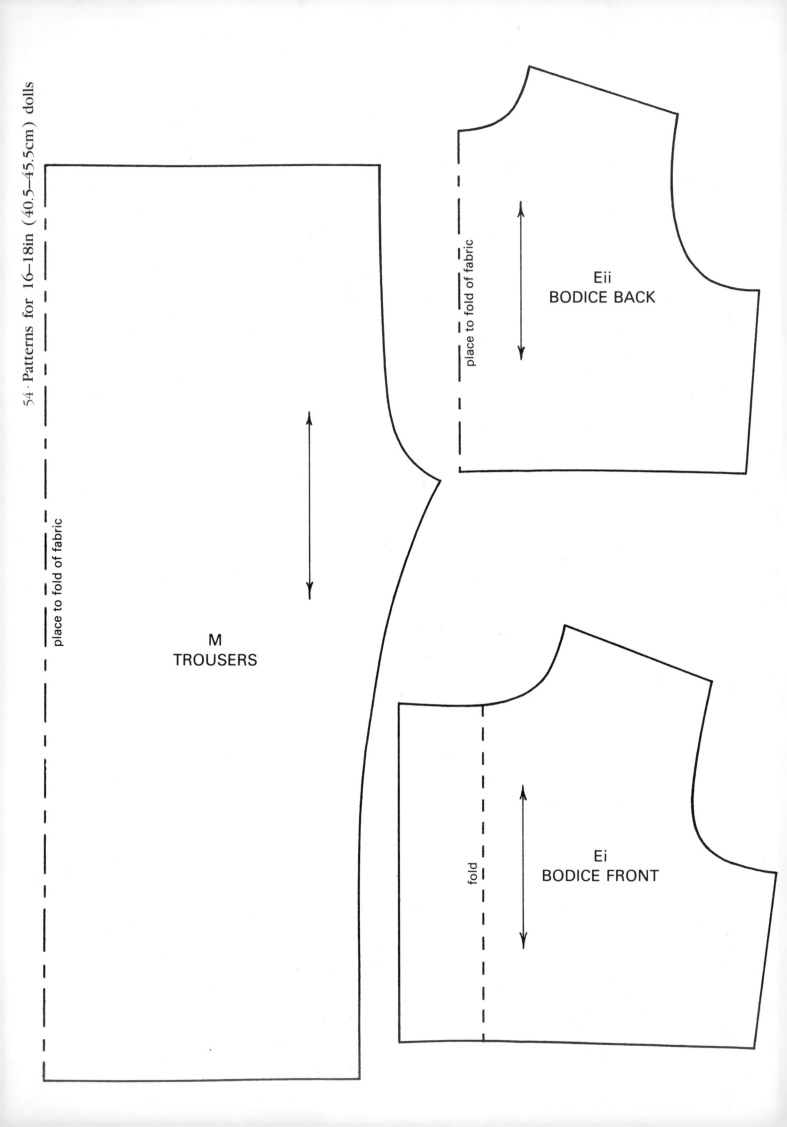

place to fold of fabric

M
TROUSERS

place to fold of fabric

Eii
BODICE BACK

fold

Ei
BODICE FRONT

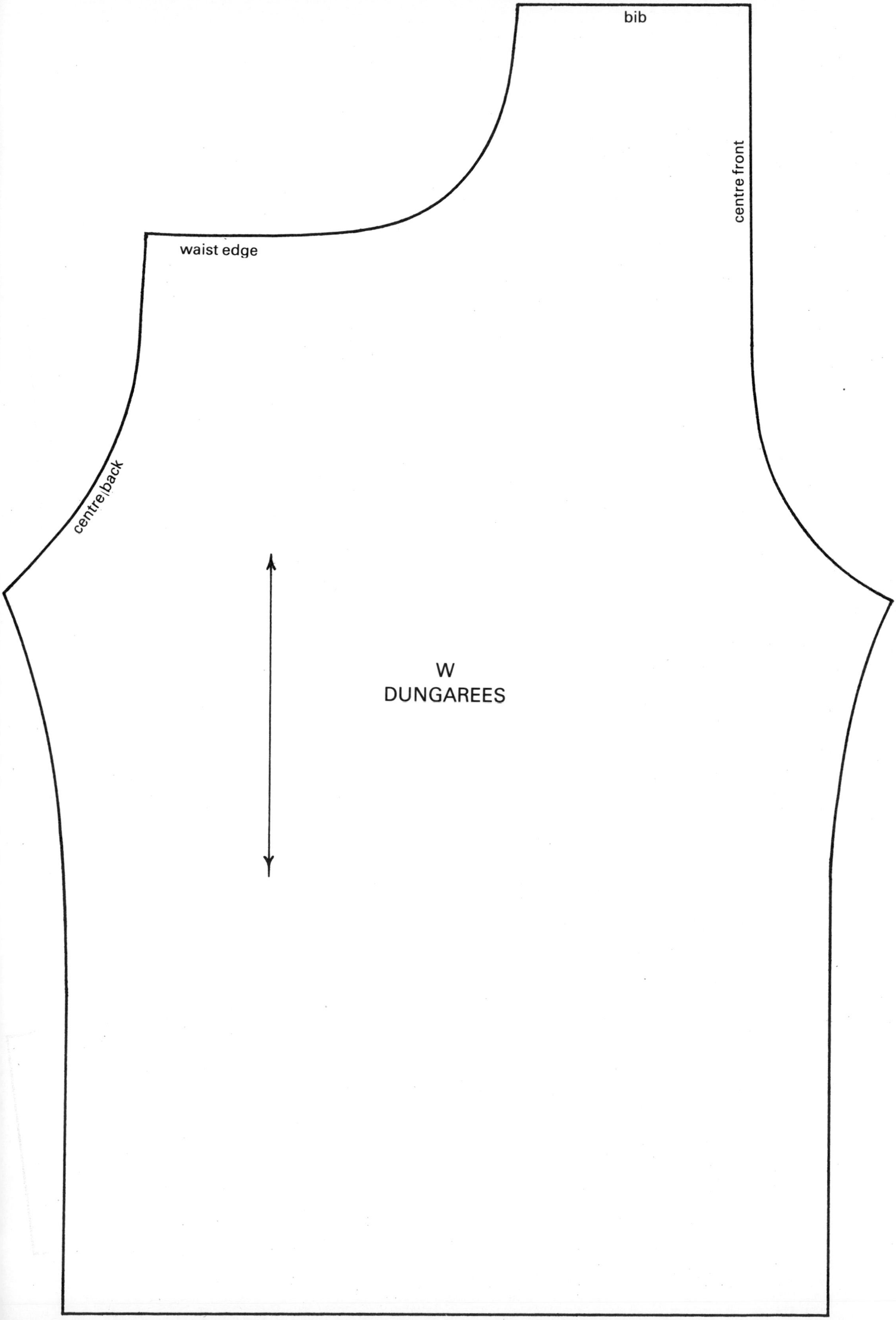

bib

centre front

waist edge

centre back

W
DUNGAREES

3 DRESSES

Simple dresses without patterns

Dolls' dresses may be made without patterns, simply by measuring the doll and cutting and gathering rectangles of fabric to fit. The sundress in Fig 10a is made by measuring the doll from chest to hem plus hem allowances and cutting a piece of fabric this length and 2½–3 times as wide. The top edge is finished with a small hem; then gathering lines are marked on the fabric with a ruler. The fabric is gathered with shirring elastic (this can be done on the sewing machine) to fit the doll's chest. The back edges are seamed together, and the lower edge is hemmed. The shoulder ties may be made from dress fabric or ribbon, stitched inside the bodice front and back at both sides and tied on the shoulders. Even more

simply, the dress may be made from ready-shirred cotton fabrics. Patch pockets might be added to the skirt.

The sundress or pinafore dress in Fig 10c is made by measuring the doll's chest and cutting a band (like a skirt waistband) to fit. The skirt is a rectangle of which one dimension is 2½ times the length of the band and the other is the required length of the dress plus hem allowance; this is gathered to fit the band. The centre-back seam is left open for 2in (5cm) below the band. Shoulder straps are stitched to the band at the back and fastened with buttons and buttonholes or press studs at the front.

Fitting notes If the dress is to be worn as a pinafore dress, measure the doll over the garment worn underneath.

Fig 10 Simple clothes for child and toddler dolls

View a Sundress made without a pattern. A rectangle of fabric, seamed at the centre back and shirred to fit the body has self-fabric or ribbon shoulder ties. Suitable for lightweight cotton fabrics or ready-shirred cotton. (Shown in colour on page 63.)

View b Rompers, adapted from drawers pattern piece B, lengthened at the waist and leg ends, shirred to fit the body and gathered into bands or frills at the ankles. Self-fabric or ribbon ties on the shoulders. Suitable for lightweight cotton fabrics.

View c Sundress made without a pattern. A rectangle of fabric is gathered to a deep band cut to fit the body and fastened at the centre back. Self-fabric straps button over the shoulders. Suitable for lightweight cotton fabrics.

View d Dungarees adapted from drawers pattern piece B, lengthened at the waist and leg ends, gathered to a deep band cut to fit the body and fastened at the centre back. Self-fabric straps button over the shoulders. Suitable for light- or medium-weight fabrics, eg cotton or needlecord. Worn over a blouse in a toning print fabric, eg cotton or Viyella.

View e Bibbed skirt, pattern piece AA, fastened with self-fabric straps crossed over from the back waist to button on the bib front. Suitable for medium-weight fabrics, eg denim or needlecord. Worn over a blouse in a toning print fabric, eg cotton or Viyella. Add pockets (pattern piece T) if required.

View f Dungarees, pattern piece W, fastened with self-fabric straps crossed over from the back waist to button on the bib front. Suitable for medium-weight fabrics, eg needlecord, denim or velveteen. Worn over a shirt in a lightweight fabric, eg cotton or Viyella. Add pockets (pattern piece T) if required. (Shown in colour on page 15.)

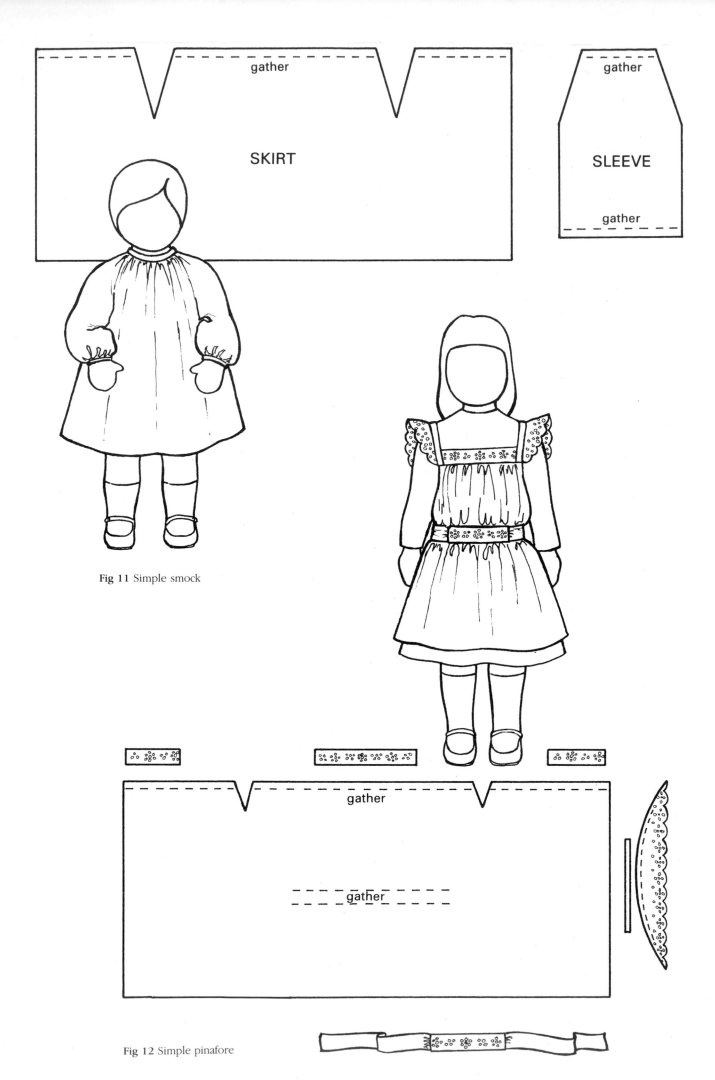

gather

SKIRT

SLEEVE

gather

gather

Fig 11 Simple smock

gather

gather

Fig 12 Simple pinafore

Smock dresses may be made by measuring the doll from neck to hem plus hem allowance and cutting a rectangle of fabric this length and 3 times as wide. Fold the fabric in half – then half again and mark. Then cut V shapes for the armholes at these marks (see Fig 11). For the sleeves, measure the doll's arm length from neck to wrist plus hem allowance and cut rectangles this length and wide enough to fit around the doll's arm (or fuller if you prefer). Cut wedge shapes from the top ends of the sleeves to correspond with the armholes. Stitch the sleeve seams, then stitch the sleeves into the armholes. Gather all around the top edge (with two threads) and pull up to fit the doll's neck. Stitch the back seam up to about 2in (5cm) below the neckline (check the size of the doll's head); then turn back the remainder of the back edges and hem as facings. Bind the neckline with bias binding or bias-cut dress fabric. Hem the sleeve ends. Full sleeves can be gathered with shirring elastic to make frills. Fasten the back with loops and buttons. Turn up the lower edge and hem. This dress is particularly good for baby dolls and looks very attractive with matching knickers or as an angel top over tights.

Simple pinafores may be made in much the same way as the dress above, omitting the sleeves (see Fig 12). Measure the doll from chest to hem, plus hem allowance, and cut a rectangle of fabric this length and 2½ times as wide. Cut out shallow armholes and roll hems around them. Hem the back edges and gather the top edges to fit the doll. Bind the gathered edges with bias binding. The yoke may be made of the type of broderie anglaise trimming that consists of a flat band with a frill along one side. Working on the doll, fold and pin the trimming to make a square yoke with four mitred corners. Cut off the excess, hem the back edges and stitch the corners. Stitch the yoke front to the bound edge of the skirt front and the back yoke pieces to the back skirt pieces. Fasten the back yoke with loops and buttons and hem the lower edge. The pinafore might have a frill of broderie anglaise to match the yoke. As an alternative, the yoke might be made of straight pieces of broderie anglaise stitched to the bound skirt edges, with gathered shoulder frills of broderie anglaise with bound edges stitched to either side at back and front. The waistline of the pinafore might be gathered at the front and trimmed with a flat band of broderie anglaise and sashes which tie in a bow at the back (see Fig 12). This type of pinafore was very popular on antique dolls, and looks very authentic if you use old broderie anglaise and white cotton lawn.

Dress bodices

All the dress bodice patterns are designed to be made up with linings. This is because lining the bodice is much simpler than hemming, binding or facing the edges and also because it gives the dress more 'body' so that it fits, and looks, better. The linings should be cut in a lighter-weight fabric than the bodice – cotton lawn is an excellent lining for most fabrics, or perhaps silk for silk and brocade fabrics. Lace dresses should be lined with net. The same patterns are used for both bodice and bodice lining. Where a stiff bodice is required, for example on an evening gown, an interlining of unbleached calico is used, working the lining and interlining as one piece.

If the bodice is to have pleats or pintucks, these are made before the pattern is cut out. Cut a piece of fabric rather larger than the bodice pattern, squarely on the grain. Mark, tack and stitch pleats or pintucks as required. Square the pattern piece carefully over the worked fabric and cut out the piece (see Fig 15). (Linings and interlinings are cut without tucks or pleats.)

Back-opening bodice
(*pattern pieces front Di and back Dii*)

Cut one bodice front and two back pieces in fabric and in lining. Stitch the shoulder seams on the fabric and the lining. With right sides facing, stitch the bodice to the lining up the back edges and around the neckline; clip, turn through and press. If the bodice is to have a bound neckline, omit the stitching around the neckline; simply sew the back edges, turn through, press, and then bind the neckline with bias-cut strip. A bound neckline looks particularly attractive with a pintucked bodice. This method is also used if the neckline is to have a band collar, which is made in the same way but cut wider than binding and on the straight grain of the fabric.

From this point on, the fabric and lining are worked as one piece. They can be stitched together all the way around the outside edge, which makes them easier to work with.

The sleeves (see 'Sleeves') are sewn into the armholes while the bodice is still a flat piece, which is much easier than setting them after the side seams are stitched. The side seams are sewn from the bodice edge through the armhole and down the sleeve all in one.

Front-opening bodice
(*pattern pieces front Ei and back Eii*)

Cut one bodice back and two front pieces in fabric and in lining. Use the selvedge (if there is one) for the front edges. Stitch the shoulder seams on the fabric and the lining. With right sides facing, stitch the fabric to the lining around the neckline, clip, turn through and press. From this point on, the fabric and lining are worked as one piece and may be stitched together all the way round. The sleeves are sewn in and the side seams stitched as above.

When the skirt is stitched to the waistline, (see 'Skirts'), the front edges of the bodice (and the top of the skirt) are turned under to form facings and hemmed to the lining.

a

b

c

d

e

f

Wrapover bodice
(pattern pieces front F and back Eii)

Cut one bodice back and two front pieces in fabric and in lining. Stitch the shoulder seams on the fabric and the lining. With right sides facing, stitch the fabric to the lining up both fronts and around the neckline, clip, turn through and press. Do not stitch the two layers together around the outside edge. Sleeves are sewn to the armholes of the fabric only. Stitch the side and sleeve seams in the fabric, and the side seam in the lining separately. This leaves the lining loose at the waistline, so that it can be hemmed over the seam to neaten when the skirt is stitched to the bodice.

Smock yoke
(pattern pieces front Gi and back Gii)

The smock yoke is made up in exactly the same way as the back-opening bodice.

Fitting notes for all bodices Check the chest measurements. Check that the back/front closure overlaps sufficiently. Check that the neckline is not too large or small – a lined neckline will be larger, a bound neckline smaller than the pattern toile. Check that the bodice is the correct length for the proposed costume, (allow for the waist seam) and shorten or lengthen as required. Check that sufficient allowance is made for side seams. Check that the armholes are deep enough. For lady dolls with slim waists, you may wish to make small darts on the front bodice. Mark the placement on the pattern toile and make darts in both fabric and lining.

Sleeveless bodice

If the bodice is to be made without sleeves, eg for a pinafore dress, stitch the bodice side seams, then bind or face the armholes with bias binding or bias-cut dress fabric, hemmed to the bodice lining.

Adapting bodice patterns
Necklines

To change the shape of the bodice neckline to scooped, square, V-shaped or heart-shaped (see Fig 17) simply fold the front-bodice pattern toile in half (so that both sides match) and cut the new neckline. Match the front to back toiles, and trim the back neckline to meet at the shoulder. Check the pattern toiles on the doll before cutting the fabric.

Waistlines

To make a higher waistline, simply trim the bottom edges of the bodice patterns.

To make a dropped waistline, lengthen the patterns, extending the sides in a slight A-line.

To make a dress with a V-shaped front waistline, make the bodice and skirt separately. Adapt the front pattern toile as shown in Fig 20. Make up the bodice as described and face the lower edge with bias binding. Make up the skirt and bind the waist with bias binding. Stitch small hooks to the inside lower edge of the bodice at the side seams, and small loops to the skirt waist to correspond. Put the skirt onto the doll and fasten. Put the bodice onto the doll, hook it onto the skirt, and fasten. (Use bodice patterns *Di* and *Dii*.)

Fig 13 Waisted, back-opening dresses using bodice pattern pieces front *Di* and back *Dii*

View a Dress and pinafore in cotton or Viyella-type fabrics. The dress has a Peter Pan collar (pattern piece *O*) and short puffed sleeves (pattern piece *J*) gathered into frills. The skirt is gathered to the waistline. The pinafore is sleeveless with a scooped neckline and patch pockets (pattern piece *T*) and the gathered skirt is cut shorter than the dress. The dress and pinafore can be in contrasting or toning print and plain fabrics, eg print dress/plain pinafore, or plain dress/print pinafore; or contrasting plain colours, eg navy dress with scarlet pinafore or brown dress with cream pinafore. (Shown in colour on page 15.)

View b Dress with bound neckline and long, full sleeves (pattern piece *J*) gathered into frills. The gathered skirt has a frill at the hem and the bodice has a square frill, both outlined with narrow ribbon. Matching wide ribbon sash. Suitable for all lightweight cotton or silk-type fabrics in plain colours or tiny prints. Ribbon trimmings to tone or contrast, eg pale-pink lawn trimmed with darker-pink ribbons, or a flower-print cotton trimmed with ribbons in the main colour of the print.

View c This dress in cotton or Viyella-type fabrics has a Peter Pan collar (pattern piece *O*), long plain sleeves (pattern piece *I*) and a pintucked bodice. The gathered skirt has a frill at the hem. Collar, bodice, sleeve ends and skirt are trimmed with narrow lace edging. The sash is self-fabric. Suitable for plain colours or tiny prints, eg plain grey or blue with white lace trimmings, or a muted pastel print with cream lace. Tiny buttons may be placed down the centre front of the bodice. (Shown in colour on page 15.)

View d This dress in crisp cotton fabrics has a Peter Pan collar (pattern piece *O*) and short puffed sleeves (pattern piece *J*) with cuffs. The gathered skirt has pintucks at the hem and two patch pockets (pattern piece *T*). The collar, cuffs and pockets are trimmed with narrow lace edging. The sash or belt is self-fabric. Suitable for gingham, plain colours or small prints, eg brown gingham with a white collar and white lace edging, or red and white spots with a white collar and lace edging. Suitable for antique German character-dolls.

View e This dress in lightweight soft fabrics, eg lawn or silk, has a band collar and pintucked bodice. The 'regency' sleeves have gathered puffs at the top (pattern piece *J*) with tight lower sleeves (pattern piece *I*), pintucked at the wrists. The gathered skirt is full length. The neckline, bodice front and sleeve ends are trimmed with narrow lace, and the sash is ribbon or self-fabric. Tiny buttons down the centre front are optional. Best in plain fabrics (to show the pintucks) in soft colours, eg pink, pale blue, sea green, coffee etc. The sash looks good one shade darker, or contrasting, eg a coffee dress with a brown satin-ribbon sash.

View f This dress in soft heavy fabrics, eg velvet or needlecord, has long plain sleeves (pattern piece *I*) and a full-length gathered skirt. The round collar and cuffs are made from old lace or crochet doilies or table mats. Best in rich, dark, plain colours, eg crimson, dark brown, blue, or dark green with cream or white lace trimmings. (See page 15.)

a   b   c

Fig 14 Dresses for lady dolls using bodice pattern pieces front *Di* and back *Dii* adapted to a scooped neckline (see Fig 17)

View a This dress with a scooped neckline edged with self-fabric or lace frill has a full-length gathered skirt and elbow-length full sleeves (pattern piece *J*) gathered into self-fabric or lace frills. A wide satin-ribbon sash and artificial flower trim the waist. Suitable for light-weight fabrics in pastel or subtle colours with a toning colour for the sash, eg a pale-pink lawn dress with self-fabric frills and a darker-pink sash and flower; or a pale-grey silk dress with grey lace frills and a grey sash with a pink flower.

View b This dress with a scooped neckline, elbow-length straight sleeves and a full-length flared skirt is trimmed with narrow lace edging at the neckline and sleeve ends and ribbon bows on the shoulders. Suitable for elaborate fabrics in light or medium weight, eg satin, heavy silk or brocade, in rich colours, eg black satin and sequins trimmed with black lace and black satin-ribbon bows, or white and gold patterned brocade with white lace and bows. Suitable for lady dolls circa 1900–10. (Shown in colour on page 187.)

View c This dress with a scooped neckline and high waistline has a full-length gathered skirt and 'regency' sleeves (pattern pieces *I* and *J*). The neckline and sleeve ends are edged with narrow lace and a self-fabric or ribbon sash ties at the back. Suitable for lightweight fabrics in plain colours or prints, eg a white dotted-swiss dress trimmed with white lace and a cherry-coloured ribbon sash, or flower-print cotton dress in blues and greens with ivory lace and a self-fabric sash.

Plate 6
The 20in (51cm) doll in the centre of the picture is a reproduction Kestner from Recollect. She wears a white cotton lawn pinafore with yoke, waistband and shoulder frills made from old broderie anglaise.

The Sasha boy and girl dolls are 16in (40.5cm) tall. The boy wears a simple T-shirt in blue and white striped stretch-cotton made from a baby's vest and blue denim shorts. His straw hat, socks and sandals are from Sasha. The girl wears a simple sundress in pink cotton with a shirred bodice and shoulder ties. Her wreath is made of artificial flowers, her basket is from GP Ceramics and her socks and shoes are from Sasha.

The baby doll is a 15in (38cm) reproduction 'Baby Gloria' from Recollect. She wears a round-yoke dress in cream silk crêpe trimmed with lace and flower motifs and a matching bonnet.

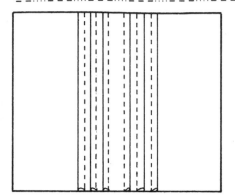
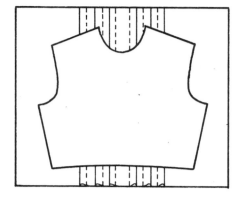

Fig 15 Making pintucks before cutting out

Fig 16 Waisted, back-opening dresses using bodice pattern pieces front *Di* and back *Dii*

View a Dress in light cotton fabrics with a Peter Pan collar (pattern piece *O*), short puffed sleeves (pattern piece *J*) with cuffs, and a pintucked bodice. The gathered skirt has patch pockets. The collar, cuffs, bodice front and pockets are trimmed with scalloped trimming. The bodice can have tiny buttons down the centre front. Best in plain colours (to show the pintucks), eg denim blue with white trimming, or brown with cream trimming.

View b This dress designed for broderie anglaise has a Peter Pan collar (pattern piece *O*), short puffed sleeves (pattern piece *J*) gathered into frills, and a gathered skirt. The sleeves and skirt are cut to use the scalloped edge of the broderie anglaise. The sash is satin ribbon in a pastel or strong colour. This dress may also be made in wide lace, perhaps worn over a coloured slip with a sash in the same colour. (Dress in lace shown in colour on page 135.)

View c This dress in soft heavy fabrics, eg velveteen or wool mixes or Viyella-type fabrics, has a long gathered skirt, long full sleeves (pattern piece *J*) gathered into lace-trimmed cuffs, and a Peter Pan collar (pattern piece *O*) made in heavy lace. The sash is in toning satin ribbon. Suitable for pastel or strong, plain colours, eg black velveteen with a cream lace collar and black satin-ribbon sash, or pale pink with a cream lace collar and darker-pink satin-ribbon sash.

View D Blouse and pinafore dress in contrasting fabrics. The blouse, in cotton or a Viyella-type fabric, has a Peter Pan collar (pattern piece *O*) and long full sleeves (pattern piece *J*) gathered into cuffs. The pinafore dress is sleeveless, has a scooped neckline and gathered skirt with patch pockets, and is made in heavier-weight fabrics, eg a blouse in a print Viyella with a needlecord pinafore in a plain colour; or a blouse in gingham with a blue denim pinafore.

View e This dress in a crisp printed cotton fabric with a plain fabric applied yoke and cuffs has a plain round neckline, long straight sleeves (pattern piece *I*), a full-length gathered skirt and a self-fabric belt. The yoke and cuffs are edged with trimming. Suitable for small geometric prints with a toning or contrasting plain yoke and cuffs. Good in 'puritan colours', eg grey, putty, rust or brown with white or black trimming.

View f This dress in lightweight cotton or silk fabrics has a bound neckline with a lace frill, short full sleeves (pattern piece *J*) gathered into frills, a three-tier frilled skirt and a ribbon sash with an artificial flower trim. Suitable for pastel colours with a toning or contrasting sash and flower, eg an apple-green silk dress with a dark-green satin-ribbon sash and pink rosebuds; or a white voile dress with a crimson satin-ribbon sash and white flowers. Suitable for antique dolls circa 1910–30.

a

b

c

d

e

f

Fig 17 Adapting a bodice neckline

Fig 18 Dresses using bodice patterns front *Di* and back *Dii*, adapted to a square neckline (see Fig 17)

View a Dress with a square neckline, long skirt and short puffed sleeves (pattern piece *J*) gathered into frills. Designed for broderie anglaise, using the scalloped edge for the skirt hem and sleeve ends. A satin-ribbon sash and artificial flower trim the waistline. The dress may also be made in lace and worn over a coloured silk slip, with a matching-colour sash. Note: This pattern is also suitable for lady dolls and made in white or ivory lace over silk or soft satin would make a wedding dress. (Shown in colour on page 86.)

View b Dress with a square neckline, short puffed sleeves (pattern piece *J*) gathered into bands, and a gathered skirt. Suitable for crisp cotton fabrics in plain strong or bright colours or small prints. Trimmed with embroidered ribbon or braid around the neckline, sleeve bands and skirt. Eg a plain green cotton dress with green, yellow and white embroidered braid; or a blue and white gingham dress with blue and white embroidered braid. Suitable for antique dolls circa 1920–30.

View c Dress with a square neckline, long full sleeves (pattern piece *J*), gathered into narrow cuffs, and a gathered skirt. Suitable for light- or medium-weight fabrics, eg Viyella or cotton, in tiny prints. The bodice and cuffs are trimmed with ribbon bands and bows and lace or self-fabric frills. Eg pastel-pink printed Viyella with pink satin ribbons and cream lace frills; or black and cream printed cotton with self-fabric frills and black ribbons.

View d Sleeveless pinafore dress with a square neckline, gathered skirt and optional patch pockets. Suitable for medium-weight fabrics, eg fine wool, needlecord or heavy cotton, in plain strong colours. Worn over a blouse or shirt in a toning print. Eg a rust needle-cord pinafore dress over a checked Viyella shirt, or a navy wool pinafore dress over a white cotton blouse. The front bodice can be trimmed with tiny buttons; the neckline and pockets can be top-stitched. (Shown in colour on page 2.)

View e This dress with a square neckline, long gathered skirt and 'regency' sleeves (pattern pieces *I* and *J*) has pintucked front bodice and pintucked sleeve ends. The neckline and sleeve ends are trimmed with narrow lace edging. The self-fabric sash is tied at the back. Suitable for lightweight fabrics, eg silk or lawn, in plain colours. Eg, a blue lawn dress edged with white lace and trimmed with tiny white buttons; or black silk edged with black lace. Note: This pattern is also suitable for lady dolls and made in ivory, cream or white silk would make a wedding dress.

View f This sleeveless dress has a square neckline and double skirt simulating an apron over a skirt. Worn over a blouse with puffed sleeves and a gathered neckline. Suitable for crisp cotton fabrics or a mixture of fabrics in one colour or several colours, eg a black velvet bodice with a mock laced front, scarlet cotton overskirt trimmed with embroidered braid, and black cotton underskirt worn over a white lawn blouse; or a mid-blue cotton bodice and overskirt over a blue and white striped underskirt and yellow blouse. Suitable for German dolls circa 1910–30.

a

b

c

d

e

f

a

b

c

d

e

f

Fig 19 Dresses using back-opening patterns front *Di* and back *Dii* (*see Fig 17 for adapting to a heart-shaped neckline or V neckline and Fig 35 for adapting the bodice to A-line*)

View a This dress has a heart-shaped neckline, gathered skirt and short puffed sleeves (pattern piece *J*) gathered to bands. The neckline, skirt hem and sleeve bands are faced with a contrasting fabric and the neckline is trimmed with embroidered flower motifs. An optional ribbon or self-fabric sash can be tied at the waistline. Suitable for crisp cotton fabrics in toning or contrasting colours, eg a lilac and white gingham dress with white facings and lilac flower trims, or a brown cotton dress with cream facings and pink flower trims. Suitable for antique dolls circa 1920–30.

View b This dress has a heart-shaped neckline, long gathered skirt and long full sleeves (pattern piece *J*) gathered into narrow cuffs. The cuffs and neckline are edged with narrow lace and the bodice front is trimmed with an artificial flower. The ribbon sash is tied at the back. Suitable for lightweight fabrics, eg silk or lawn, in pale colours or pastel prints with toning or contrasting colours for the sash and flower, eg a white dotted-swiss dress with white lace, a green satin-ribbon sash and yellow flower, or a pastel-pink print lawn with cream lace, a cream sash and pink flower. Note: This dress may also be made for a lady doll, and as a wedding dress in white or ivory silk or soft satin.

View c This ballet tutu has cut-away shoulders replaced with ribbon straps and full gathered skirts. The bodice should be made in satin (lined with lawn) with matching satin ribbon for the shoulder straps and net tulle for the skirts. The dress may have an artificial flower at the centre of the front neckline.

View d This dress bodice adapted to A-line has a deep V neckline filled with a ruched plastron (pattern piece *Niii*), elbow-length straight sleeves (pattern piece *I*) and a dropped waistline with a pleated skirt. The V neckline and sleeve ends are trimmed with lace. The dress can be made in one fabric, eg silk or taffeta, or in two or three different fabrics – eg a silk plastron, velvet bodice and sleeves, and taffeta skirt – in plain strong colours or brocaded patterns. Eg a dark-green velvet bodice and sleeves, and a medium-green taffeta plastron and skirt with cream lace; or a mid-blue brocade bodice, sleeves and skirt with a matching blue silk plastron and beige lace. Suitable for antique French bébé dolls circa the 1880s.

View e Dress bodice adapted to A-line has a deep V neckline filled with a lace over fabric 'bib', long plain sleeves (pattern piece *I*) and a gathered skirt. A large sash is tied at the side front and the V neckline and sleeve ends are trimmed with heavy lace or braid. The dress can be made all in one fabric – eg velveteen or fine wool, with lace over a matching lining for the vest – or in several fabrics, eg a velvet bodice, a silk skirt, and the lace over silk bib. The sash should be in a lightweight fabric such as silk or in wide ribbon. Eg a brown velvet bodice, sleeves and skirt, with cream lace over brown silk vest, and a brown silk sash and heavy cream lace trimming; or a crimson brocade bodice and sleeves, a crimson taffeta skirt, cream lace over crimson silk bib, a crimson silk sash and black braid trimming. Suitable for antique French bébés circa the 1880s.

View f Sleeveless pinafore dress, bodice adapted to A-line with V neckline, dropped waist and pleated skirt. Suitable for medium-weight fabrics, eg fine wool, needlecord or heavy cotton, in plain colours. Worn over a shirt (pattern pieces *Ki, Kii, Kiii*) with a round collar (pattern piece *P*). Eg a grey flannel pinafore dress worn over a pink and white striped cotton shirt, or a brown needlecord pinafore dress over a cream Viyella shirt.

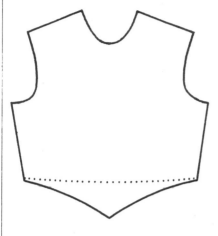

Fig 20 Making a V-shaped waistline

Fig 21 Dresses for lady dolls using bodice pattern pieces front *Di* and back *Dii* adapted to a V-shaped waistline (see Fig 20) – bodice and skirt made separately

View a This bodice with a scooped neckline and elbow-length full sleeves (pattern piece *J*) gathered into lace frills is worn with a matching gathered skirt with a looped, lace-trimmed overskirt. The bodice and skirt are trimmed with ribbon bows and artificial flowers. Suitable for lightweight fabrics, eg lawn or silk, or lace over silk, in pastel colours. Eg a pale-pink lawn dress trimmed with white lace, pale-blue ribbon bows and pink and blue flowers; or cream lace over silk dress with cream ribbon bows and pink flowers. Suitable for antique dolls circa 1850–60. (Shown in colour on page 187.)

View b This bodice with a plain round neckline, long straight sleeves (pattern piece *I*) and a full-length gathered skirt in matching fabric is worn with a fichu tied around the shoulders. The dress is trimmed with ribbon or braid bands at the sleeve ends and skirt hem, and edged with narrow lace at the neck and wrists. Suitable for medium-weight fabrics, eg

Viyella, fine wool or cotton, in plain strong or subtle colours or prints. The fichu is in lightweight fabric to tone or contrast. Eg a grey Viyella dress trimmed with black braid and white lace worn with a white muslin fichu; or a chestnut-brown wool dress trimmed with brown velvet ribbon and cream lace worn with a brown silk fichu. Suitable for antique dolls circa 1850–60.

View c Bodice with a plain round neckline has a Peter Pan collar (pattern piece *O*) trimmed with lace frills, long full sleeves (pattern piece *J*) gathered into narrow, lace-trimmed cuffs, and a long gathered skirt with a frill at the hemline. The neckline is trimmed with a ribbon bow. Suitable for light- or medium-weight fabrics in plain colours or prints, eg a beige Viyella dress with beige lace trimming and a rose-pink bow, or a tiny print cotton on a dark ground with ivory lace and a black bow.

a　　　　　　　　b　　　　　　　　c

a

b

c

d

Fig 22 Wrapover styles using bodice pattern pieces front *F* and back *Eii*

View a Dress with a wrapover bodice tied with a self belt, gathered skirt, shawl collar (pattern piece *S*) and short puffed sleeves (pattern piece *J*) with cuffs. The collar and cuffs are trimmed with scalloped edging. Suitable for crisp cottons in plain or patterned fabrics with a matching or contrasting collar and cuffs. Eg a navy blue cotton dress with a white collar and cuffs trimmed with white lace edging, or a small geometric print cotton dress with toning plain collar, cuffs and trimming.

View b Dress with a wrapover bodice tied with a ribbon sash, flared skirt and full sleeves (pattern piece *J*) gathered into narrow bands. The neckline, front edge of the dress and sleeve bands are bound with narrow binding. There are lace frills on the sleeve ends and a lace insert inside the neckline. Suitable for medium-weight fabrics, eg velveteen or wool, with matching or contrasting trimmings. Eg a crimson velvet dress with the edges bound with crimson satin bias binding, a crimson satin-ribbon sash and cream lace frills and insert; or a dark-green wool dress with pale-green silk binding and sash, and white lace frills and insert.

View c Wrapover sleeveless pinafore dress with a button fastening and gathered skirt. Suitable for medium-weight fabrics, eg needlecord or wool flannel, in plain colours. Worn over a blouse with a Peter Pan collar and long sleeves. Eg a rust needlecord pinafore dress over a checked blouse; or a grey flannel pinafore over a pink and white striped blouse.

View d Coat (pattern adapted to A-line – see Fig 35) with a shawl collar (pattern piece *S*) and long straight sleeves (pattern piece *I*) with a button fastening. Suitable for medium-weight fabrics, eg velveteen or wool flannel, in plain strong or subtle colours, trimmed with top-stitching or narrow braid in a matching or contrasting colour. Eg a navy blue coat with red braid trimming and navy buttons; or a grey velvet coat with grey top-stitching and silver metal buttons. Suitable for antique dolls circa 1900–10.

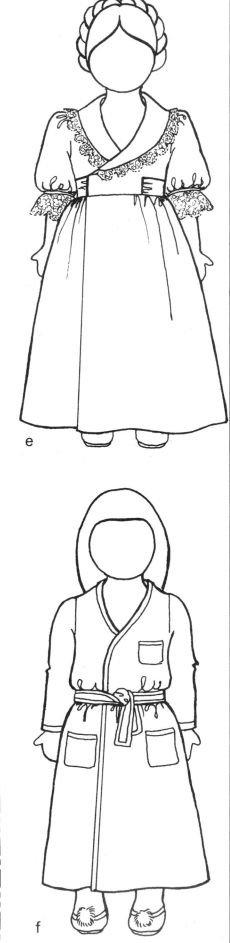

Fig 22 Wrapover styles using bodice pattern pieces front *F* and back *Eii*

View e Dress with a wrapover bodice with a shawl collar (pattern piece *S*) and full sleeves (pattern piece *J*) gathered to lace frills. The collar is trimmed with lace to match. The dress is tied with a self-fabric belt and has a long gathered skirt. Suitable for light- or medium-weight fabrics, eg silk, satin or velveteen, in plain strong or subtle colours. The collar is in a matching or contrasting fabric or colour. Eg an old-gold heavy-silk dress with a cream satin collar and cream lace frills; or a brown velvet dress with a white muslin collar and white lace frills. Note: This dress is also suitable for lady dolls, and in white or ivory silk or satin will make a wedding dress. (Shown in colour on page 135.)

View f Dressing gown (patterns adapted to A-line) with long straight sleeves (pattern piece *I*) and a self-fabric tie belt. Suitable for most fabrics, eg towelling, fleece fabric or cotton. Trimmed with top-stitching and patch pockets.

Fig 23 Square-yoked smock dresses using pattern pieces front *Gi* and back *Gii*

View a This smock dress with a gathered skirt, Peter Pan collar (pattern piece *O*) and long full sleeves (pattern piece *J*) gathered into cuffs, has optional patch pockets and a bow tied at the neckline. Suitable for light- or medium-weight fabrics, eg cotton, Viyella or fine wool, in strong or subtle plain colours with a matching or contrasting fabric for the collar, cuffs and ribbon bow. Eg a navy blue cotton dress with a white cotton collar and cuffs and a red and white dotted ribbon bow; or a dark-green Viyella dress with a cream Viyella collar and cuffs and a dark-green satin-ribbon bow.

View b Smock dress with a bound neckline, gathered skirt and short puffed sleeves (pattern piece *J*) gathered into narrow bands. Suitable for lightweight fabrics, eg silk or lawn, in plain pastel colours trimmed with a flower braid in toning or contrasting colours, eg an eau-de-Nil silk dress with pink flower braid trim, or a pale-blue or pink lawn dress with blue or pink flower braid trim. Suitable for antique dolls circa 1910–30.

View c This smock dress has a pintucked front yoke, bound neckline, long straight sleeves (pattern piece *I*) with pintucks at the sleeve ends, and a gathered skirt with pintucks above the hem. The neckline, wrists and bodice front are trimmed with narrow lace and optional tiny buttons on the bodice front. Suitable for lightweight fabrics, eg cotton, lawn or dotted swiss, in plain subtle colours. Eg, a white dotted-swiss dress with white lace and buttons; or a grey cotton dress with black lace and buttons. Suitable for antique dolls circa 1900–10. (Shown in colour on page 167.)

View d This smock dress has a pintucked front yoke, a band collar, long full sleeves (pattern piece *J*) gathered into cuffs and a full-length gathered skirt with a frill at the hemline. The collar and cuffs are trimmed with narrow lace edging and the yoke is outlined with a self-fabric or lace frill. Suitable for lightweight fabrics in plain pastel colours or soft prints, eg lawn, cotton or silk. Eg a pale-pink or blue lawn dress with white lace edging; or a pastel-print lawn dress in pinks with cream lace edging.

View e Smock dress with a round neckline, gathered skirt, long full sleeves (pattern piece *J*) gathered into cuffs, and a detachable sailor collar (pattern piece *R*). Suitable for crisp cotton fabrics in plain strong or bright colours trimmed with ribbon or braid in a contrasting colour, eg a rust cotton dress and collar trimmed with black ribbon, or a white cotton dress with a mid-blue collar trimmed with white braid.

View f Smock dress with a round neckline, full-length gathered skirt and long full sleeves (pattern piece *J*) gathered into frills at the wrist, with shoulder frills. The neckline, wrists and shoulder frills are trimmed with narrow lace edging. Suitable for lightweight fabrics, eg cotton, lawn or silk, in plain pastel colours or prints. Trimmed with ribbon bands and rosettes on the yoke in toning or contrasting colours. Eg a white lawn dress with white lace and deep-rose-pink ribbon trimmings, or a pastel-pink print dress with pink ribbons. The dress may also be made in sheer fabric and worn over a coloured slip with matching ribbon trimmings, eg a white organdy dress over a dark-green silk slip with dark-green ribbons.

a

b

c

d

e

f

73

Pouched front

To make a dropped pouched-front waistline (see Fig 24), the bodice patterns *Di* and *Dii* are lengthened to A-line. The front waistline is cut in a curve, as shown in Fig 24, in the dress fabric, but not in the lining. The curved lower edge in the fabric is gathered, pulled up to fit, and tacked to the lining – forming the pouch.

Bib bodice

Fig 25 shows how to cut a bib bodice from the bodice pattern, for use with a basic skirt to make a pinafore or pinafore dress. The bib may be cut for the front only with straps at the back – or as front and back bodice. To make the bib bodice, cut the front and two back

pieces in fabric and in lining. Stitch the shoulder seams on the fabric and the lining. With right sides facing, stitch the fabric to the lining down the back edges, around the neckline and down both sides. Clip, turn through (by pushing the backs through the shoulders to the front) and press. Stitch the front to the inside of the centre front of the skirt waistband and stitch the back pieces inside the back waistband.

Applied yokes

Fig 27 shows how to cut a yoke from the bodice pattern. The yoke is made in contrasting fabric or lace, and put on top of the bodice fabric during, or after, making up. Add any lace frills etc to the yoke before stitching it to the bodice.

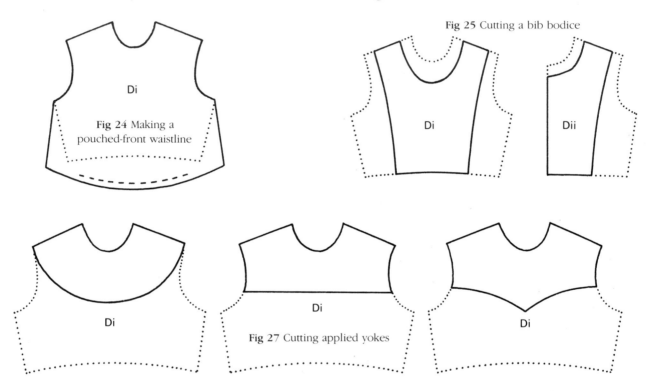

Fig 24 Making a pouched-front waistline

Fig 25 Cutting a bib bodice

Fig 27 Cutting applied yokes

Fig 26 Gathered skirts

View a Simple gathered skirt with a waistband. The waistband is cut to fit the doll's waist. The skirt is cut three times as wide as the waistband and to the length required plus hem allowance, and gathered to the waistband. Suitable for most light- or medium-weight fabrics.

View b Gathered skirt with a waistband and frill at the hemline. The waistband is cut to fit the doll's waist. The skirt is cut twice as wide as the waistband and the frill is cut 1½ times as wide as the skirt. The skirt and frill are cut to the length required plus seam and hem allowance. The frill is gathered to the skirt and the skirt is gathered to the waistband. Suitable for most medium- and lightweight fabrics.

View c Gathered skirt with a waistband and straps. The skirt is made up as View a.

The straps, made in self-fabric, are stitched inside the back waistband, crossed at the back over the shoulders and fastened with buttonholes to buttons on the front waistband. Patch pockets are optional. Suitable for most light- or medium-weight fabrics.

View d Pinafore designed for wide broderie anglaise edging. The skirt is made up as View a (without the hem allowance), using the scalloped edge at the hem, and leaving the (hemmed) back edges open. The straps are made of frilled broderie anglaise edging and the bib is stitched between the straps at the front. The bib and straps are stitched inside the front waistband, the straps are not crossed at the back and are stitched inside the back waistband. (Shown in colour on page 39.)

View e Pinafore with a gathered skirt,

waistband and bib front with straps and shoulder caps. The skirt is made up as View a, but the back seam is left open. The bib is cut from pattern piece *Di* (see Fig 25). The straps are cut to fit the bib shoulders. The sleeve caps (optional) are hemmed semi-circles of fabric stitched to the bib front and straps over the shoulders. The straps are buttoned to the back waistband. Suitable for most light-weight fabrics.

View f Pinafore dress with a gathered skirt, waistband and bib front and back. The skirt is made up as View a. The bib front and backs are cut from patterns front *Di* and back *Dii* (see Fig 25). The back bib pieces are sewn to the back waistband, the front bib to the front waistband. The back fastens with buttons and buttonholes and there are optional mock button fastenings on the shoulders. Suitable for most light- or medium-weight fabrics.

Fig 28 Dresses using back-opening pattern pieces front *Di* and back *Dii*
(*for pouched-front adaption see Fig 24; for applied yokes see Fig 27*)

View a Dress cut with a hip-length pouched front has full, elbow-length sleeves (pattern piece *J*) gathered into narrow bands, and a gathered skirt. The top of the bodice and sleeves and the skirt are overlaid with lace and a ribbon sash is tied at the low waistline. Suitable for lightweight fabrics, eg silk or soft satin, in plain strong or pastel colours. The sash might be in a matching or contrasting colour. Eg a dark-green silk dress, overlaid with white lace, with a dark-pink ribbon sash; or a pale-pink satin dress, overlaid with cream lace, with a pink sash. Suitable for antique dolls circa 1900–10. (Shown in colour on page 163.)

View b This dress cut with a hip-length pouched front has short puffed sleeves (pattern piece *J*) gathered into bands, and a gathered skirt trimmed with tucks and lace. Lace bands trim the bodice front and back with frills over the shoulders. A wide ribbon sash is tied at the low waistline. Suitable for lightweight fabrics, eg silk, lawn or dotted swiss, in white or pastel colours with a matching or contrasting sash. Eg a white dotted-swiss dress with white lace and a pale-blue sash; or a pale-lilac dress with ivory lace and a dark-lilac

sash. Suitable for antique dolls circa 1895–1910.

View c This dress cut with a hip-length pouched front has long straight sleeves (pattern piece *I*), a round neckline, pleated skirt and detachable sailor collar (pattern piece *R*). The neckline, sleeve ends and collar are trimmed with contrasting ribbon or braid. Suitable for medium-weight fabrics, eg fine wool or heavy cotton, with the collar in a matching or contrasting fabric. Eg a dress and collar in dark-red wool trimmed with black braid; or a dress in navy blue cotton with a white piqué collar trimmed with navy blue ribbon. Suitable for antique dolls circa 1890–1910.

View d Waisted dress with a round neckline, gathered skirt and plain long sleeves (pattern piece *I*), with an applied square yoke with shoulder ruffles and cuffs in a contrasting fabric. Suitable for light- or medium-weight fabrics, eg Viyella, cotton or fine wool, in strong colours. The yoke is especially suitable for broderie anglaise or lace. Eg a tartan Viyella dress with a white broderie anglaise yoke and cuffs; or a dark-green cotton dress with a cream

lace yoke and cuffs. (Shown in colour on page 127.)

View e This waisted dress with a gathered skirt and long full sleeves (pattern piece *J*) gathered into cuffs has an applied heart-shaped yoke and band collar and cuffs in lace with lace frills. A ribbon sash is tied at the waistline. Suitable for lightweight fabrics, eg silk or lawn, with matching or contrasting lace and sash. Eg a cream silk dress with a cream lace yoke and cuffs and a coffee satin-ribbon sash, or a pale-green lawn dress with a white lace yoke and cuffs and a dark-green satin-ribbon sash.

View f This waisted dress with a gathered skirt and short puffed sleeves (pattern piece *J*) gathered into bands has an applied round yoke in contrasting fabric with a frilled edge to match the sleeve bands. Suitable for light- or medium-weight fabrics, eg cotton or Viyella, in a print for the dress and a toning or contrasting plain fabric for the yoke and cuffs. Eg a small-print cotton in blue and red for the dress with a white cotton yoke and cuffs, or a pastel-print Viyella dress with a toning plain Viyella yoke and cuffs.

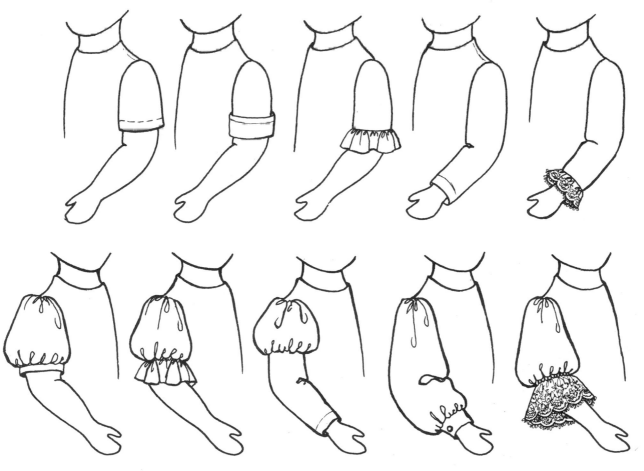

Fig 29 Sleeve styles

Sleeves (Fig 29)

Straight sleeves
(*pattern piece I*)

The straight sleeve may be used with any of the dress bodice patterns and cut to any length required. For dresses, sleeves are usually unlined, but if lining is required, use the same fabric as for the bodice lining and make up the sleeve and lining as one piece. Pintucks should be worked before cutting out. Measure the sleeve length against the under part of the doll's arm, ie armpit to wrist (or elbow etc), and add the hem allowance. Cut two sleeves (ensuring that any pattern matches on both sleeves). Gather the sleeve head with two threads ½in (1.2cm) apart, pull up the gathers to fit the bodice armhole, spreading the gathers evenly; pin or tack, then stitch the sleeve into the armhole. Remove the gathering threads. The seam may be neatened by stitching several times and trimming, or by blanket stitching, machine zigzag or binding. Stitch the side seam of the bodice through the armhole and down to the end of the sleeve. Turn up the sleeve end and hem. Trim if required. (Flat bands of trimming are easier to apply before the sleeve is seamed.)

Fitting notes Check that the sleeve is long enough and wide enough, especially at the upper arm, and that the lower end is wide enough to fit easily over the doll's hand.

Full sleeves
(*pattern piece J*)

The full sleeve may be used with any of the dress bodice patterns and cut to any length required. If lining is required, see above. Full sleeves are made with frills or cuffs to draw in the fullness. For frills, cut the sleeve sufficiently long to allow a deep hem. Measure the doll's underarm, ie armpit to wrist (or elbow etc), and add the hem allowance. Cut two sleeves, ensuring that any pattern matches on both sleeves. Gather the sleeve head with two threads ½in (1.2cm) apart, to fit the armhole. Spread the gathers evenly, pin or tack, and then stitch the sleeve into the armhole. Stitch the side seams and sleeve seams. Turn up deep hems on the sleeve ends. Gather just above the hems with doubled shirring elastic and pull up to fit the doll's arm. Strengthen by weaving more shirring elastic over and under the gathering stitches (see Fig 3).

Fitting notes Check that the sleeves are long enough. They may be pushed up a little, but do not look attractive if pulled down too far as they lose the puff effect.

When making sleeves with cuffs, cut the cuff to fit the doll's arm. Check that the cuff will slip easily over the doll's hand. (If not, consider shirt sleeves – see Chapter 5, 'Shirts'.) Measure the sleeve length required against the doll's underarm. Gather the lower

Plate 7
The large doll in the centre of the picture is a 20in (51cm) reproduction AM 1894 from GP Ceramics. She wears a pale-pink embroidered lawn dress with a Peter Pan collar, long full sleeves and a long skirt. The sashes, stitched to either side of the front waist, tie at the back. The matching poke bonnet has a frilled brim and is trimmed with artificial flowers.

The 14in (35.5cm) doll on the left is made from a kit from Hello Dolly. She wears a French dress in pink lawn with full sleeves and a gathered skirt trimmed with ivory lace and pink ribbon bows. The matching shirred hat is worn as a bonnet, tied under the chin. Her beige leather buttoned boots are from Recollect.

The 16in (40.5cm) doll on the right is also made from a kit from Hello Dolly. Her printed lawn dress has a high waist-line, long gathered skirt and 'regency' sleeves and is trimmed with white lace and artificial flowers. The matching bonnet has a poke brim and gathered circular crown. The bag is gathered at the top edge and has a cord handle.

The baby doll, also made from a kit from Hello Dolly, is 14in (35.5cm) tall. He wears a white broderie anglaise dress with a pintucked bodice, long full sleeves and a gathered skirt. The bodice is trimmed with broderie anglaise frills and ties with satin ribbons.

edge of the sleeve and stitch to one long edge of the cuff. Gather the sleeve head, stitch the sleeve into the armhole and stitch the side seam through the armhole, down the sleeve to the end of the cuff. Turn up the cuff on the inside and hem over the raw edge of the sleeve/cuff seam. Trim as required.

Fitting notes It is essential that the cuff fits over the doll's hand.

The 'regency' sleeve (see Fig 29, middle of the bottom row) is made by using the top third of the full sleeve, pattern piece *J*, and the lower two-thirds of the straight sleeve, pattern piece *I*, plus seam and hem allowance. Gather the lower edge of the full upper sleeve, and stitch it to the top edge of the straight lower sleeve. Neaten this seam, then proceed as above.

Skirts

Skirt patterns are not given in the book because the pieces are too big to fit onto the page, and because both gathered and pleated skirts are simple rectangles of fabric and flared skirts are a simple shape cut to fit the doll. Instructions given here are for dresses, but also apply to skirts with a waistband. All skirts may be made with a lining, in which case fabric and lining are worked as one piece. Lining is recommended for long skirts on lady dolls.

Gathered skirt

Measure the length of skirt required and the waistline of the dress (or waistband of the skirt). Cut a rectangle of fabric of which one dimension is the length required (plus waist seam and hem allowance) and the other is 2½–3 times the length of the waistline (or waistband). Neaten and turn in ½in (1.2cm) at the back edges. Gather the top edge with two threads ½in (1.2cm) apart and pull up to fit the waistline. Spread the gathers evenly and stitch to the waistline. The seam may be neatened by sewing several rows of stitches and trimming, or by machine zigzag, blanket stitch, or bias binding. Stitch the back seam to 2in (5cm) below the waistline. Turn up and hem the lower edge. (See also the notes with Fig 26.)

Skirt frill

Most gathered skirts might have a frill at the hemline. If the fabric is suitably lightweight (eg lawn or silk), the frill may be made in double (folded) fabric, so that the folded edge becomes the hem. On heavier fabrics, this method makes the frill too bulky, so the lower edge should be hemmed. To measure the frill, decide how deep you want it. As a general rule this should be one-third or less of the overall length of the skirt. For a folded frill, allow twice the required depth plus seam allowance. For a single thickness, allow the required depth plus seam and hem. The fabric cut for the frill should be 1½ times the length of the bottom edge of the skirt. When making a doubled frill, fold the fabric in half along the length and press. Work the double thickness as one piece. The frill may be stitched to the skirt before the skirt is made up, or added onto a skirt already made (without a hem). A single-thickness frill should be hemmed after the back seam is stitched. To make the frill, gather the top edge – on two threads ½in (1.2cm) apart – and pull up the gathers to fit the skirt. Spread them evenly and stitch. The seam should be neatened by sewing several times and trimming, or blanket stitching, machine zigzag, or binding.

Fig 30 Overskirts

Overskirt

If the dress is to have an overskirt, it is best to make the skirt and bodice separately so that the waist seam is not too bulky. The overskirt may be sewn to the bodice or to the skirt waistband, depending on the style of the dress. Cut the overskirt as wide, or a little wider than the skirt and to the length required (allow for the frill or hem). Fig 30 shows several styles; a front-opening, an 'apron' front and a lace overskirt, which are all made up in the same way as the skirts above. The looped effects are made by gathering the overskirt at the sides and pulling up the gathers. This is more easily done when the skirt is on the doll to judge the best effect. Gather the top edge of the overskirt and stitch it to the dress bodice, or – with the skirt – to the skirt waistband. Put the garment on the doll. Use pins to mark the places you want to gather – this is usually in line with the bodice side seams. Remove the skirt and, with tiny stitches, make lines of gathering, leaving the needle and thread in the skirt. Put it back onto the doll and pull up the gathering to make the effect you want. Fasten off securely.

Train

The Victorian train was cut as an extension to the back of the skirt – all in one – but by Edwardian times, the detachable train had become fashionable. This is rather like an apron, worn at the back. It may be rectangular or oval and is cut somewhat longer than the skirt in matching fabric. It may be hemmed, lined or edged with trimming, and the top edge is gathered to fit the back waist, and bound with a strip of dress fabric. This bound edge has small hooks at each end which fasten the train to small worked loops on either side of the bodice at the back waistline. (See the black gown in the plate on page 187.) As the train is detachable, the dress may be worn with or without it – the small worked loops on the bodice do not show when the train is removed. Trains are only suitable for lady dolls wearing formal ball gowns or wedding dresses (Fig 31).

Fig 31 Detachable train

Pleated skirt

Measure the waistline of the dress (or waistband of the skirt) and cut a rectangle of fabric 3 times this length. In lightweight fabrics, this may be in double thickness (folded) fabric so there will be no need to make a hem. In heavier-weight fabrics, allow for the waist seam and hem. Turn up the hem allowance and press; tack the hem in place. Mark the pleats – knife pleats or box pleats (see Fig 32) as you prefer – measuring with a ruler and marking fold lines with tailor's chalk. Fold and pin the pleats. Check the pleated length against the waistline and ensure that the back seam will be concealed under a pleat – adjust if necessary. Tack the pleats in place with three threads along the length, and press. Loosen the tacking at the back, and stitch the centre-back seam (on a skirt, leave about 2in (5cm) open at the top). Stitch the skirt to the waistline (or band). Remove the tacking threads and stitch the hem. Press the pleats again if necessary. Pleated skirts 'sit' particularly well on bodices with dropped waistlines, eg the French dress (see instructions below).

Flared skirt

The flared skirt is cut to fit the doll, and may be slim or full, and gathered or not. Measure the doll's waist, and add a seam allowance. Measure the length from waist to hem and add a seam and hem allowance. Cut one front and two back pieces (reverse for front opening) as shown in Fig 34. The waistline may be cut to fit the lower edge of the bodice (or waistband), or cut wider and gathered to fit. For some styles, the front skirt is

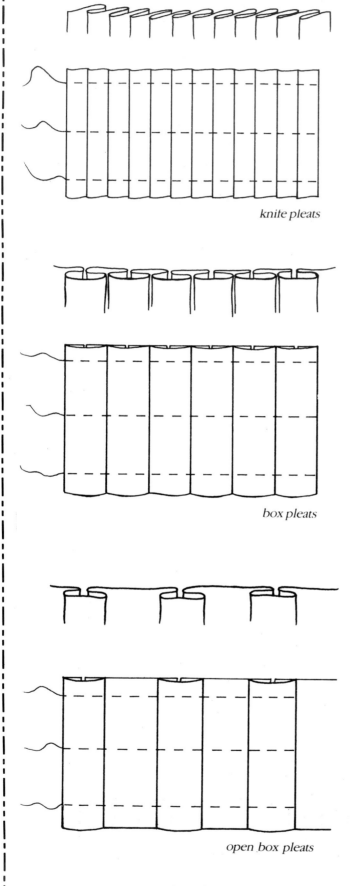

knife pleats

box pleats

open box pleats

Fig 32 Making pleats

Fig 33 Dresses using bodice pattern pieces front *Di* and back *Dii* adapted to a dropped waistline

View a Dress with a dropped waistline, Peter Pan collar (pattern piece *O*), short puffed sleeves (pattern piece *J*) gathered into sleeve bands, and a gathered skirt. A fabric belt is buttoned at the front of the low waistline. Designed for crisp cotton fabrics with a contrasting collar, sleeve bands and belt. Eg a brown gingham dress with white cotton collar, cuffs and belt; or a blue cotton dress with a cream collar, cuffs and belt. Suitable for antique dolls circa 1920–30.

View b This French dress made from pattern pieces front *Ni* and back *Nii* has a ruched plastron (pattern piece *Niii*) which may be made in one piece with the dress bodice or separately. The elbow-length straight sleeves (pattern piece *I*) and dress fronts are trimmed with lace and the skirt may be gathered or pleated. The dress may be made all in one lightweight fabric, eg lawn or silk, or in two different fabrics, eg a dark-green velvet bodice and sleeves, eau-de-Nil silk skirt and plastron with cream lace trimming; or a pale-blue lawn dress and plastron with white lace trimming. Suitable for French bébés circa the 1880s. (Shown in colour on page 163.)

View c Dress with a dropped waistline, bound neckline, short puffed sleeves (pattern piece *J*) gathered into frills and a gathered skirt. Designed for broderie anglaise, using the scalloped edge for the skirt and sleeve hems. The dress is trimmed with narrow ribbon slotted through broderie anglaise insertion on the bodice front and back. Eg a white broderie anglaise dress and trimming with pastel pink or blue ribbons.

View d Dress with a dropped waistline, elbow-length straight sleeves (pattern piece *I*) and a pleated skirt. Suitable for medium-weight fabrics, eg heavy cotton or taffeta. The dress is trimmed with contrasting ribbon bands and lace on the bodice front and sleeve ends. Eg a coffee-coloured cotton dress with pale-blue satin ribbon and cream lace trimming; or a dark-green taffeta dress with pink satin ribbon and cream lace trimming. Suitable for French bébés circa 1885–95 – in strong or subtle colours.

View e Dress with a dropped waistline, pleated skirt and long straight sleeves (pattern piece *I*) suitable for medium-weight fabrics, eg fine wool, velveteen or heavy cotton, in plain strong colours. The square collar (pattern piece *Q*) is in heavy lace and lace trims the sleeve ends. Eg a crimson wool dress with a cream lace collar; or a black heavy-cotton dress with a white lace collar. Suitable for antique dolls circa 1895–1910.

View f Dress with a dropped waistline, elbow-length full sleeves (pattern piece *J*) gathered into narrow bands, and a two-tier pleated skirt. The neckline and sleeve bands are trimmed with narrow lace, the top skirt is overlaid with lace, and a ribbon sash is tied at the side front. The dress may be made all in one lightweight fabric, eg silk, or in two toning fabrics, eg taffeta for the bodice and silk for the skirt, in plain strong or subtle colours or woven patterns. Eg the bodice and sleeves in mid-blue brocade, and the skirt and sash in mid-blue silk with ivory lace; or the bodice, sleeves and skirt in coffee taffeta with coffee lace and a brown ribbon sash. Suitable for antique dolls circa 1890–1910.

a

b

c

d

e

f

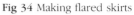

Fig 34 Making flared skirts

plain and the back skirt is gathered. The hem of the flared skirt is a gentle curve – not straight – and it is often easier to face it with bias instead of making an ordinary hem.

Fitting notes Check that the angle of the side seams is the same on both sides on back and front.

The bibbed skirt, pattern piece *AA*, is a simple flared skirt, cut with centre-front and back seams. To make the skirt, stitch centre-front and back seams. Make a small hem all the way around the top edge and a larger hem on the lower edge. The skirt fits loosely around the body, and has straps stitched inside the back waistline and buttoned to the bib front (see Fig 10e).

Peplum

The peplum is an extension to the bodice which is virtually a very short skirt. It is made up in the same way as the flared skirt, and stitched to the bodice (or jacket) waistline. The lower edges may be shaped to curve, and on a front-opening bodice the front edges of the peplum may be shaped into points (see Fig 47).

A-line dresses
(pattern pieces front Vi and back Vii)

The A-line dress pattern is given in smaller sizes – for larger sizes adapt bodice patterns front *Di* and back *Dii* as shown in Fig 35, cutting to the length required.

The A-line dress may be made very simply, or cut in pre-tucked or pleated fabrics to make a variety of styles

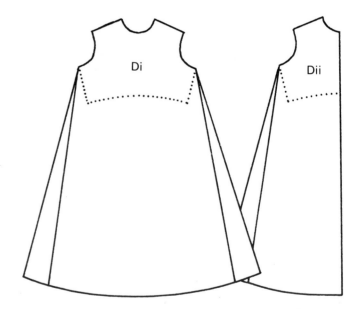

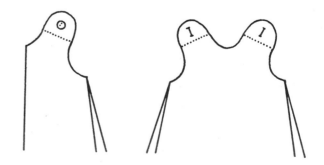

Fig 35 A-line and buttoned-shoulder adaptations for larger sizes

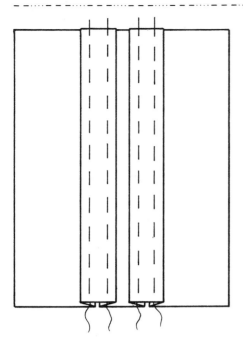
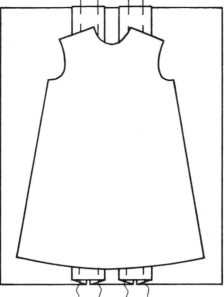
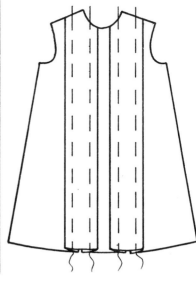

(see Fig 37). The lining should be of lighter-weight fabric, eg lawn, and cut as a simple A-line, whether the dress fabric is pleated or tucked or not.

To make a simple A-line dress, cut one front and two back pieces in fabric and in lining. (Cut sleeves as required.) Stitch the shoulder seams on the fabric and the lining. With right sides facing, stitch the fabric to the lining around the neckline and down the back edges for approximately one-third of the length. Clip, turn through and press. From this point, fabric and lining are worked as one piece and may be stitched together. Stitch the sleeves into the armholes; then stitch the side and sleeve seams. Stitch the back seam on the lower two-thirds of the skirt (stitch the lining and fabric separately on this seam). Hem the lower edge. The back bodice fastens edge-to-edge with buttons and loops or hooks and eyes or, on larger sizes, a zip.

To make a pleated or pintucked A-line dress (Fig 36), cut a piece of fabric rather larger than the pattern piece and squarely on the grain. Make the pleats or pintucks as required, tack and press. Centre the pattern carefully over the worked fabric and cut the piece. Cut the lining from the pattern; then make up as above.

Fitting notes Check that the angles of the sides are the same on both sides, back and front. Check that the dress will close easily edge-to-edge, without pulling.
Note Both sleeve patterns *I* and *J* may be used with the A-line dress. (See also Chapter 4, 'Collars'.)

The French dress
(pattern pieces front Ni, back Nii and plastron Niii)

The French dress (Fig 33b) has a gathered front panel (plastron) which may be made as part of the bodice front, as shown in the 14–15in (35.5–38cm) pattern or separately as shown in the larger sizes. The skirt may

Fig 36 Cutting a pleated A-line dress

be gathered or pleated and is stitched to the low waistline. The dress may be made all in one light-weight fabric, or in two or three different fabrics, but the plastron must be in a lightweight fabric to make the gathering.

To make the dress with the bodice and plastron in one piece (for larger-size patterns, tack the edges A–B together on the pattern before cutting), first cut one bodice front and two back pieces in fabric and two back pieces and one A-line front in lining. Stitch the shoulder seams on the fabric and lining. Make the plastron gathering on the lines marked on the pattern and pull up to fit the doll, fastening off. With right sides facing, stitch the fabric to the lining at the back edges. Turn through, press, and then bind the neckline with bias strip. From this point, fabric and lining are worked as one piece and may be stitched together. Sew the sleeves into the armholes and stitch the side and sleeve seams. Lap one back edge over the other and secure at the lower edge. Make up the skirt and stitch to the waistline. (The skirt will not need a back opening.) The back bodice fastens with buttons and buttonholes or press-studs.

To make the French dress with a contrasting plastron (for size 14–15in (35.5–38cm) pattern, cut at line A–B on the pattern). Work the gathering on the plastron and tack the plastron to the bodice front edges. Fit on the doll, pull the gathering up to fit and fasten off. Stitch the plastron to the bodice fronts, then proceed as above.

Fitting notes Check the bodice length – the bodice should be hip-length, so that the skirt is short. When the plastron gathers are pulled up, the bodice should fit well, but not tightly. Check that there is sufficient overlap for the back closure.
Note Both sleeve patterns *I* and *J* may be used with the French dress. (See also Chapter 4, 'Collars'.)

a   b

Fig 37 Dresses in A-line style (*Pattern pieces front Vi and back Vii; for sizes 14–15in/35.5–38cm and 16–18in/40.5–45.5cm given full-length; for larger sizes adapt patterns front Di and back Dii, see Fig 35*)

View a This dress has two box pleats at front and back, long plain sleeves (pattern piece I), a square collar (pattern piece Q) and a self-fabric belt worn at hip level. Suitable for medium-weight fabrics, eg fine wool, velveteen or heavy cotton, with the collar and belt in matching or contrasting fabrics in plain strong or subtle colours, eg a black cotton dress with a cream collar, or a rust wool dress with a matching collar. The collar, sleeve ends and belt may be trimmed with top-stitching. Suitable for antique dolls circa 1900–20.

View b The front of this dress is pintucked to yoke level and has a bound neckline and short puffed sleeves (pattern piece J) gathered into narrow bands. The neckline and sleeve bands are trimmed with narrow lace edging. Suitable for light-weight fabrics, eg silk or cotton, in a plain colour or a print. Eg a plain yellow silk dress with white lace; or a pink flower-print cotton with cream lace edging.

Plate 8
Recollect's 20in (51cm) reproduction Bru wears a coat and hat in white fur fabric. The coat fastens edge-to-edge with loops and buttons, and the hat is a simple pillbox. The white leather buttoned boots are also from Recollect.

The 16in (40.5cm) Sasha boy doll wears a simple collarless jacket and matching trousers in dark-green velvet with a white silk lace-trimmed shirt. His bow tie is dark-pink satin ribbon and he has an artificial flower pinned to his jacket.

The 16in (40.5cm) Sasha girl doll wears a white broderie anglaise dress with a square neckline, short puffed sleeves and a long gathered skirt. Her sash is dark-green satin ribbon and she carries a posy of artificial flowers.

The 15in (38cm) baby doll is a reproduction 'Dream Baby' from Recollect. He wears a long baby gown in ivory cotton lawn with full sleeves and a front panel trimmed with pintucks, ivory insertion lace and blue satin ribbons. The matching bonnet has a small brim and full circular crown.

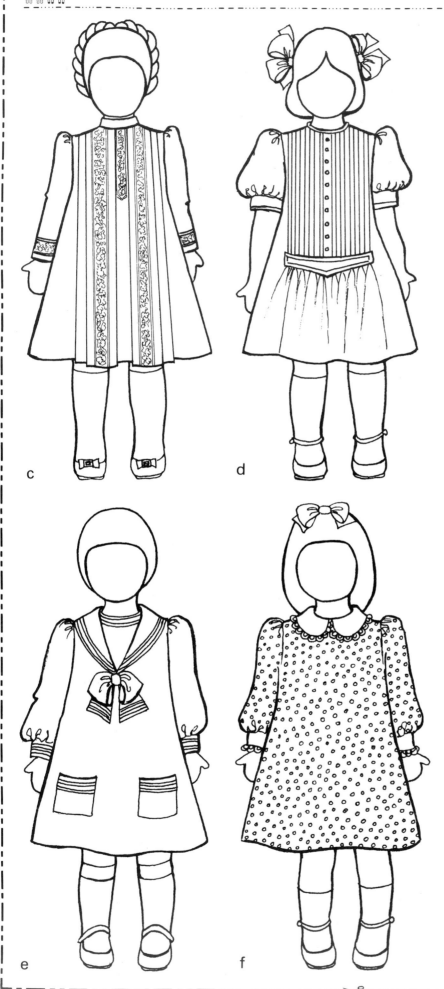

c

d

e

f

Fig 37 Dresses in A-line style (*Pattern pieces front Vi and back Vii; for sizes 14–15in/35.5–38cm and 16–18in/40.5–45.5cm given full-length; for larger sizes adapt patterns front Di and back Dii, see Fig 35*)

View c This dress has two box pleats with a knife pleat each side at front and back, a band collar, long plain sleeves (pattern piece *I*) and a lace or braid trimming on the dress front, back and sleeve ends. Suitable for medium-weight fabrics, eg heavy cotton or fine wool, in plain subtle colours. The lace or braid is in toning or contrasting colours. Eg a Wedgwood-blue cotton dress trimmed with white lace; or a green wool dress trimmed with yellow and green embroidered braid. A ribbon or self-fabric belt can be slotted through the trimming at hip level. Suitable for antique dolls circa 1900–20. (Shown in colour on page 6.)

View d Dress has pintucks at the front to hip level with a shaped, stitched band, bound neckline and short puffed sleeves (pattern piece *J*) gathered to sleeve bands. Suitable for light- or medium-weight fabrics, eg cotton, Viyella or fine wool, in plain subtle colours. The front can be trimmed with tiny buttons, and the sleeve and waistband with top-stitching. Eg lilac cotton, pale-blue Viyella or brown wool. (Shown in colour on page 6.)

View e This simple A-line dress has long full sleeves (pattern piece *J*) gathered into cuffs, patch pockets and a detachable sailor collar (pattern piece *R*). Suitable for medium-weight fabrics, eg heavy cotton or fine wool, with a matching or contrasting fabric for the collar, eg a scarlet dress and collar trimmed with navy blue ribbon, or a brown dress with a cream ribbon trim and a cream collar with a brown ribbon trim.

View f This simple A-line dress has long full sleeves (pattern piece *J*) gathered into cuffs, and a Peter Pan collar (pattern piece *O*). Suitable for medium-weight fabrics, eg heavy cotton or fine wool, in small prints on a strong- or bright-coloured background with a contrasting fabric for the collar and cuffs with a narrow scalloped trim. Eg a cotton print, red with white spots, and a white collar and cuffs trimmed with white lace; or a printed wool with a collar and cuffs of silk of the dominant colour in the print.

The round-yoke dress

(pattern pieces front yoke Hi, back yoke Hii and sleeve Hiii)

To cut the skirt for the round-yoke dress, see Fig 38. Measure the doll from chest to hem and cut a rectangle of fabric this length plus hem allowance and 2–3 times as wide. Cut the armholes as shown, using the sleeve armhole as a guide, and cut the top edge of the skirt in shallow curves down to centre front and back.

   To make the dress, cut one front and two back yokes in fabric and in lining, and two sleeves and one skirt in fabric. Stitch the shoulder seams on the fabric and the lining. Stitch the fabric to the lining (right sides facing)

up the back edges and around the neckline; clip, turn through and press. Stitch the sleeve seams, and stitch the sleeves into the armholes. Neaten the back edges of the skirt and turn under ½in (1.2cm). Gather all the way around the top edge (skirt and sleeves) with two threads ½in (1.2cm) apart; pull up, spreading the gathers evenly, and stitch to the yoke fabric. Hem the yoke lining over the seam. Stitch the centre-back seam to 2in (5cm) below the yoke. Hem the skirt and finish the sleeve ends as required. Fasten the back yoke with buttons and buttonholes or press-studs.

Fitting notes The sleeves may be long or short, and cut wider or narrower than the pattern. (For frills, cuffs, etc, see 'Sleeves' above.)

Note Only sleeve *Hiii* will fit this pattern. (See also Chapter 4, 'Collars'.)

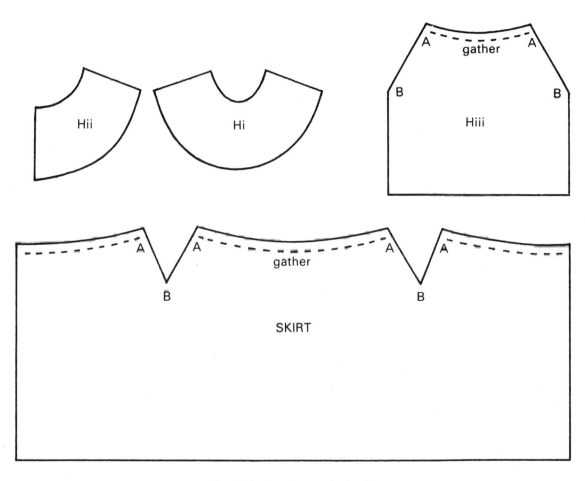

Fig 38 Cutting the round-yoke dress

a

b

c

d

e

f

Fig 39 Dresses using round-yoke pattern pieces front *Hi*, back *Hii* and sleeve *Hiii*

View a Dress with a band collar and short puffed sleeves gathered into bands. The yoke, neck band and sleeve bands are in a contrasting fabric and trimmed with a narrow scalloped edging. Optional patch pocket. Suitable for cotton and Viyella – dress in a patterned fabric; yoke, neck band and sleeve bands in a plain fabric. Eg a tiny geometric print on a dark-navy or brown background with a white yoke; or a pastel flower print in pink or blue with a plain pink or blue yoke.

View b Dress with a lace over fabric yoke, lace over fabric cuffs on long, full sleeves and a deep lace frill outlining the yoke. Suitable for lightweight fabrics, eg silk, soft satin or lawn, in pastel or subtle colours. Eg a pink, cream, lemon or blue dress with white, cream or ivory lace. Suitable for antique dolls circa 1890–1900. (Shown in colour on page 163.)

View c Dress with a band collar and full sleeves gathered into cuffs, with a deep flounce outlining the yoke. The neck band, cuffs and flounce are trimmed with ribbon or braid bands. Suitable for medium-weight fabrics, eg Viyella or fine wool, in plain subtle colours with a contrasting trim. Eg a navy blue wool dress trimmed with red ribbon; a black dress trimmed with cream ribbon; or a cream dress trimmed with navy blue braid. Suitable for antique dolls circa 1900–10.

View d Dress with a pintucked yoke, bound neckline and short puffed sleeves gathered into frills. The skirt has a frill at the hemline, and the yoke, sleeves and skirt are trimmed with flower braid. Suitable for lightweight fabrics, eg silk or lawn, in pastel colours with a contrasting or toning trim. Eg a pale-yellow silk dress with a pink and green flower braid trim;

or a pale-blue dress with a blue and green flower braid trim. Suitable for antique dolls circa 1900–20.

View e Dress with a plain round neckline, mock button fastening on the shoulder seams and three-quarter length sleeves gathered into frills. Cut extra long and bloused over a wide self-fabric sash. Suitable for fine fabrics, eg silk, or medium-weight fabrics, eg Viyella in plain subtle colours or small prints. Eg a plain rust-colour silk, or Viyella with a tiny print on a navy ground. The buttons match the colour of the dress. Suitable for antique dolls circa 1900–10.

View f Sleeveless pinafore designed for broderie anglaise using the scalloped edge for the hem. It has ruffles of narrow broderie anglaise instead of sleeves. Worn over a printed dress with a Peter Pan collar. (See Fig 13.)

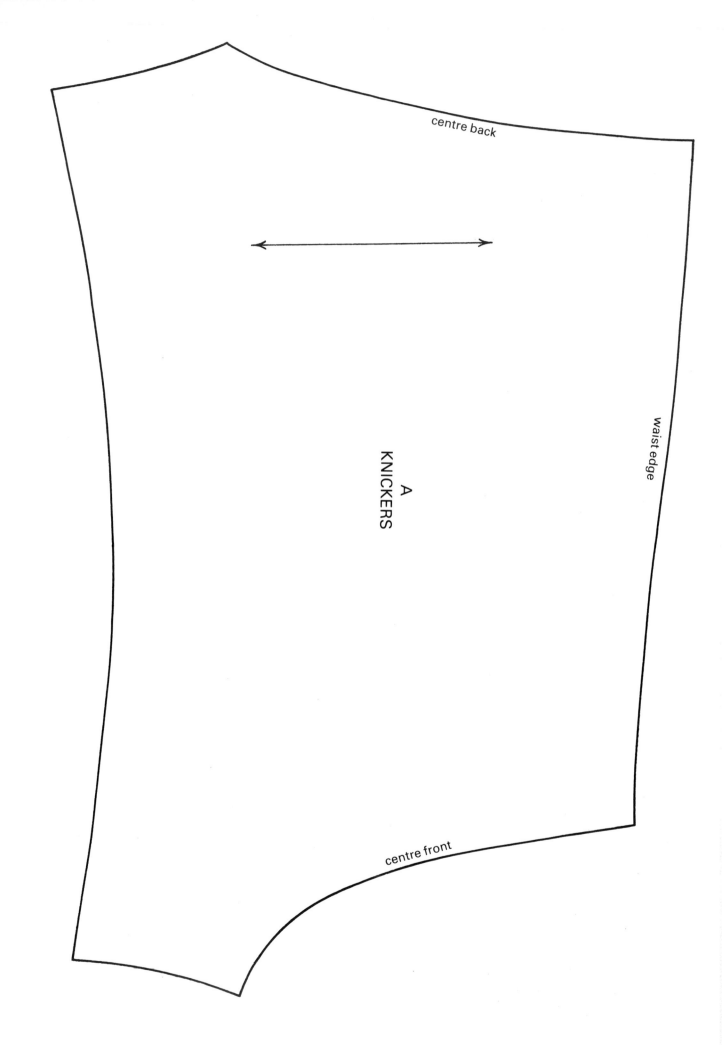

centre back

waist edge

A
KNICKERS

centre front

fold of fabric

waist edge

B
DRAWERS

centre front

centre back

R
SAILOR COLLAR

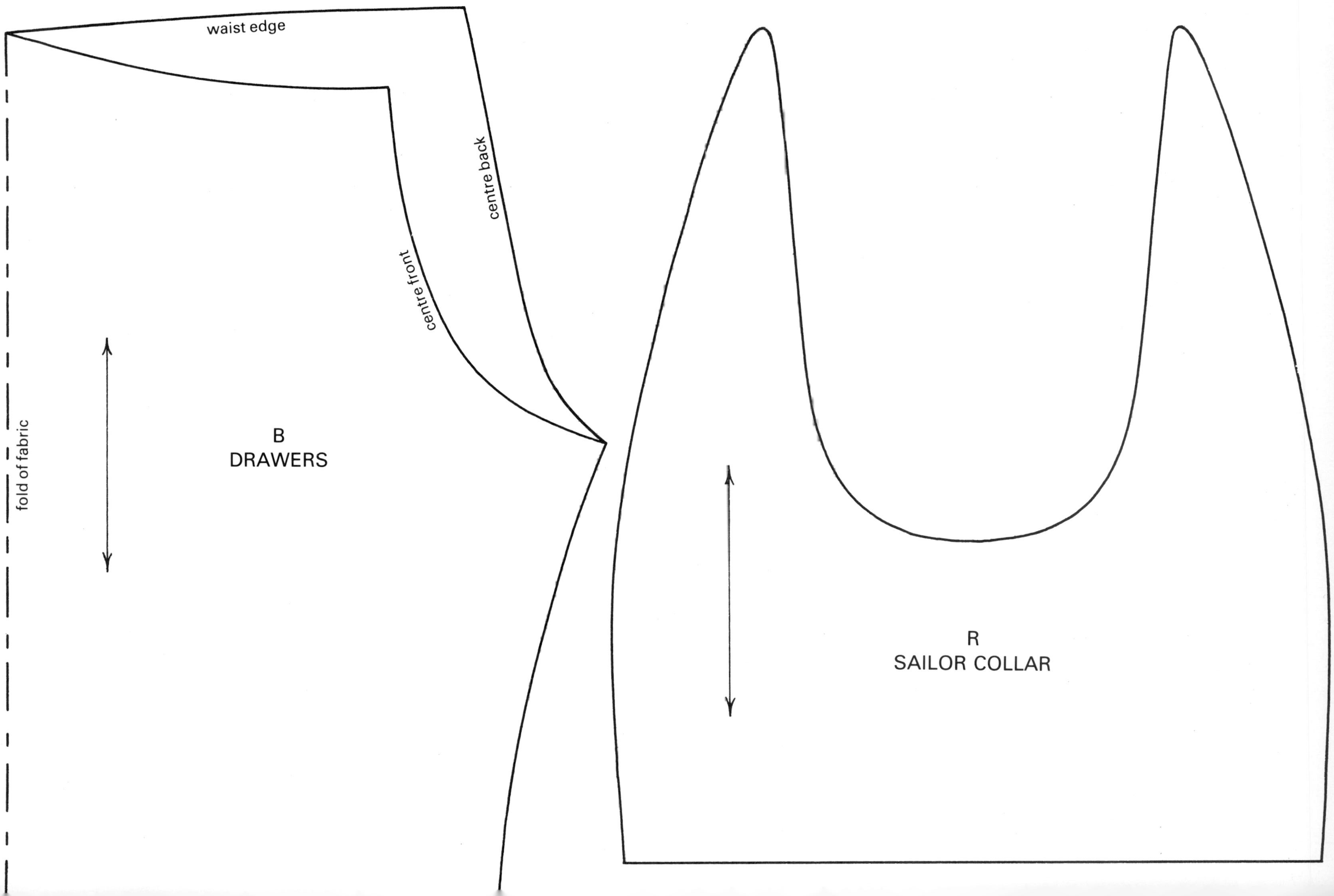

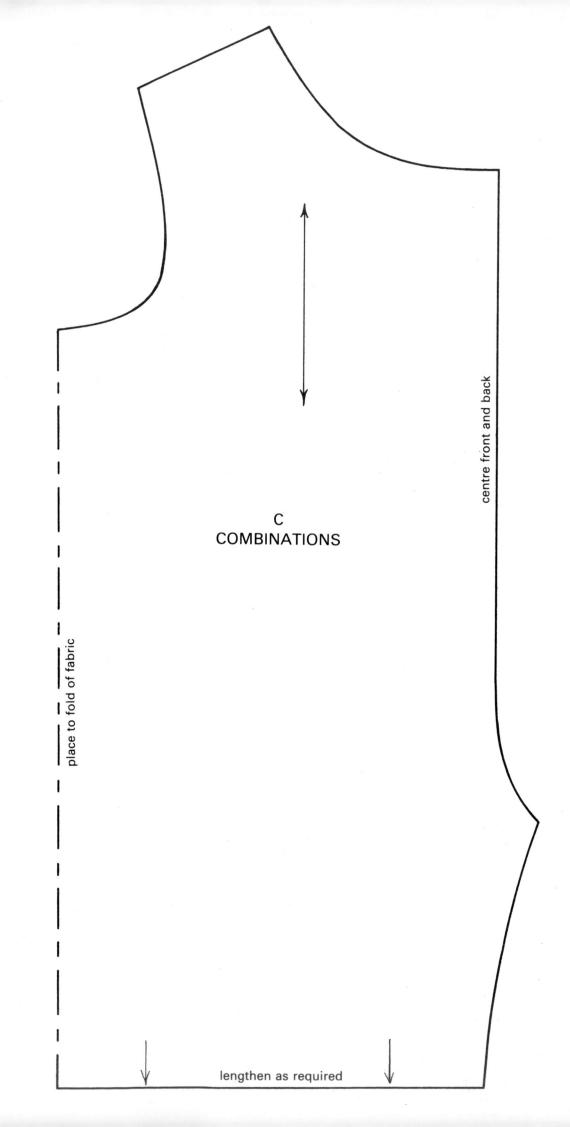

C
COMBINATIONS

centre front and back

place to fold of fabric

lengthen as required

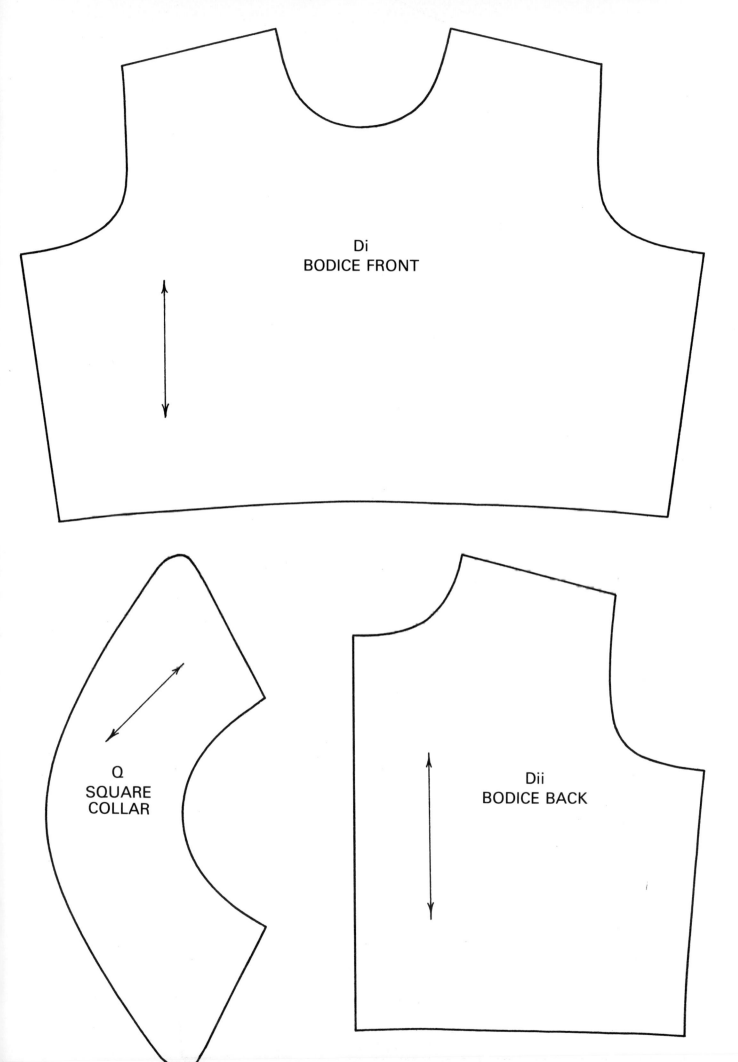

Di
BODICE FRONT

Q
SQUARE
COLLAR

Dii
BODICE BACK

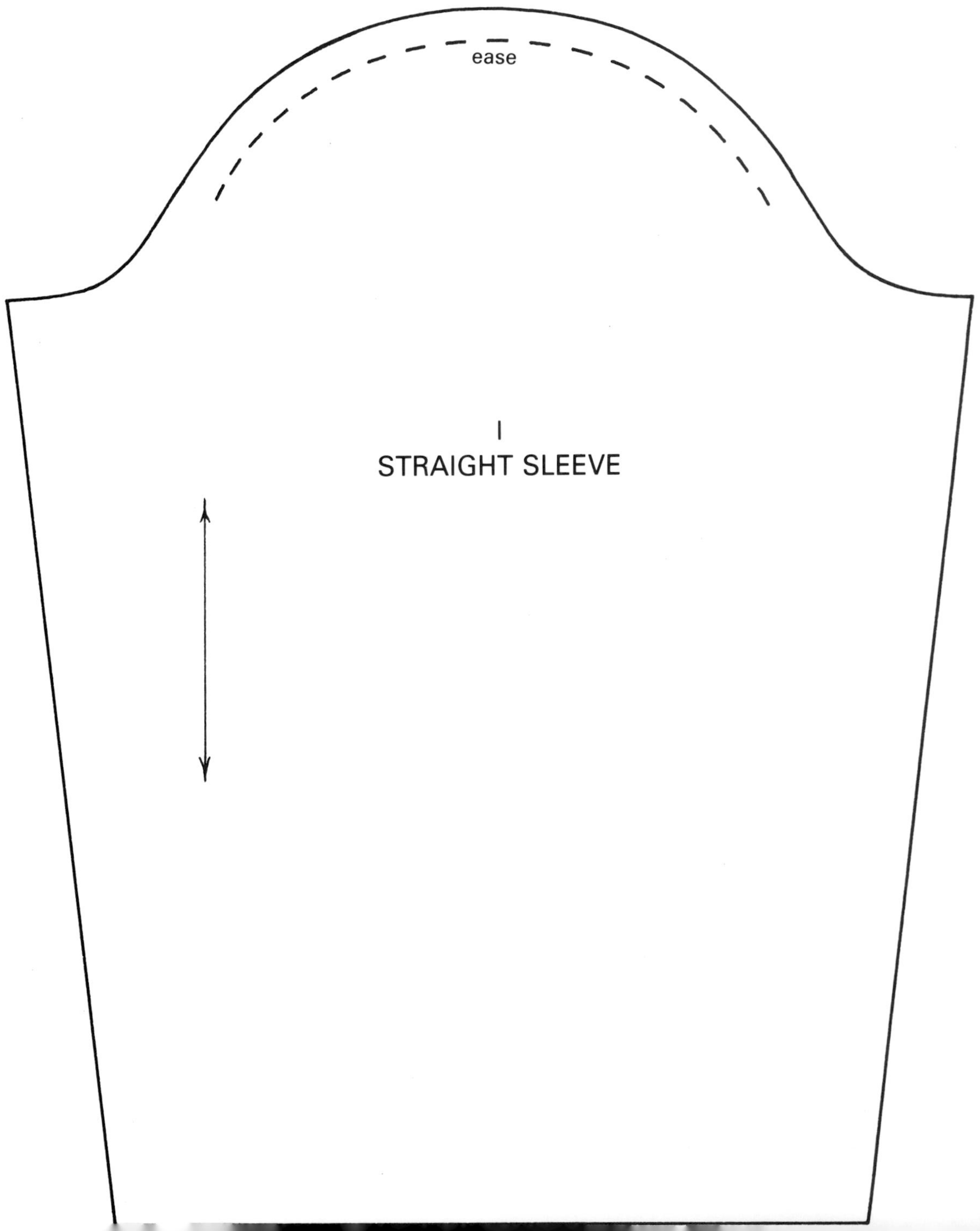

ease

I
STRAIGHT SLEEVE

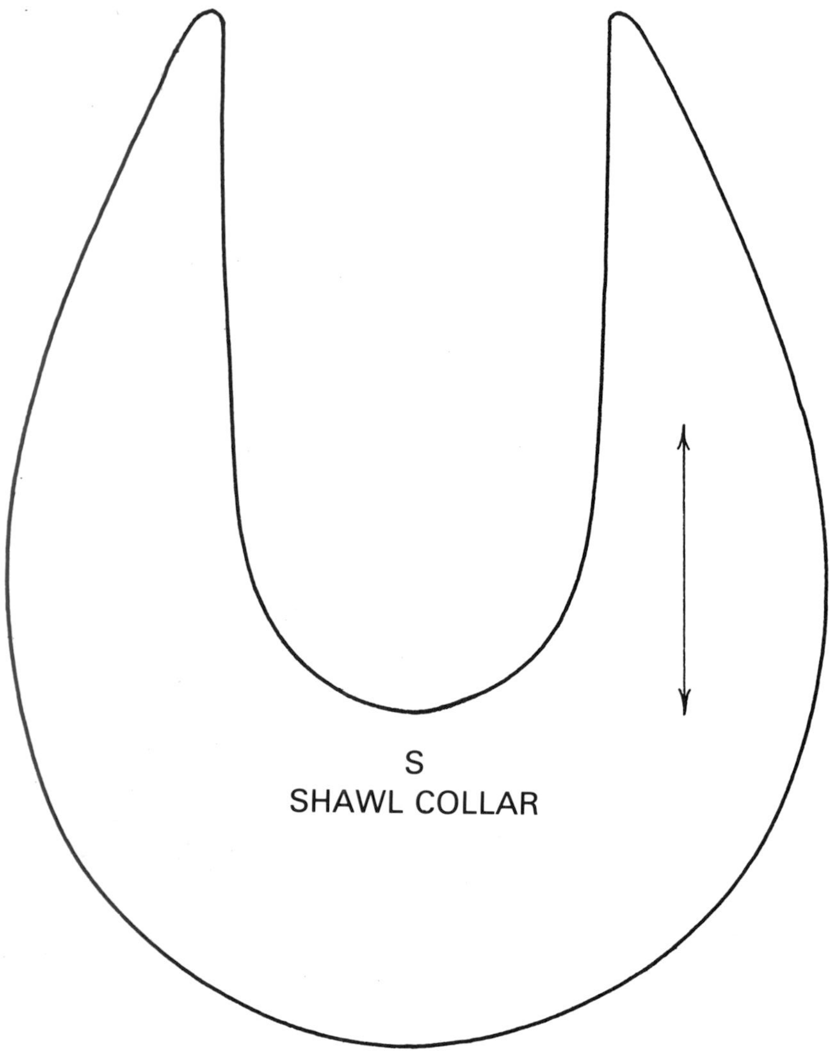

S
SHAWL COLLAR

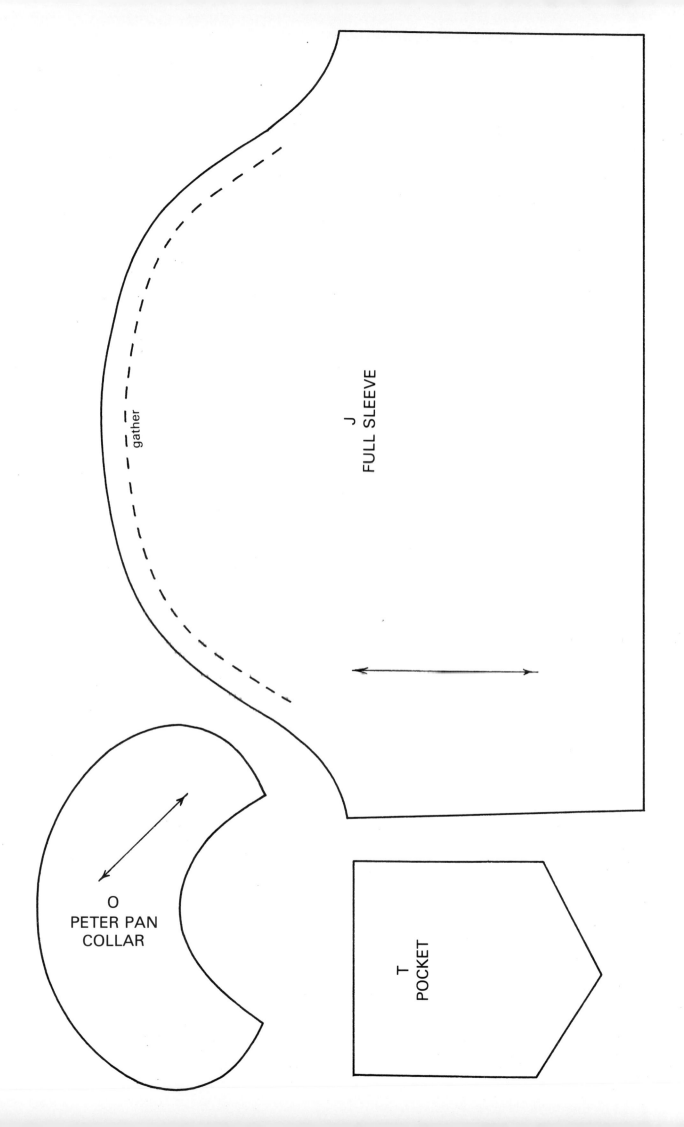

gather

J
FULL SLEEVE

O
PETER PAN
COLLAR

T
POCKET

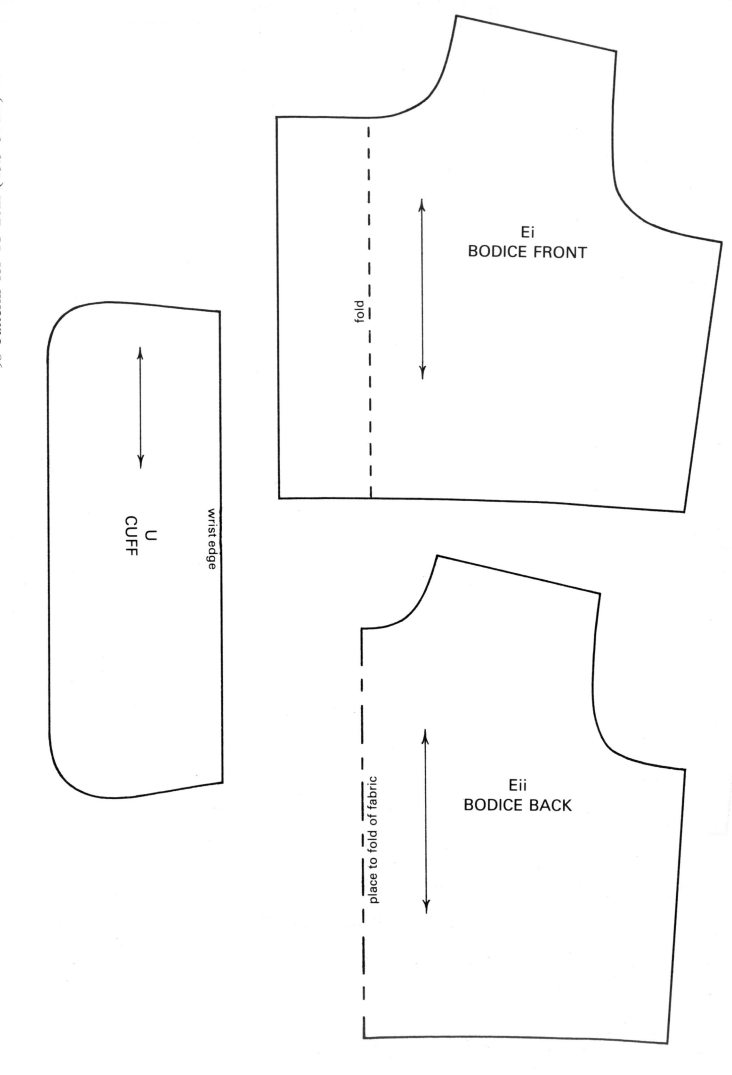

Ei
BODICE FRONT

fold

U
CUFF

wrist edge

Eii
BODICE BACK

place to fold of fabric

Gi
SMOCK-YOKE FRONT

Gii
SMOCK-YOKE BACK

F
WRAPOVER BODICE FRONT

P
ROUND COLLAR

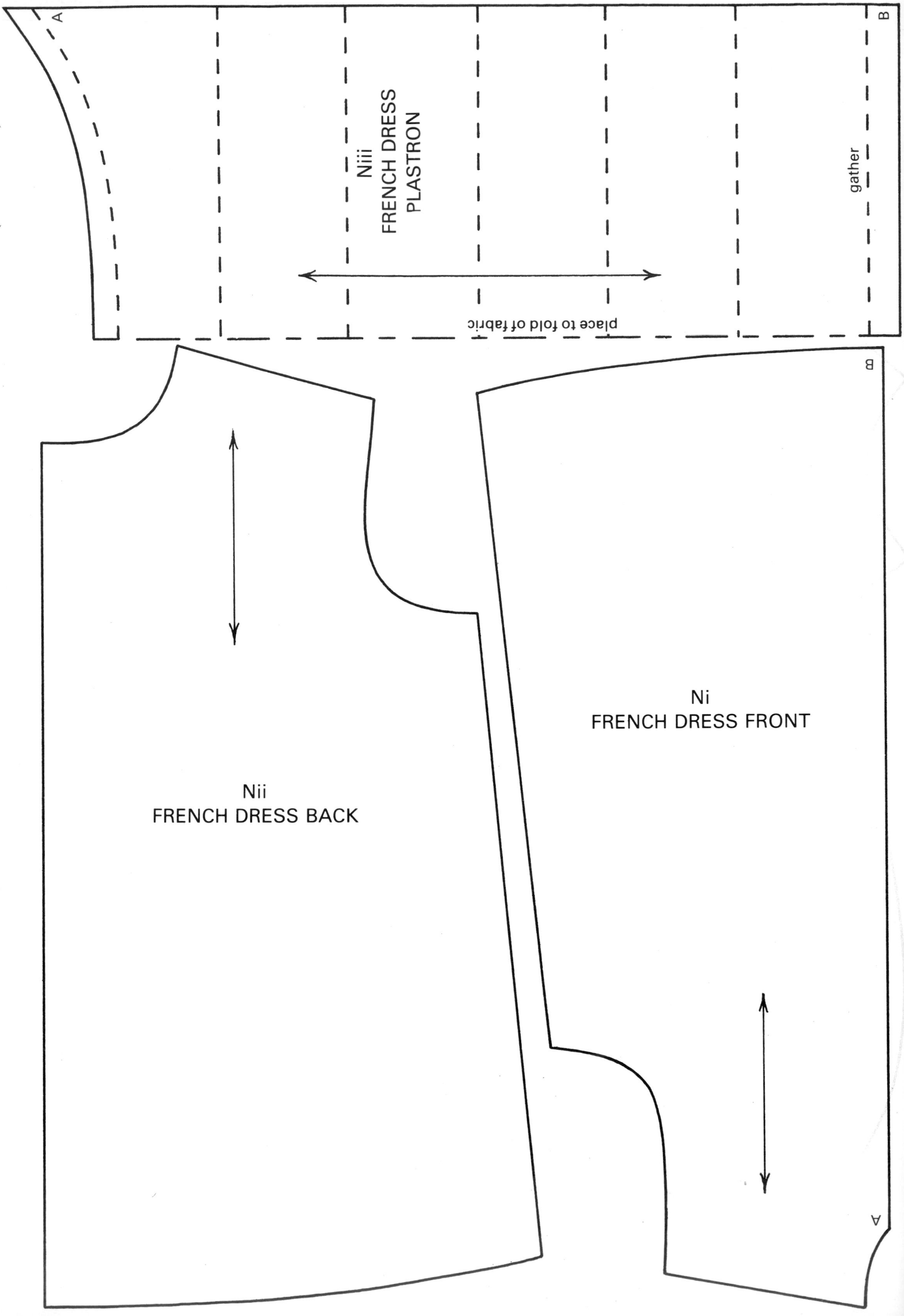

Niii
FRENCH DRESS
PLASTRON

place to fold of fabric

gather

Nii
FRENCH DRESS BACK

Ni
FRENCH DRESS FRONT

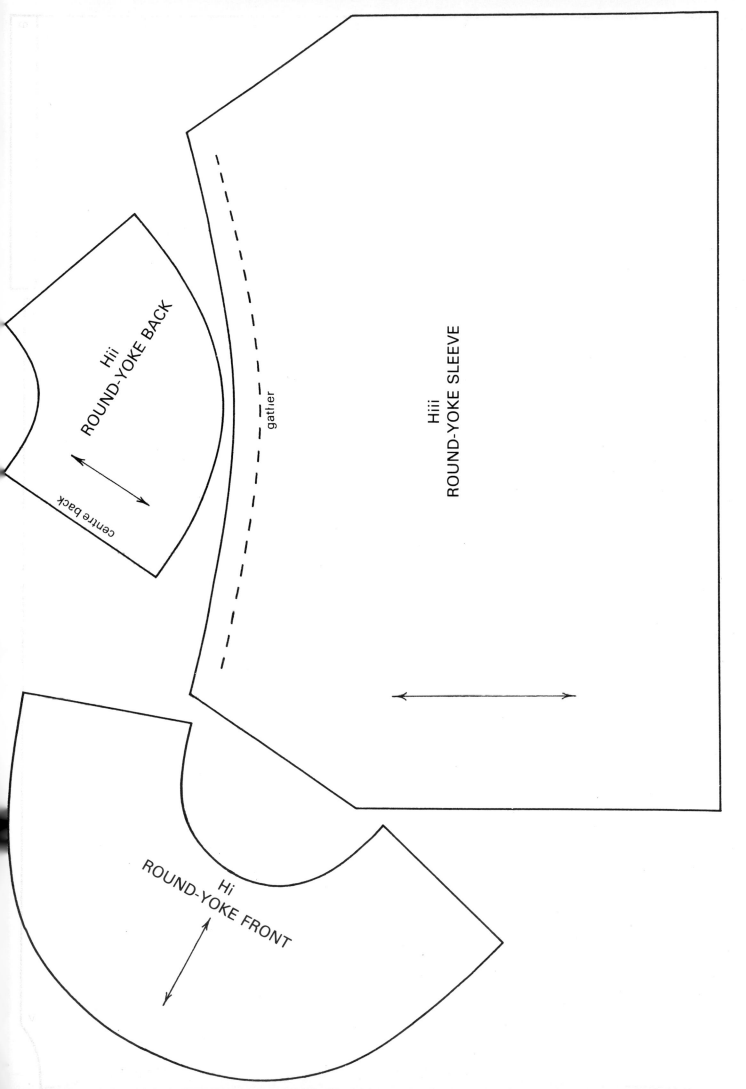

Hii
ROUND-YOKE BACK

centre back

gather

Hiii
ROUND-YOKE SLEEVE

Hi
ROUND-YOKE FRONT

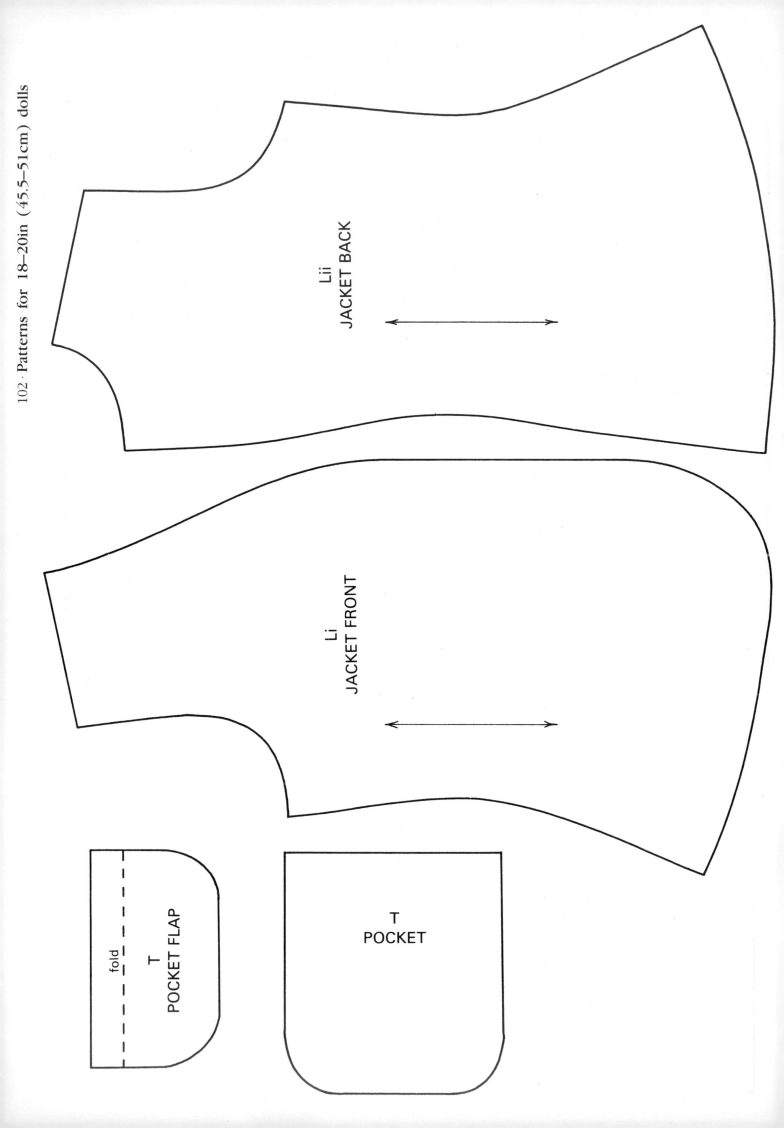

Lii
JACKET BACK

Li
JACKET FRONT

fold

T
POCKET FLAP

T
POCKET

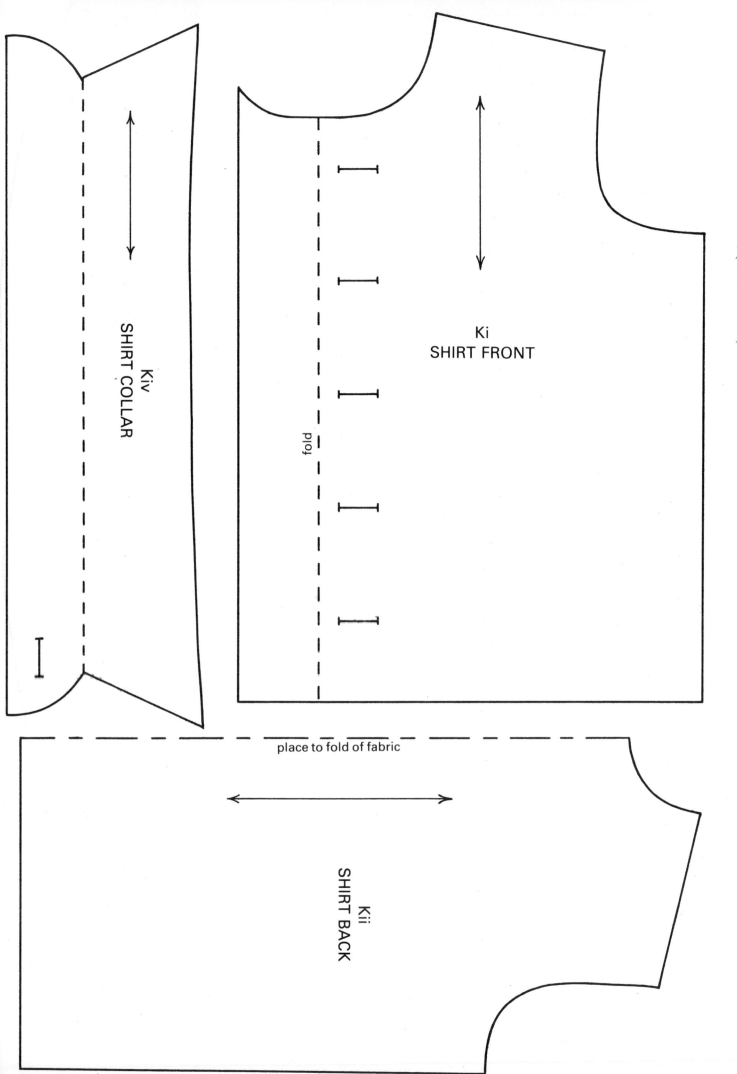

Kiv
SHIRT COLLAR

Ki
SHIRT FRONT

fold

place to fold of fabric

Kii
SHIRT BACK

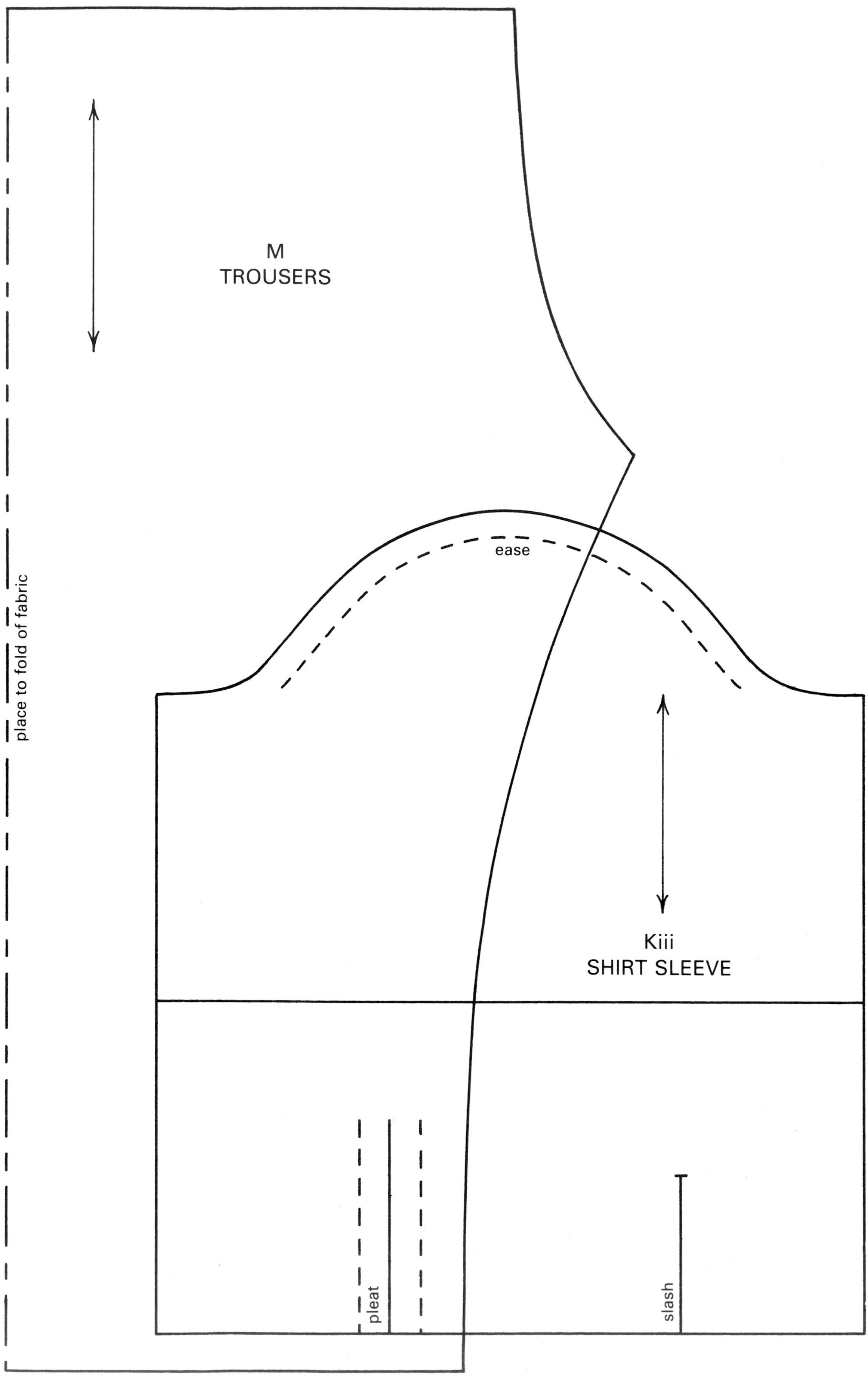

place to fold of fabric

M
TROUSERS

ease

Kiii
SHIRT SLEEVE

pleat

slash

4 COLLARS, CUFFS AND POCKETS

Collars

All the collars are made separately and stitched to the garment after making-up. If the collar needs stiffening, use lightweight iron-on Vilene. Lace, or self-fabric frills should be made up and sewn into the collar edge as the collars are made, or whipped-on narrow lace edging may be added after making-up. For self-fabric or lace frills, allow 1¼ times the length of the outside edge of the collar.

Fit the pattern toile on the garment, on the doll (allowing for seams) and make any adjustments necessary.

Collars should be lined in self-fabric, unless it is heavyweight, in which case, cut linings in matching lightweight fabric. Collars may also be made in lace, lined with net. Follow the grain lines on the patterns. The collar patterns are given in each size; use the size which corresponds to the bodice pattern size.

Peter Pan collar
(*pattern piece O*)

Cut two collar pieces and two lining pieces. With right sides facing, stitch each collar piece to a lining piece around the outside edge (sandwiching any gathered trimming). Trim the edges to ¼in (6mm), clip the curves, turn through and press. Tack the collars together loosely where they meet at the front or back neckline. Bind the raw edges of the collars with one length of matching bias binding. Press the bound edge to the inside of the collar. Slip the bound edge of the collar inside the dress neckline, matching the centre front or back and hem to the dress lining. This collar may be used with any round-neck bodice pattern – front or back opening.

Round collar
(*pattern piece P*)

Cut one collar in fabric, one in lining – with lightweight fabrics use an interlining, worked as one piece with the lining. With right sides facing, stitch the fabric to the lining around the outside edge, sandwiching any gathered trimming. Trim the seam to ¼in (6mm), clip the curves, turn through and press. Bind the raw edges with matching bias binding and press the binding to the underside. Slip the bound edge inside the dress neckline, matching centre fronts, and hem it to the dress lining. This collar may be used with any front-opening, round-neck pattern.

Square collar
(*pattern piece Q*)

This collar is cut and made up in the same way as the Peter Pan collar (above). Cut off the corner points before turning through. It may also be used with any round-neck pattern – back or front opening.

Sailor collar
(*pattern piece R*)

The sailor collar may be sewn into the dress (jacket or coat) neckline if the neckline is V-shaped and front opening (see Fig 40), or wrapover style, or it may be made as a detachable collar and worn over a round or band neckline.

To make the sewn-in collar, cut one piece in fabric and one in lining. With right sides facing, stitch the fabric to the lining around the outside edge. Trim the seam, clip the curves and corners, turn through and press. Any ribbon or braid trimming should be stitched to the collar at this stage, mitring the corners at the back and matching at the front edges. Bind the raw edges of the collar with matching bias binding, and press the binding to the underside. Slip the bound edge inside the neckline, matching centre fronts and back and hem to the lining. Trim with a ribbon bow to match the collar trimming. To make the detachable collar, cut one piece in fabric and one in lining (use interlining if the fabric is lightweight). Stitch any braid or ribbon trimming to the fabric at this stage (allowing for a ½in/1.2cm seam all the way around), mitring the corners at the back and matching at the front edges. With right sides facing, stitch the fabric to the lining all the way around the piece – leaving a small gap to turn through at the back edge. Trim the seam, clip the curves and corners, turn through and press. Use slipstitch to close the opening. Sew a small hook and loop to either end of the fronts or make two small loops and fasten the collar with a ribbon drawn through the loops and tied in a bow. The collar may be secured with a tiny gilt safety pin from the inside of the garment through the bow.

Shawl collar
(*pattern piece S*)

The shawl collar is made in the same way as the round collar (above) and may be used with any V-neck, front-opening garment. The shape may be changed by squaring off the front ends (see Fig 46b). The collar may also be used with wrapover bodice styles (see Fig 22).

Note Pretty collars may also be made from lace or crochet table mats. Cut out a circle from the centre of the mat large enough to fit the doll's neck. Slash an opening at the back. Hem the opening, bind the neck with bias binding and sew into the dress neckline.

Cuffs
(*pattern piece U – designed for straight-sleeve pattern I*)

The cuffs are lined with matching lightweight fabric, and made up in virtually the same way as the collars above. Try the pattern toile on the garment on the doll (allowing for a ½in/1.2cm seam all the way around) and make any adjustments. The cuff pattern is given in each size and, untrimmed, makes a deep jacket (or coat) cuff. Trim the pattern if required.

Cut pairs of cuffs in fabric and lining. With right sides facing, stitch each fabric piece to a lining piece (sandwiching gathered trimming if required) around the curved edge of the cuff. Trim, clip, turn through and press. Face the straight edge of the cuff with matching bias binding and press the binding to the underside. Slip the binding inside the sleeve end and hem to the lining.

Plate 9
The 22in (56cm) lady doll is a reproduction Bru from Creations Past. She wears a jacket with a squared shawl collar, elbow-length sleeves and a peplum in printed lawn. The matching full, frilled skirt has a looped, frilled overskirt. The jacket and skirts are trimmed with narrow silk ribbon and cream lace edging. The jacket belt is stiffened at the front and ties in a bow at the back. The hat is made from plaited raffia and trimmed with ribbon, artificial flowers and a feather. The doll carries a handbag and cream lace parasol.

The 18in (45.5cm) doll in the centre of the picture is 'Emily', made from a kit from Ridings Craft. She wears a dropped-waist dress in pink satin trimmed with cream lace, with a three-tier skirt made from pleated lace and satin ribbon trimming from GP Ceramics. The dress has elbow-length straight sleeves, lace shoulder-frills and a bound neckline.

Reflect's 18in (45.5cm) reproduction KR 117 on the right wears a white cotton lawn pinafore with a square yoke made from broderie anglaise trimming and a broderie anglaise frill at the hem.

The seated 16in (40.5cm) doll (author's collection) wears a high-waisted dress in printed cotton from Village Fabrics. The dress has a pin-tucked bodice, puffed sleeves and a gathered skirt and is trimmed with narrow silk ribbon, cream lace and tiny pearl bead 'buttons'. Her teddy is made in gold velveteen and has a ribbon bow.

Turn-back cuffs
(for straight sleeves)

If the turn-back cuff is to be in the same fabric as the sleeve, simply cut the sleeve long, make a deep hem and turn back the hem. For turn-back cuffs in contrasting fabric, cut a piece the same width as the sleeve end and twice the depth of the finished cuff plus seam allowance. Seam the piece to form a tube. With right sides facing, stitch one edge of the cuff to the sleeve end. Hem the other edge over the seam on the inside. Fold up the cuff. (See also Chapter 3, 'Sleeves'.)

Note If collars, pocket flaps and cuffs are to have bound edges, stitch the fabric to the lining with the *wrong sides* facing and a slightly larger seam allowance. Trim, then bind the edges as required, and proceed as above.

Pockets
and pocket flap *(pattern piece T)*

Pocket patterns are given in each size in two shapes; the making-up method is the same for both shapes.

Cut the pocket in fabric. Turn under and tack ½in (1.2cm) around the outside edge. Turn under and hem the top edge. Press. Pin and top stitch or slipstitch the pocket in place and remove the tacking. The pocket flap may be used with a pocket, or on its own. Cut one piece in fabric and one in lightweight lining for each flap. With right sides facing, stitch the fabric to the lining all the way around, leaving a small gap on the top edge to turn through. Trim, turn through, press and close the opening. Trim if required and top stitch or slipstitch in place.

Fig 40 Sailor blouse/jacket ▶

5 MAINLY FOR BOYS

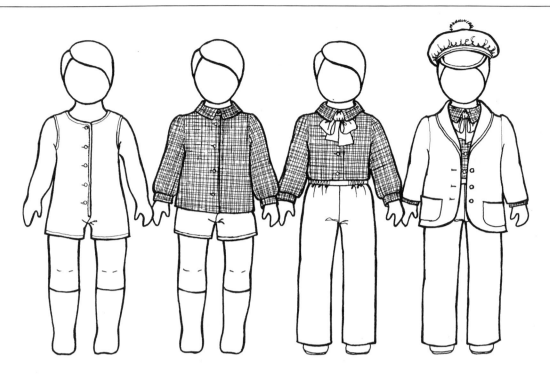

Shirt

(*pattern pieces front Ki, back Kii, sleeve Kiii and collar Kiv*)

The shirt pattern is given in each size. It is designed for light- or medium-weight fabrics. The collar (and cuffs) should be stiffened with lightweight iron-on Vilene.

To make the shirt, cut one back, two front pieces, two sleeves, and two collar pieces, one stiffened and one unstiffened. Cut two cuffs to fit the doll's wrists with button and buttonhole fastening.

Stitch the shoulder and side seams. Neaten and turn back the front edges to form facings, tack and press. Slash and hem the sleeve openings. Stitch the sleeve seams. Pleat the sleeve ends and stitch to the cuffs. Gather the sleeve heads, to ease and stitch the sleeves into the armholes. With right sides facing, stitch the collar pieces together around the outside edge, trim, clip, turn through and press. With right sides facing, stitch the stiffened collar edge to the outside neckline; hem the other collar edge to the inside. Hem the lower edge of the shirt. Make buttonholes on the shirt front and cuffs; sew on buttons.

Fitting notes Check the chest measurement and back length. Check the sleeve length on the doll's underarm. Check that the collar fits the doll's neck, and that the neck is long enough for the collar to 'sit' well.

Note The round collar, pattern piece *P*, may be used instead of the shirt collar – made up as above. Sleeves may also be short, with or without turn-back cuffs. Sleeve pattern *J* may be used instead of the shirt sleeve (see Chapter 3, 'Sleeves').

A back-opening blouse may be made by lengthening the bodice patterns front *Di* and back *Dii* with sleeves *I, J* or *Kiii* and Peter Pan or square collars (*O* or *Q*) or band collar.

A front-opening blouse may be made by using the shirt pattern (above) with Peter Pan (*O*), square (*Q*) or round collars and full-sleeve pattern *J*.

The sailor-blouse (Fig 40) is made by adapting the front-opening bodice patterns to V-neckline, and lengthening in a slight A-line. The sailor collar (*R*) is sewn into the neckline, and the blouse may be lined. It is worn over a sleeveless, back-opening blouse with band collar.

Trousers

(*pattern piece M*)

The trousers are designed to have an elastic casing at the waistline. If the pattern in the doll's height size is not large enough at the waist, use a larger size. Also check that the back waist-to-crotch seam is long enough (allow for casing) especially if your doll has a big bottom – lengthen at the top edge if necessary. Also check the inside-leg measurement.

To make the trousers, cut two pieces. Stitch the leg seams, then stitch the centre-front seam, through the crotch to the centre back. Hem the leg ends, and make a casing at the top edge. Thread elastic to fit the doll's waist.

Knickerbockers are made by cutting the pattern leg just below knee-length, and gathering to bands cut to fit the doll's leg.

The pattern may be used for shorts or underpants simply by cutting the legs off as required.

Note This pattern may also be used to make simple pantalettes, or shortened to make drawers, trimmed with lace or broderie anglaise.

Dungarees
(*pattern piece W*)

The pattern is given in smaller sizes – for larger sizes, adapt pattern *M*, using a smaller dungarees pattern as guide.

The dungarees are designed to pull up the body and fit loosely at the waist. Check that the pattern fits around the doll's waist. Check also that the back waist-to-crotch and inside-leg measurements are long enough.

To make the dungarees, cut two pieces. Stitch the centre-front and centre-back seams. Stitch the inside-leg seam, up one leg, through the crotch and down the other leg. Make a narrow hem all round the top edge and hem the leg ends. Cut and make up straps to fit from the back waist, crossed, over the shoulder to the bib. Stitch the straps inside the back waist and button (or clip – see Fig 4g) to buttons on the bib.

This pattern may also have the legs shortened to knee length – or cut long, with deep hems, turned back at the leg ends. Pockets (pattern piece *T*) may be used with trousers, shorts or dungarees – use pocket patterns one size smaller than trouser patterns.

Jackets and tunics

The bodice patterns may be used to make jackets and tunics for boy dolls.

The simple jacket shown in Fig 48b is made from the front-opening patterns *Ei* and *Eii* with sleeve pattern *I*. The bodice patterns are lengthened in a slight A-line, and the front edges trimmed to meet edge-to-edge. The jacket is lined in a lightweight matching fabric. To make the jacket, make up in the fabric and lining, separately. Stitch the shoulder seams; gather the sleeve heads to ease and stitch the sleeves into the armholes. Stitch the side seams through the armhole to the sleeve end. With right sides facing, stitch the fabric to the lining all the way around the edge, leaving a small gap at the lower back edge to turn through. Clip the curves and corners, turn through, slipstitch the opening closed and press. Turn up the sleeve ends and hem; hem the sleeve linings to the sleeves.

The tunic shown in Fig 48c is also made from patterns *Ei* and *Eii*, and the shirt sleeve *Kiii*. The bodice patterns are cut to thigh length, in a slight A-line. The tunic is unlined. To make up, stitch the side and shoulder seams. Neaten and turn back the front edges to make facings. Face the neckline with bias strip. Slash and hem the openings in the shirt sleeves and pleat the sleeve ends to fit cuffs cut to fit the doll. Stitch the sleeve seams; gather the sleeve heads to ease and stitch the sleeves into the armholes. Hem the lower edge of the tunic and work buttonholes down the front and on the cuffs; sew on buttons. The square collar (pattern piece *Q*) may be made in contrasting fabric – trimmed or untrimmed – and is made up as described in 'Collars' (Chapter 4), and stitched inside the neckline. Make self-fabric or leather belt.

The lined 'Norfolk' jacket (Fig 48f), is also cut from lengthened patterns *Ei* and *Eii* and sleeve *I*. The neckline is adapted to a V-shape, and a shawl collar (pattern piece *S*) is made in the same fabric. Cut rectangles of fabric, squarely on the grain, rather larger than the pattern front and back pieces. Make large box pleats on either side of the front and back, and tack to hold. (The pleats may be top-stitched.) Centre the patterns carefully over the pleated fabric, and cut the back and front pieces. The lining is cut without pleats, from the same patterns. Make up both fabric and lining, separately. Stitch the shoulder seams. Gather the sleeve heads to ease and stitch the sleeves into the armholes. Stitch the side seams, through the armholes to the sleeve ends. With right sides facing, stitch the fabric to the lining, up the front edges and around the neckline; clip, turn through and press. Hem the lower edge of the jacket, and hem the lining to the jacket with loose stitches. Hem the sleeves and hem the linings to the sleeves. Make up the shawl collar as described in Chapter 4, and stitch it inside the jacket neckline. Make buttonholes and sew on buttons. Make a self-fabric buttoned belt, and thread through loops worked on the jacket side seams.

Fitting notes Check the chest measurement and back length. Check the sleeve length against the doll's underarm. The jackets and tunic may be worn with matching trousers or knickerbockers.

T-shirt

A simple T-shirt may be made from stretch-cotton fabric (cut from a child's T-shirt or vest) using patterns front *Di* and back *Eii* and sleeve *I* (long or short). Cut back, front and sleeves to the length required and scoop out the neckline to fit over the doll's head. If your doll has a very large head, slash and hem a small opening at the centre back. Stitch the shoulder seams. Gather the sleeve heads to ease and stitch the sleeves into the armholes. Stitch the side seams through the underarms to the sleeve ends. Bind the neckline and (short) sleeve ends with bias-cut fabric. Hem the lower edge (and long sleeves). If the back opening is slashed, fasten with a loop and button.

For boys' clothes, see also Chapter 7, 'Jackets, coats and cloaks'.

P
ROUND COLLAR

waist edge

centre back

centre front

place to fold of fabric

A
KNICKERS

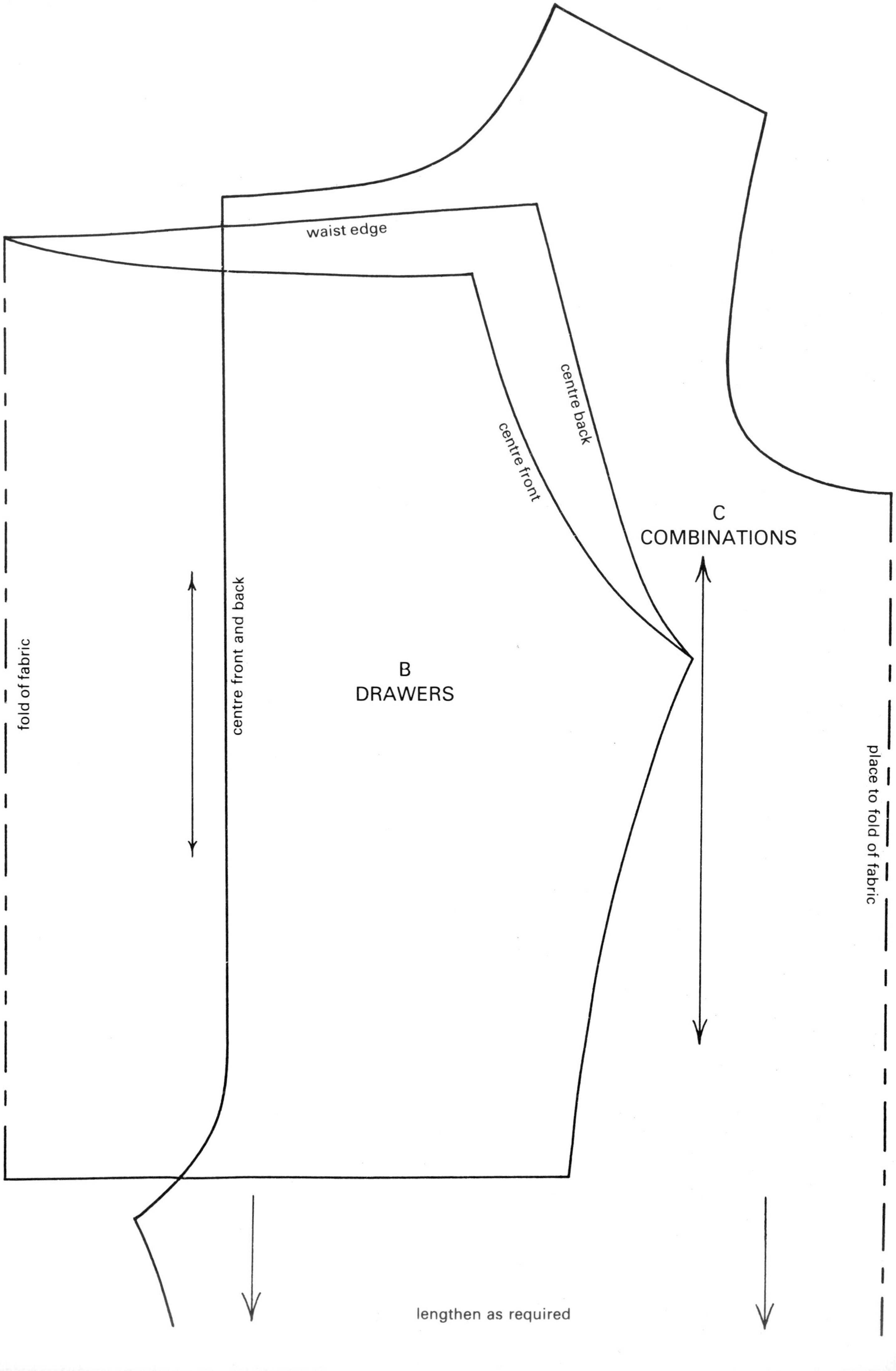

fold of fabric

waist edge

centre back

centre front

centre front and back

B
DRAWERS

C
COMBINATIONS

place to fold of fabric

lengthen as required

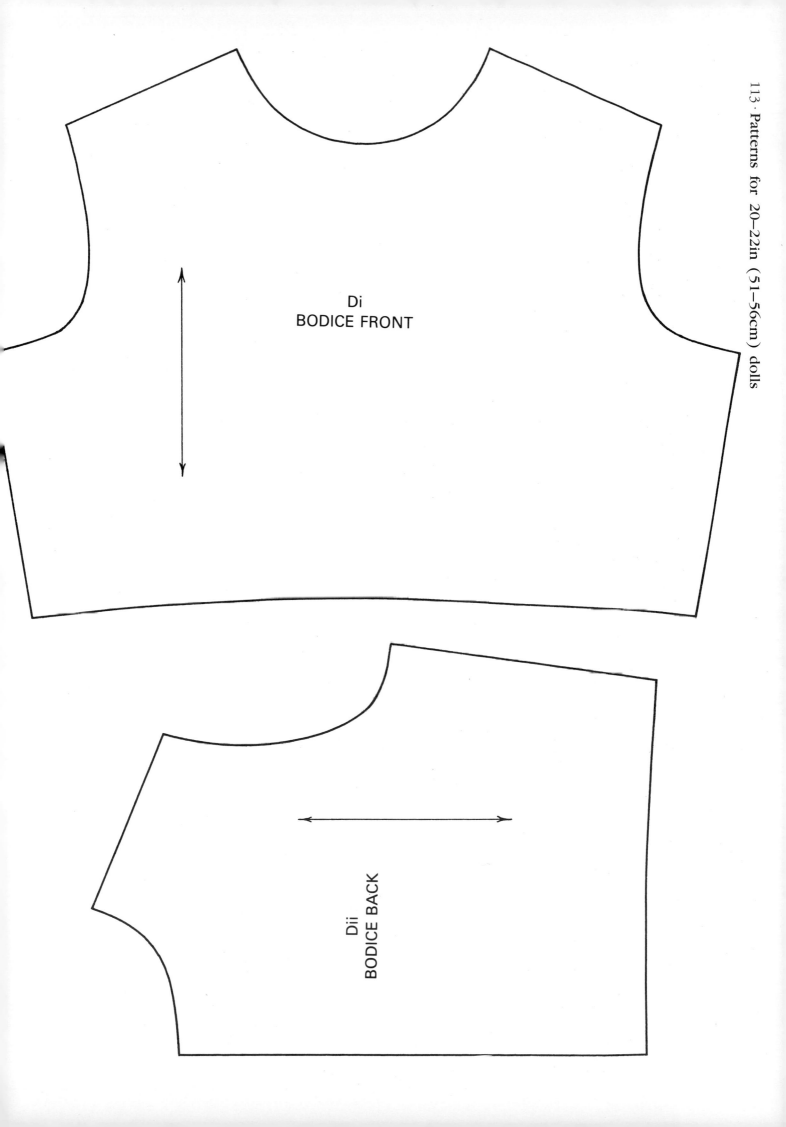

Di
BODICE FRONT

Dii
BODICE BACK

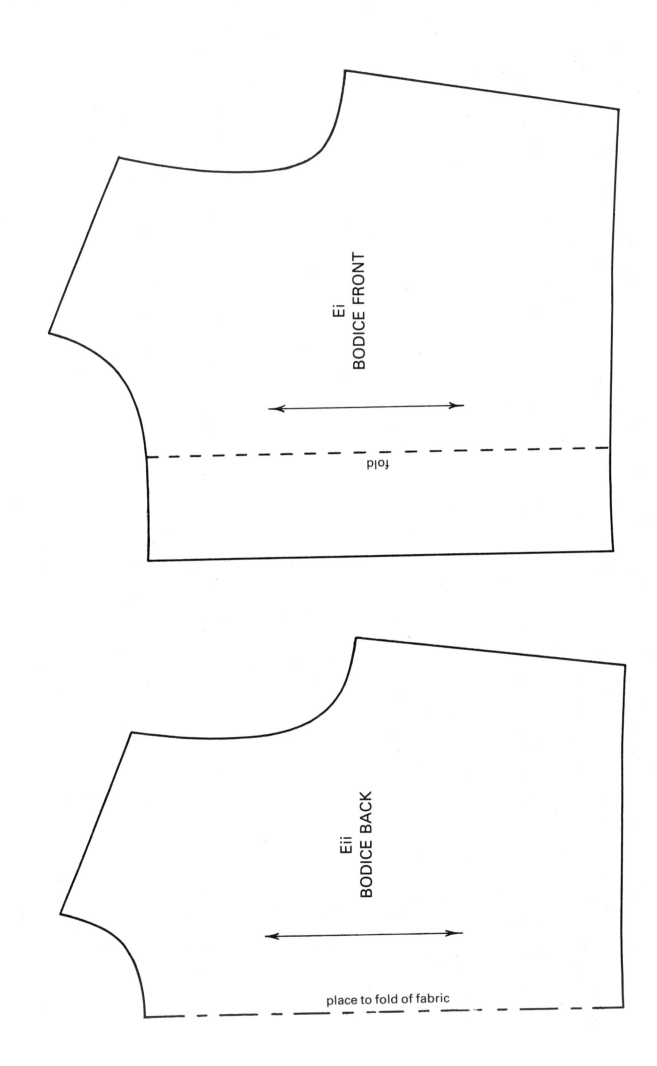

Ei
BODICE FRONT

fold

Eii
BODICE BACK

place to fold of fabric

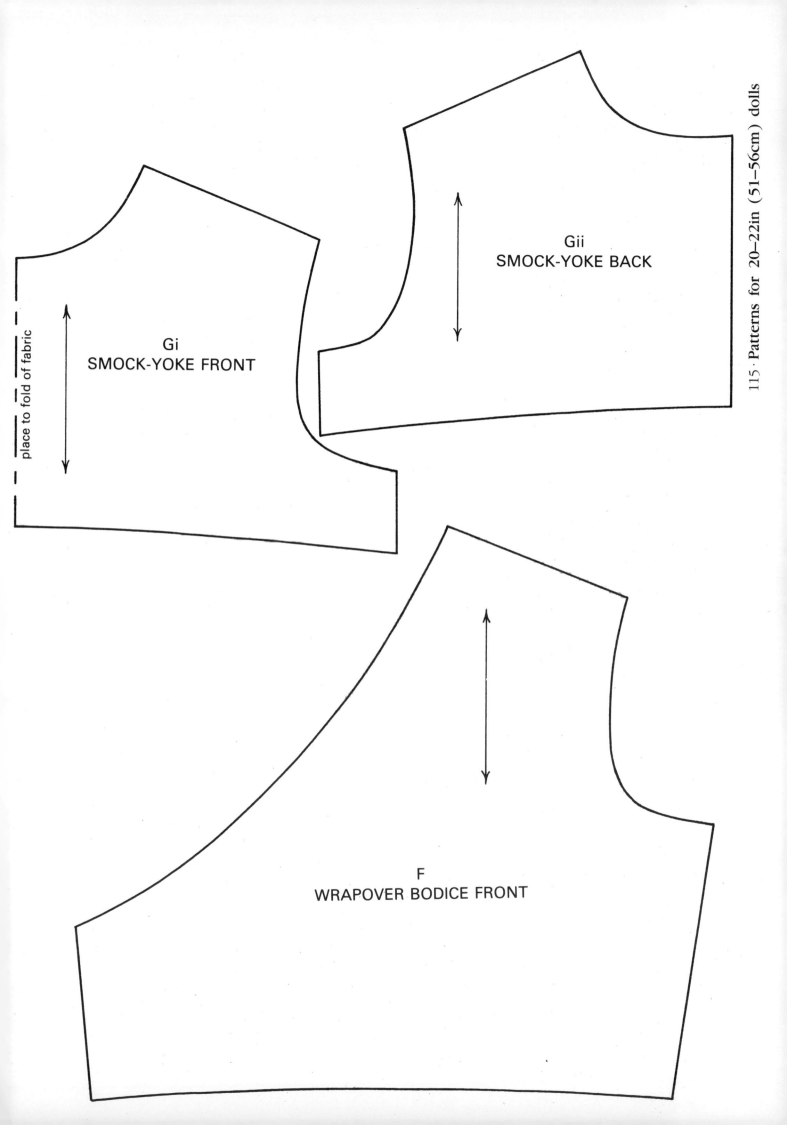

place to fold of fabric

Gi
SMOCK-YOKE FRONT

Gii
SMOCK-YOKE BACK

F
WRAPOVER BODICE FRONT

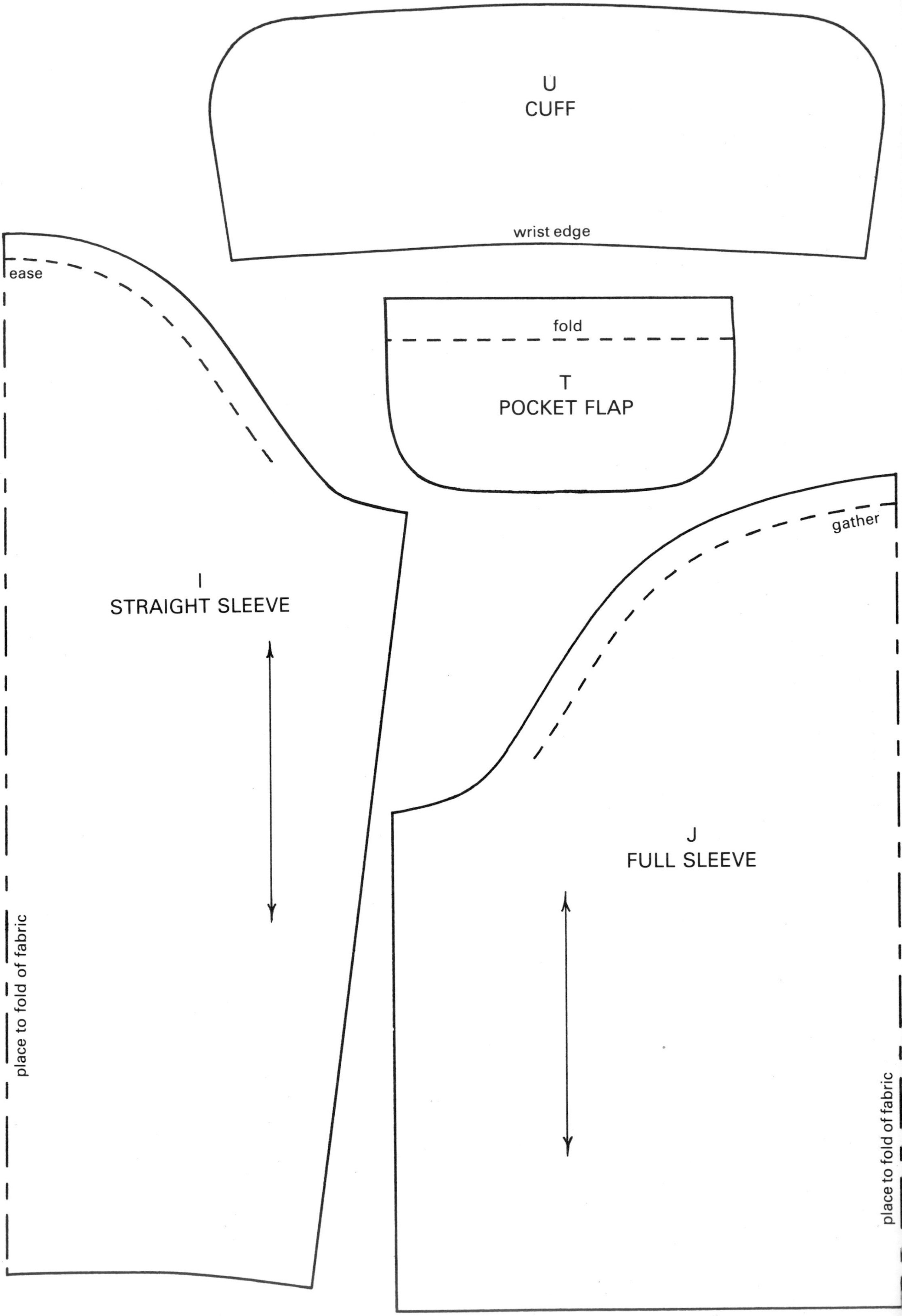

U
CUFF

wrist edge

fold

T
POCKET FLAP

ease

I
STRAIGHT SLEEVE

gather

J
FULL SLEEVE

place to fold of fabric

place to fold of fabric

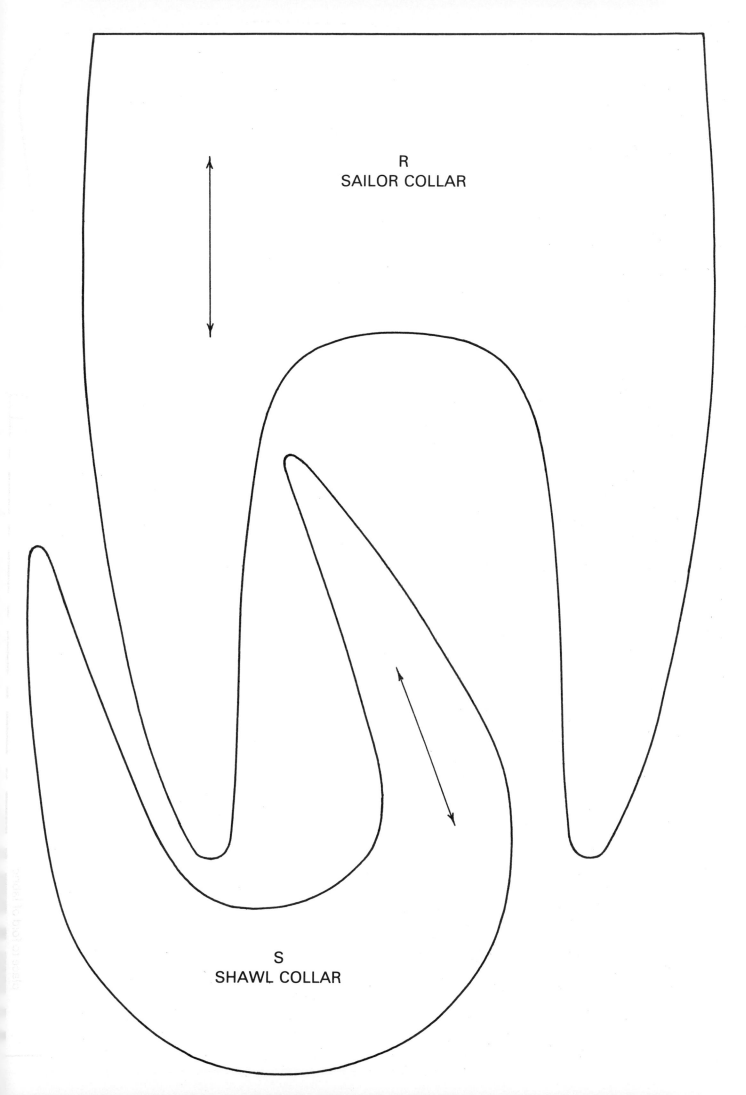

R
SAILOR COLLAR

S
SHAWL COLLAR

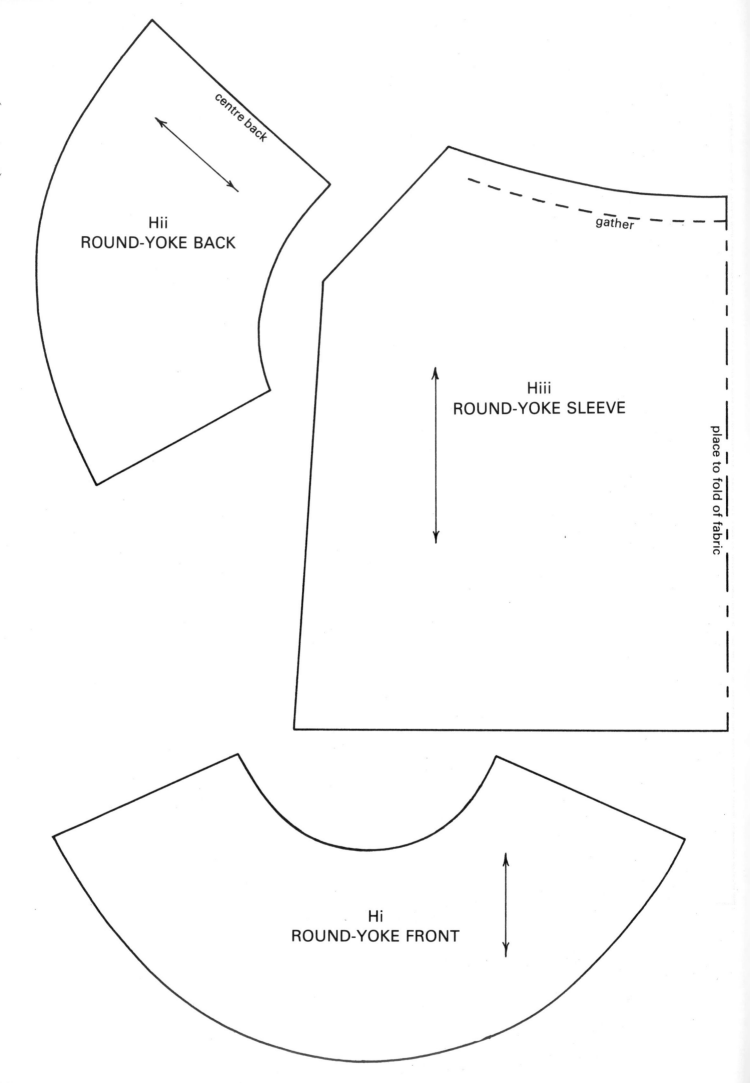

Hii
ROUND-YOKE BACK

centre back

gather

Hiii
ROUND-YOKE SLEEVE

place to fold of fabric

Hi
ROUND-YOKE FRONT

centre back

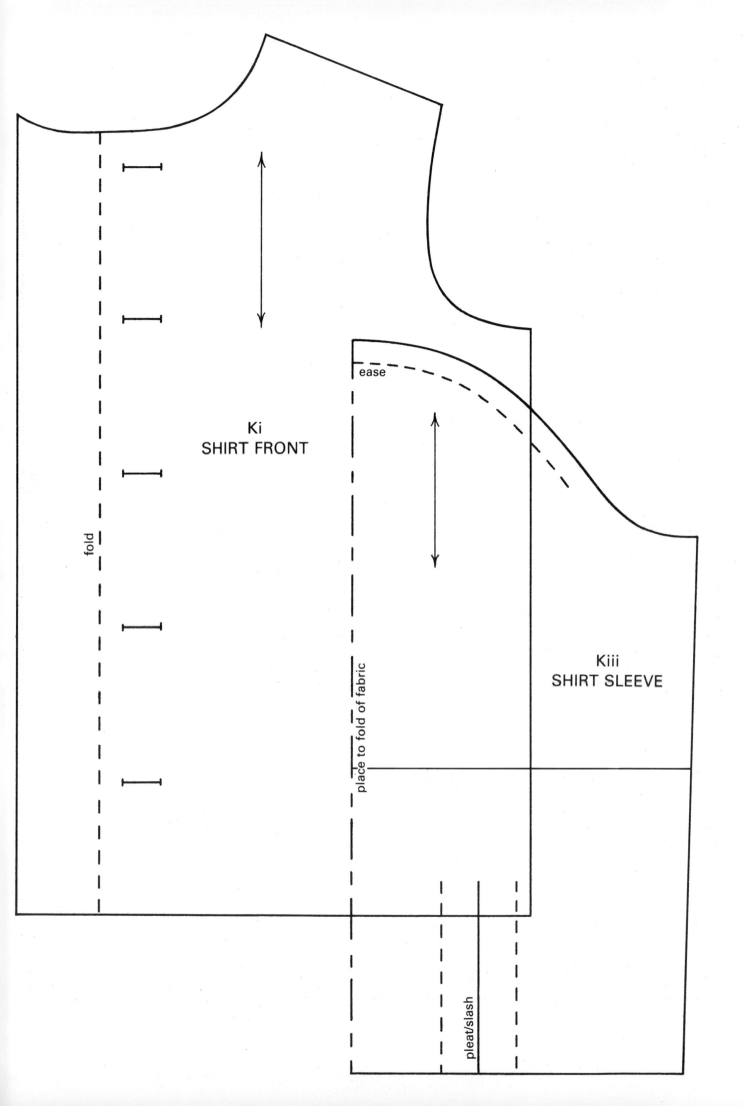

fold

Ki
SHIRT FRONT

ease

place to fold of fabric

Kiii
SHIRT SLEEVE

pleat/slash

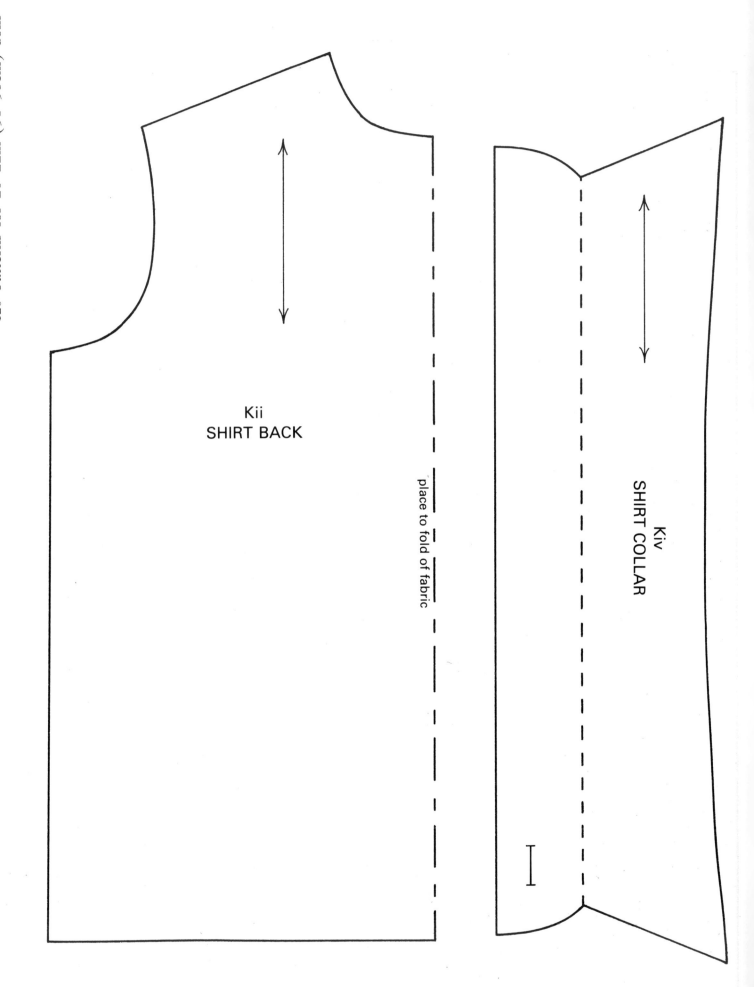

Kii
SHIRT BACK

place to fold of fabric

Kiv
SHIRT COLLAR

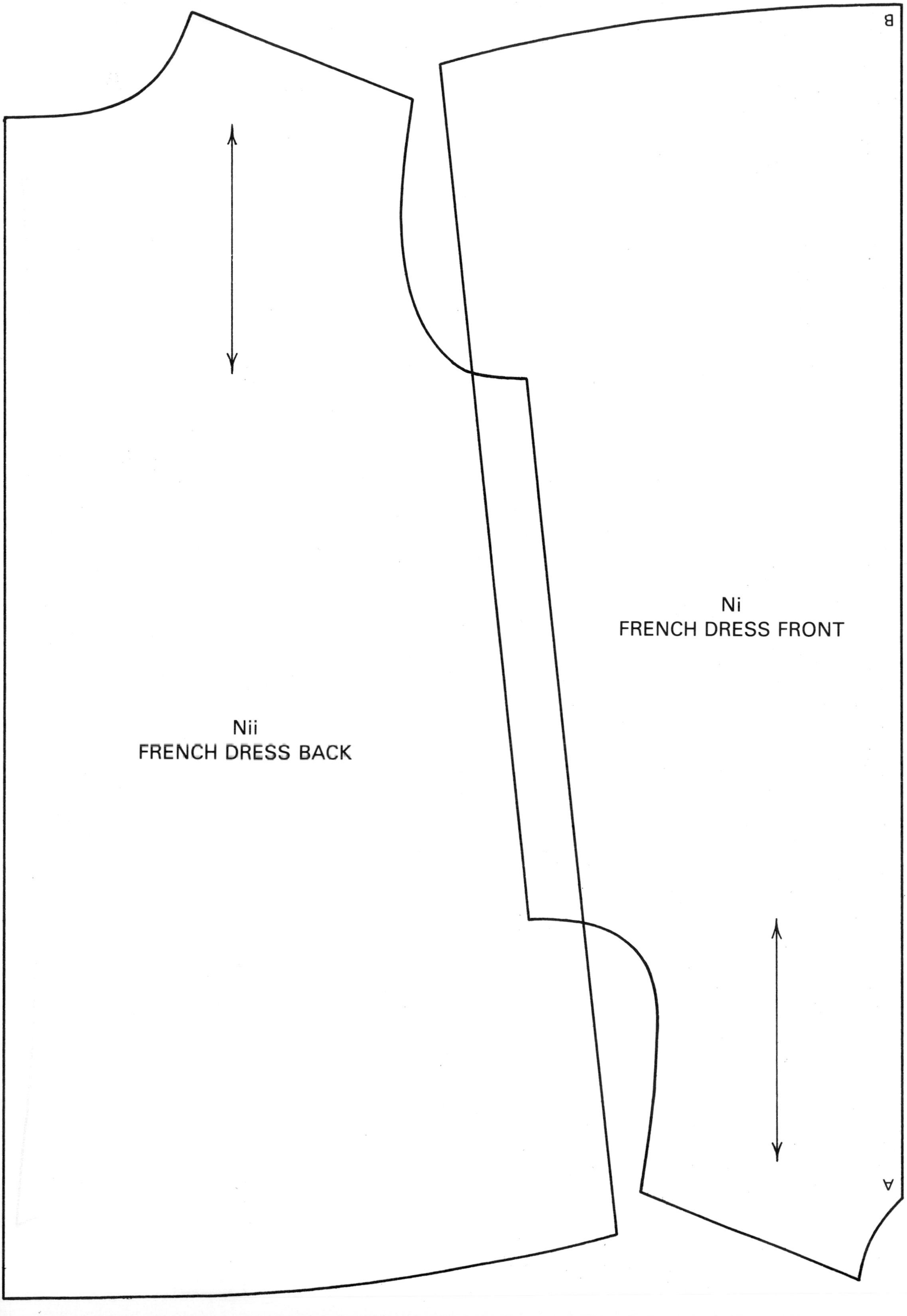

Ni
FRENCH DRESS FRONT

Nii
FRENCH DRESS BACK

B

A

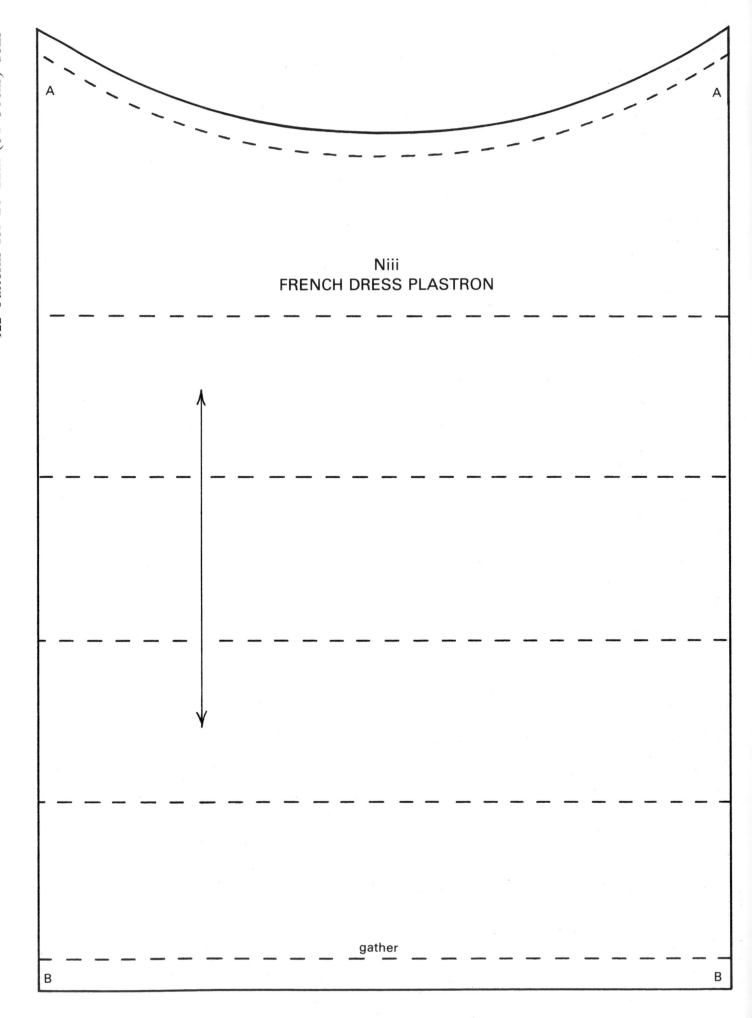

A

A

Niii
FRENCH DRESS PLASTRON

gather

B

B

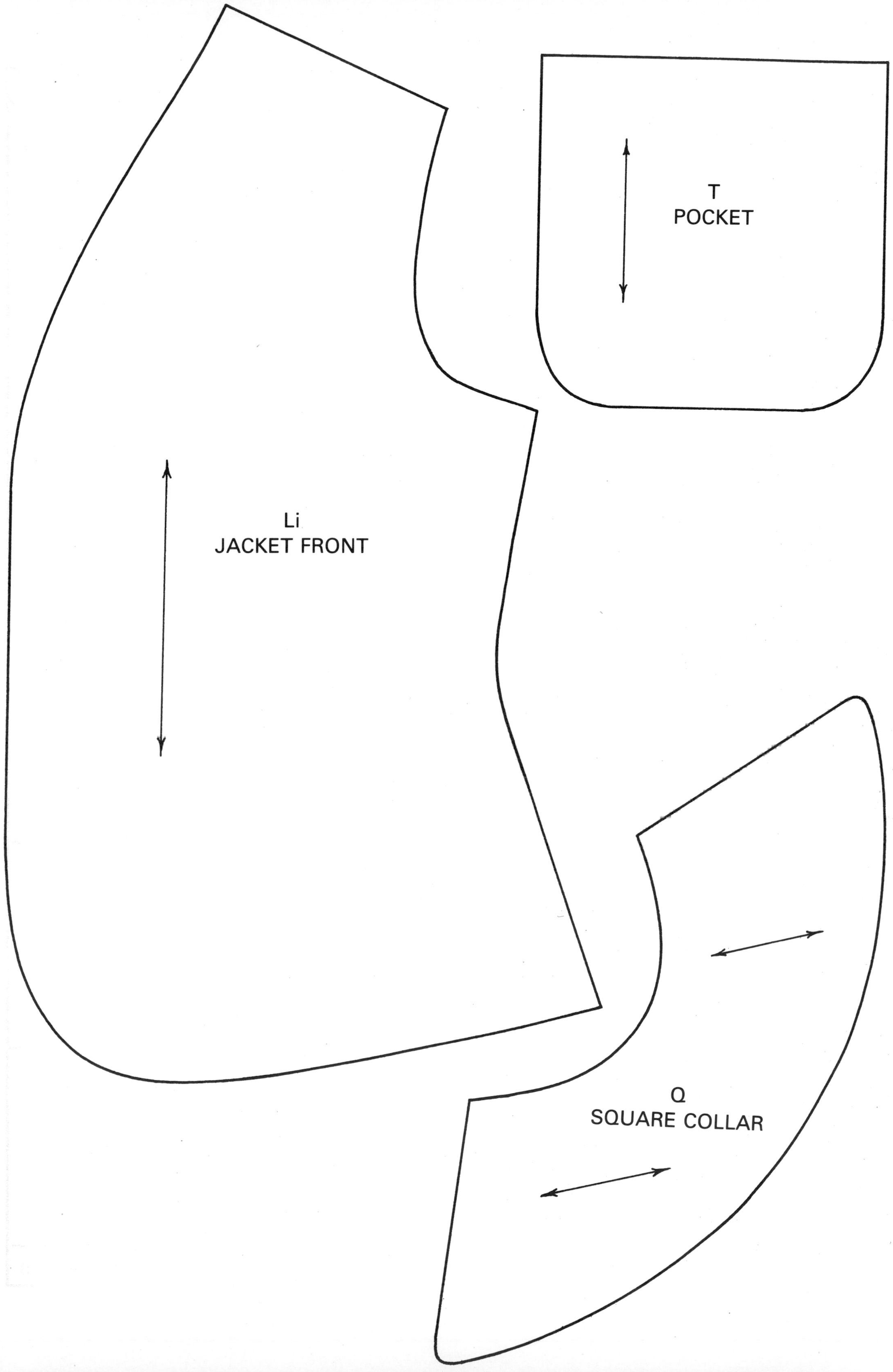

T
POCKET

Li
JACKET FRONT

Q
SQUARE COLLAR

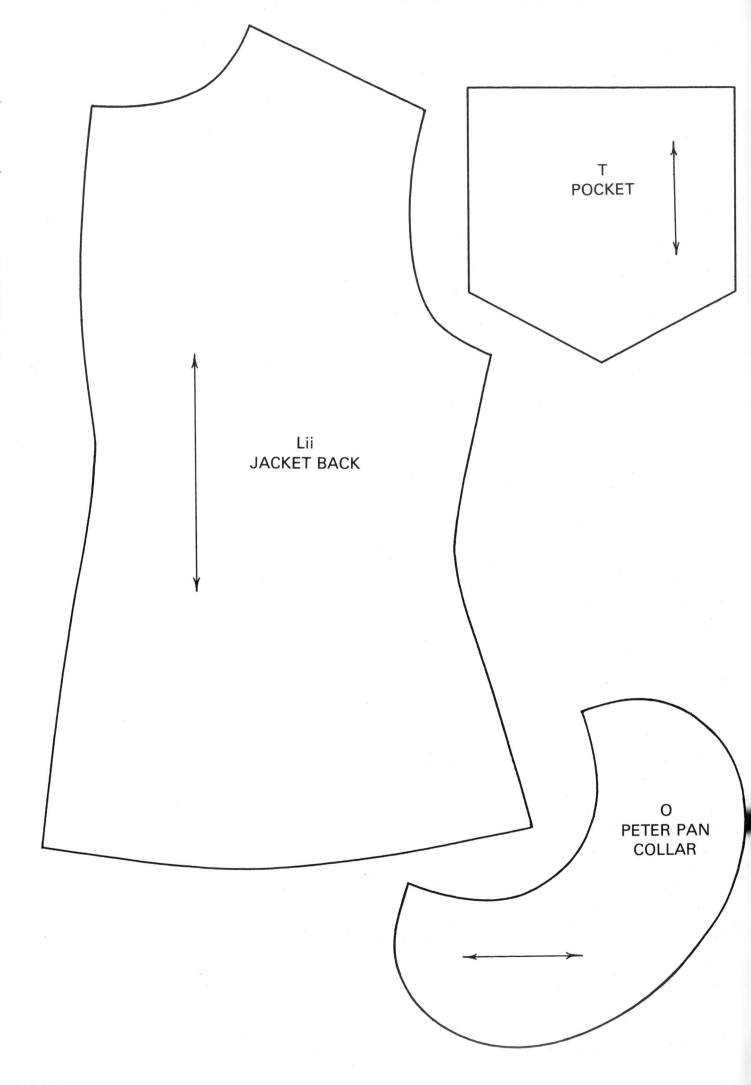

T
POCKET

Lii
JACKET BACK

O
PETER PAN
COLLAR

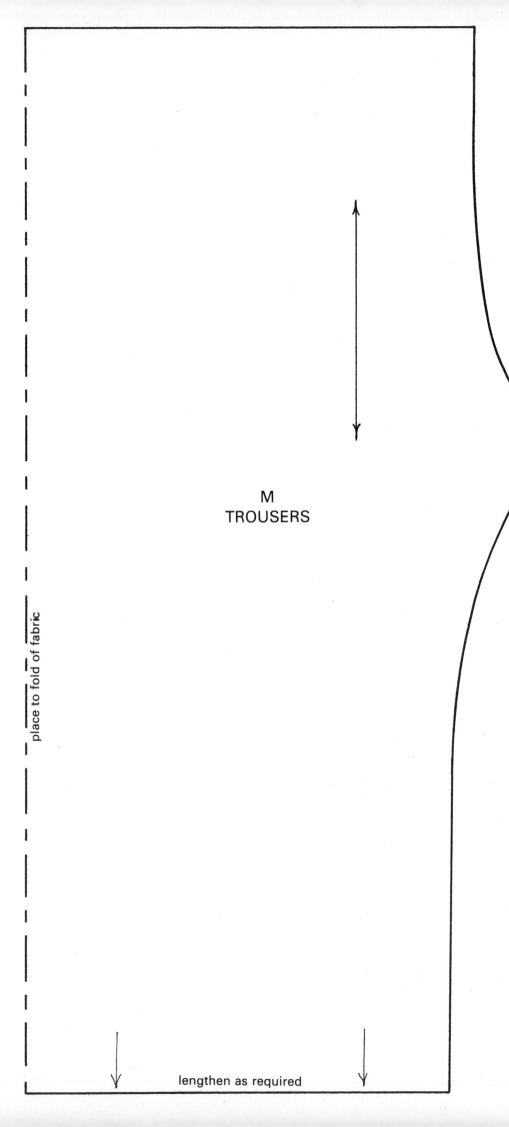

M
TROUSERS

place to fold of fabric

lengthen as required

6 BABY CLOTHES

Underwear

The baby's nappy is described in Chapter 2, as are knickers, which may also be made for baby dolls. Simple nappies may be made from hemmed towelling or, for small dolls, a white face-flannel, cut diagonally and the raw edge hemmed or bound with white bias binding. Dolls' plastic pants can be made from life-size ones by using the knickers pattern (piece *A*), following the instructions in Chapter 2.

Babies may have liberty bodices, socks and chemises, all described in Chapter 2.

Petticoats for baby dolls might have high waistlines – made from pattern pieces *Gi* and *Gii* (smock yoke) with gathered skirts or A-line (pattern pieces *Vi* and *Vii*) depending on the style of the dress. Follow the instructions for petticoats in Chapter 2.

Dresses

For baby dolls, with their short, plump bodies, the best patterns for dresses are the smock yoke *Gi* and *Gii* (which make a high waistline on babies), with the full sleeve pattern *J* (long or short), and the round-yoke patterns *Hi, Hii* and *Hiii*. Both of these styles can be made up in a variety of ways (see Figs 41 and 44), and trimmed as simply or elaborately as you please. Full making-up instructions are given for both styles in Chapter 3.

When making baby gowns with long skirts, measure the length required plus hem allowance, and cut the skirt at least twice this width. As baby dolls' necks are usually very short, the styles are shown without collars, but if you prefer, the Peter Pan collar (pattern piece *O*) may be used with either pattern (see Chapter 4). Short baby dresses may have matching knickers.

For baby bonnets, see Chapter 9. See also the knitting and crochet patterns in Chapter 8.

Plate 10
The 20in (51cm) doll in the centre of the picture is 'Collette', made from a kit from Ridings Craft. She wears a navy blue wool collarless jacket with a matching gathered skirt and a white blouse with a Peter Pan collar. Her bow tie is made from red and white spotted cotton and matches the hatband on the straw hat from GP Ceramics. Her shoulder-bag is brown leather, her stockings blue and white striped stretch-cotton. The spectacles are from Ray Cornford.

The 14in (35.5cm) doll (author's collection) on the left wears a red tartan dress with long plain sleeves, a round neck and a gathered skirt. The white broderie anglaise applied yoke has a band collar and shoulder frills and is trimmed with a black ribbon bow and tiny black bead 'buttons'. The sleeve ends are trimmed with white broderie anglaise turn-back cuffs.

The 16in (40.5cm) doll on the right is a reproduction 'Hilda' from GP Ceramics. She wears a cream cotton jacket with a sailor collar and long full sleeves with cuffs trimmed with navy blue ribbon over a matching sleeveless blouse with a band collar. Her pleated skirt is navy blue fine wool, and a navy blue ribbon bow trims the front of the blouse. The straw hat is from GP Ceramics; the navy wool socks are made from a child's sock.

The 10in (25.5cm) doll (author's collection) at the front of the picture wears a hooded cloak made in red felt, the neckline tied with red satin ribbons.

a

b

c

d

e

f

Rompers
(*using drawers pattern piece B*)

The drawers pattern piece *B* is extended at the top edge to reach the doll's armpits, and cut straight across. Legs may be short or long as preferred. This garment is designed for lightweight fabrics.

Shirred rompers
(*Fig 10b*)

Cut two drawers pieces, stitch the centre-front seam and hem the top edge. Mark gathering lines and gather with shirring elastic to fit the doll's body. Stitch the centre-back seam and the inside leg seam. Make casings at the leg ends and thread elastic to fit the doll's legs. Make fabric or ribbon straps and stitch to the back and front top edges to tie on the shoulders.

Rompers with band top
(*Fig 10c*)

Cut a band (like a deep waistband) to fit the doll's body. Cut two drawers pieces and stitch the centre-front seam. Stitch the centre-back seam, leaving a small opening with hemmed facings. Stitch the inside leg seam. Gather the top edge and stitch to the band. Fasten the back band with buttons and buttonholes or loops. Make casings at the leg ends and thread elastic to fit the doll's legs. Make fabric or ribbon straps and sew to the band top back and front.

Rompers with yoke and sleeves
(*smock-yoke patterns front Gi and back Gii and sleeve pattern J – long or short*)

Make up the smock yoke and sleeves as described in 'Dress bodices' in Chapter 3. Make up the drawers as

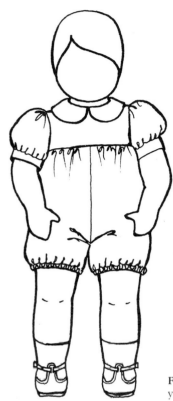

Fig 42 Rompers with yoke and sleeves

Fig 41 Dresses for toddler and baby dolls using smock-yoke pattern pieces front *Gi* and back *Gii*

View a Short dress with a gathered skirt, bound neckline and short puffed sleeves (pattern piece *J*) gathered into narrow bands. The neckline and sleeve ends are trimmed with gathered lace frills. Suitable for lightweight fabrics, eg cotton, silk or Viyella, in plain colours or tiny prints. A ribbon sash is tied around the high waistline. Plain strong or pastel colours, eg a pink cotton dress with white lace and pink satin ribbon, or a dress in tiny print with a red or blue ground, white lace and plain red or blue ribbon.

View b Short dress with a gathered skirt, plain round neckline and long full sleeves (pattern piece *J*) gathered into cuffs, in plain or patterned fabrics with a toning or contrasting ribbon or braid trimming on the cuffs and outlining the yoke front. Suitable for lightweight fabrics, eg a navy blue plain Viyella dress with a scarlet ribbon trim, or a dress in a tiny-flower-print cotton with a plain-colour ribbon trim.

View c Coat dress (pattern adapted to a

front opening) with a gathered skirt, round collar (pattern piece *P*) and long straight sleeves (pattern piece *I*) and a front button fastening. Suitable for medium- or lightweight fabrics, eg fine wool, needlecord or velveteen, in plain colours. Trimmed with top-stitching on the collar and sleeve ends. Eg a navy blue wool coat with red top-stitching; or a pale-blue velveteen coat with matching top-stitching.

View d This long baby gown has a pintucked bodice, short puffed sleeves (pattern piece *J*) gathered into narrow bands, and a pintucked gathered skirt. Fine-gathered lace trims the neckline and sleeve bands; wider lace trims the bodice centre front, the skirt and the skirt hem. A ribbon sash is tied around the high waistline. Suitable for lightweight plain pastel fabrics, eg silk or lawn; also for sheer fabrics worn over a white or coloured slip. Eg a cream silk gown trimmed with cream lace, with a cream sash; or a white voile gown with white lace worn over a pale-blue slip with a blue ribbon

sash. Suitable for antique baby dolls circa 1900.

View e Long baby gown with a pintucked yoke, long full sleeves (pattern piece *J*) gathered into narrow cuffs, and a long, full, gathered skirt with a centre panel of lace, ribbon insertion and pintucks outlined with lace. There is fine lace edging at the neck and wrists and there are tiny buttons on the bodice front. Suitable for lightweight fabrics, eg lawn or silk, trimmed with lace and coloured satin ribbon. Eg a white lawn gown with pink ribbons; or an ivory silk gown with blue ribbons. (Shown in colour on page 86.) Suitable for antique baby dolls circa 1850.

View f Long baby gown with a bound neckline, short puffed sleeves (pattern piece *J*) gathered to broderie anglaise frills, and a full skirt with a broderie anglaise frill at the hem. A broderie anglaise frill outlines the square yoke. Suitable for lightweight cotton fabrics, eg lawn, in white or pastel colours. May also be made entirely in broderie anglaise and perhaps worn over a coloured slip.

for band-top rompers and stitch to the yoke. Make casings at the leg ends and thread elastic to fit the doll's legs. Fasten the back yoke with buttons and buttonholes or press-studs (Fig 42).

Fitting notes Check that the shoulder-to-crotch measurement is long enough. Peter Pan or square collars, (pattern pieces O and Q) may be used with the rompers (match size to smock-yoke size).

Bunnysuit
(*pattern pieces X*)

The all-in-one bunnysuit is designed for fleece fabrics with slight stretch. It has an optional hood, given in the smaller size (enlarge pattern if required), and fastens with a small zip at the centre front. Before cutting, check the chest measurement, the back neck-to-crotch, and inside leg measurements. Also check the sleeve length (underarm) allowing for the hem.

To make the bunnysuit, cut two body pieces and two soles (and one hood if required). Stitch the centre-back body seam. Stitch the centre-front body seam from the crotch up for 1–2in (2.5–5cm), turn back the remainder of the front edges and sew in the zip. Stitch the side seams from wrist to foot. Stitch the inside leg seam. Stitch the soles into the feet. Hem the sleeve ends. Fold the hood piece in half and stitch the centre-back seam. Hem the front edge, and gather the back neck edge to fit and stitch to the neckline. (Or face the neckline with bias binding.) Ease any trapped pile

from the seams, and clip, if necessary, around the zip (Fig 43).

Note The bunnysuit pattern may be used to make a stretch-towelling all-in-one, facing the neckline and front edges with bias binding. Fasten with press-studs.

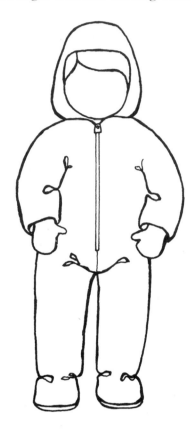

Fig 43 Bunnysuit

Fig 44 Dresses for toddlers and baby dolls using round-yoke dress pattern pieces front *Hi*, back *Hii* and sleeve *Hiii*

View a Short dress with a plain round neck and short puffed sleeves with bound ends. Made in plain-colour, lightweight fabrics, eg cotton lawn or silk in pastel colours, trimmed with embroidery or an embroidered motif on the yoke. Eg a pale-pink silk dress with pale-pink, green and cream embroidery; or a golden-yellow cotton dress with a white-daisy-and-green-leaf embroidered motif. Suitable for antique baby/toddler dolls circa 1920. (Shown in colour on page 131 as a baby gown.)

View b Short dress with a bound neckline and long full sleeves with bound ends. Trimmed with a self-fabric frill around the yoke, lace at the neckline and wrists, and tiny buttons on the yoke front. Suitable for printed or plain fabrics, cotton or Viyella-type; for larger dolls also needlecord.

View c Short dress with a yoke and overskirt made in broderie anglaise to simulate a pinafore has short puffed

sleeves gathered into frills and a skirt. Suitable for lightweight fabrics. Plain colours for the yoke lining, skirt and sleeves to contrast with white broderie anglaise for the skirt and yoke, eg pink, blue or yellow cotton, or navy, red or brown Viyella. Note: This may be made as one garment, or as two separate garments, making up the dress in the plain fabric and a sleeveless overdress in broderie anglaise.

View d This long baby gown has a plain round neckline and short puffed sleeves gathered into frills. The whole dress is made in lace over silk, using the two layers of fabric as one, and concentrating the lace pattern on the yoke, sleeves and skirt hem. The lining may be in the same colour as the lace, eg white lace over white silk, or in a contrasting pastel colour, eg white lace over blue silk, or cream lace over pink silk. Suitable for antique baby dolls.

View e Long baby gown with a plain round neckline, pintucked yoke, short puffed sleeves gathered into cuffs, and a frilled skirt hem. Trimmed with narrow satin ribbon slotted through lace or broderie anglaise insertion on the yoke front, cuffs and skirt. Suitable for lightweight silk or cotton fabrics in white or pastel colours with pastel-coloured ribbons. Also in sheer fabrics, eg organdy or voile, over a pastel-coloured slip with matching ribbons. Eg a white organdy dress with white lace insertion and pale pink ribbons over a pale pink silk slip. Suitable for antique baby dolls circa 1920.

View f Long baby gown with a plain round neckline and long full sleeves gathered into deep lace frills. There is a deep gathered lace frill around the yoke. Suitable for all lightweight silk or cotton fabrics, and for soft satin, eg a cream satin gown with cream lace trim, or a white silk gown with white lace trim. Suitable for antique baby dolls.

a

b

c

d

e

f

7 JACKETS, COATS AND CLOAKS

Jackets and coats are made in light-, medium- or heavier-weight fabrics, depending on the size of the doll. They should be lined with a matching lightweight fabric, and where more stiffening is required, an un-bleached-calico interlining is used.

The basic jacket

(*pattern pieces front Li, back Lii and sleeve I, with optional collar and cuffs*)

To make the jacket, cut two back pieces, two front pieces and two sleeves in fabric and in lining. Make up the fabric and lining separately. Stitch the centre-back seam. Stitch the shoulder seams. Gather the sleeve heads to ease and stitch the sleeves into the armholes. Stitch the side seams through the armhole to the sleeve ends. Clip all curves and press the seams open. If the jacket is to have bound edges, stitch with *wrong sides* facing. Pull the lining sleeves down the fabric sleeves. Stitch the fabric to the lining all the way around the outside edge, trim and bind with bias-cut fabric. If the jacket is to have unbound edges, stitch with right sides facing, all the way around the outside edge leaving a gap at the centre-back lower edge. Clip, trim the seam and turn through. Slipstitch the opening closed and press. Turn up the sleeve ends and slipstitch in place. Hem the lining over the turned-up sleeve ends. The jacket may be fastened edge-to-edge or with an overlap.
Fitting notes Check the chest measurement. Check the back length. Check the sleeve length against the doll's underarm. Check that sufficient overlap is allowed for front closure.

Jacket and coat variations on the basic jacket

The shawl collar, pattern piece *S*, or the sailor collar, pattern piece *R* and cuff, pattern piece *U*, may be used with the jacket if required (see 'Collars' in Chapter 4). The full sleeve, pattern piece *J*, with a cuff may also be used with the jacket pattern (see 'Sleeves' in Chapter 3). Both pocket patterns *T* and cuff pattern *U* may be used with this jacket.

The jacket front edges may be cut back, perhaps to show a mock waistcoat front, or squared. The patterns may be lengthened to make a dress or coat (see Fig 47) by extending the centre-front, centre-back and side seams.

Jackets and coats may also be made from front-opening bodice patterns *Ei* and *Eii*, used with sleeve *I*. The pattern will make a waisted coat with a gathered or flared skirt (see Fig 41c) or may be lengthened in A-line to full-length. The round collar, pattern piece *P*, and cuff *U* may be used with this pattern.

Bodice patterns back *Eii* and front *F* may be used to make wrapover-style coats, either waisted with gathered or flared skirt, or extended to full-length A-line. The shawl collar (*S*) or the sailor collar (*R*) may be used with this pattern (see Fig 22).

Jackets and coats with overlapping front edges can be fastened with buttons and buttonholes or with hooks and eyes and 'mock' buttons. The wrapover style can have a double-breasted fastening. Edge-to-edge fastenings may be with buttons and loops, hooks and eyes or frog fastenings. On large dolls, small toggles might be used. Consider trimming coats with fur collars and cuffs.

a

b

c

d

Fig 45 Dresses, jackets and coats using jacket pattern pieces front *Li* and back *Lii* with shawl collar *S* and sleeve pattern *I*

View a Jacket with a shawl collar and cuffs (pattern piece *U*) and pocket flaps (pattern piece *T*) in a firm, medium-weight fabric, eg wool, brocade or velvet. There is a trimming on the collar, jacket, cuffs and pocket flaps of bias binding, heavy lace or braid. The jacket is lined, and fastened with buttons and worked buttonholes. It is worn over a sleeveless dropped-waist dress (adapt patterns *Di, Dii*) with a box-pleated skirt in medium-weight fabrics, eg taffeta or satinised cotton. The bodice can be overlaid with gathered lace. The jacket and dress may be made in matching or contrasting subtle colours, eg a medium-green taffeta dress with a darker-green velvet jacket, and the pocket flaps, collar and cuffs in the dress fabric, or an ivory brocade jacket with a pink taffeta dress. (Shown in colour on page 167.) Suitable for French bébés circa the 1880s.

View b Jacket (patterns shortened), with a shawl collar made in medium-weight fabric, eg wool or velveteen, and lined. The jacket is fastened with buttons and worked buttonholes, and worn over a blouse with a Peter Pan collar in a lightweight silk or cotton fabric and a gathered skirt in fabric to match the jacket. Suitable for plain strong or subtle colours or prints, eg a jacket and skirt in printed needlecord with a toning plain-colour blouse, or a jacket and skirt in plain navy wool over a white blouse. (Shown in colour on page 127.)

View c Coat (jacket patterns lengthened – see Fig 47), in a medium-weight fabric, eg wool or velvet. It has a shawl collar and patch pockets (pattern piece *T*) trimmed with heavy lace, and is fastened with buttons and worked buttonholes. The coat is lined. Suitable for plain fabrics, eg grey velvet with white lace trimming, or brown wool with cream lace trimming.

View d This dress (jacket patterns lengthened), made without the collar, has three-quarter length sleeves and a pleated skirt. The bodice and sleeves are in a medium-weight fabric, eg brocade or velveteen, and the dress is trimmed with ribbon around the neckline and sleeve ends and down the bodice front. There is lace at the neckline and sleeve ends. The sash and pleated skirt are in lightweight fabrics, eg silk, and button and buttonhole fastenings are used. Suitable for plain or patterned fabrics in toning strong or subtle colours, eg a crimson velvet bodice and sleeves, with a rose-pink sash and skirt, crimson satin ribbon and cream lace trimmings, or a brown brocade bodice and sleeves, with a cream taffeta skirt and sash, brown velvet ribbon and cream lace trimmings. Suitable for French bébés circa the 1880s.

e

f

Fig 45 Dresses, jackets and coats using jacket pattern pieces front *Li* and back *Lii* with shawl collar *S* and sleeve pattern *I*

View e Dress (jacket patterns lengthened), with a shawl collar, three-quarter length sleeves with turn-back cuffs, and a pleated skirt. Worn over a ruched front. The bodice and sleeves are in a medium-weight fabric, eg brocade or velvet; the skirt, collar and cuffs are in a lightweight fabric. There is a trimming of gathered lace on the collar, cuffs and skirt, and a large sash of the skirt fabric. The fastenings are buttons and buttonholes. Suitable for subtle or strong colours in plain or patterned fabrics, eg a mid-blue brocade bodice and sleeves with a paler-blue skirt, collar, sash, cuffs and ruched inset with cream or white lace, or a dark-grey velvet bodice and sleeves with a crimson silk collar, cuffs, sash, skirt and ruched inset with grey lace trimming. Suitable for French bébés circa the 1880s.
View f Coat (jacket patterns lengthened), made with a shawl collar, cuffs (pattern piece *U*) and pocket flaps (pattern piece *T*) in a medium-weight fabric, eg wool or tweed, patterned or plain. The coat is trimmed with top-stitching on the collar, cuffs and pocket flaps. It has button and buttonhole fastenings and buttons on the pocket flaps and cuffs.

Plate 11

The 22in (56cm) lady doll at the centre of the picture is a reproduction Bru made from a kit from Reflect Reproduction Dolls. She wears a gold silk dress with a wrapover bodice, elbow-length full sleeves and a long gathered skirt. The shawl collar and cuffs are made of embroidered organdy. The dress fastens with sashes, stitched to either side of the front bodice and tied at the back. The picture hat is made of black hat felt and trimmed with black satin ribbon and a peacock feather. The doll carries a walking stick and a black velvet handbag.

The 14in (35.5cm) doll (author's collection) at the front wears an ivory lace dress with full sleeves, a band collar and a gathered skirt. The sash is golden-yellow satin ribbon trimmed with artificial flowers, and the cameo pendant is from GP Ceramics.

The 18in (45.5cm) reproduction KR 117 from Reflect Reproduction Dolls on the left wears a collarless jacket with edge-to-edge fastening and a peplum in black printed needlecord with a matching flared skirt. The jacket and skirt are trimmed with narrow black velvet ribbon and worn over a beige lace blouse with a band collar and frilled cuffs. The doll has a pillbox hat and muff made in dark-brown fur-fabric and a brooch made from a life-size earring.

Recollect's 20in (51cm) reproduction Kestner on the right of the picture wears a white dotted-swiss smock dress with full sleeves and a frilled hem. The dress is trimmed with insertion lace. The straw hat from GP Ceramics is trimmed with artificial flowers.

a   b   c

Fig 46 Suits for lady dolls using jacket pattern pieces front *Li* and back *Lii* and sleeve pattern *I*

View a This collarless jacket edged with gathered lace frills is fastened at the centre front with buttons and buttonholes or hooks and eyes. It is worn with a flared skirt in a matching fabric cut with a front panel trimmed with lace to match the jacket. Suitable for medium-weight fabrics, eg taffeta, fine wool or velvet, in plain strong colours. Eg a green velvet suit trimmed with heavy cream lace; or a grey taffeta suit trimmed with grey lace. Note: Made in white or ivory taffeta or satin this pattern would make a wedding dress. Suitable for antique dolls circa the 1870s.

View b This jacket with a shawl collar (pattern piece *S*) has button and button-hole front fastenings and a lace edging on the collar and sleeve ends. Worn with a full-length gathered skirt in matching fabric. Suitable for medium-weight fabrics, eg fine wool, velveteen or needle-cord, in plain strong colours with a collar in matching or contrasting fabric. Eg a brown wool suit and collar with cream lace trimming, or an olive-green needle-cord suit with a white lawn collar and white lace.

View c This collarless jacket with bound edges and deep cuffs (pattern piece *U*) has button and buttonhole or hook and eye front fastenings. The neckline and cuffs are trimmed with lace. It is worn with a gathered full-length skirt and a lace-trimmed looped overskirt. Suitable for medium- or lightweight fabrics, the jacket and skirt may be made in the same fabric or in toning fabrics, eg a jacket and underskirt in plum-colour velvet, an over-skirt and cuffs in plum brocade, and the jacket edges bound with plum brocade and black lace trimming, or a jacket, overskirt and underskirt in beige silk trimmed with beige lace. Note: Made in heavy silk or taffeta in white or ivory trimmed with matching lace, this pattern is suitable for a wedding dress. Suitable for antique dolls circa 1875–85.

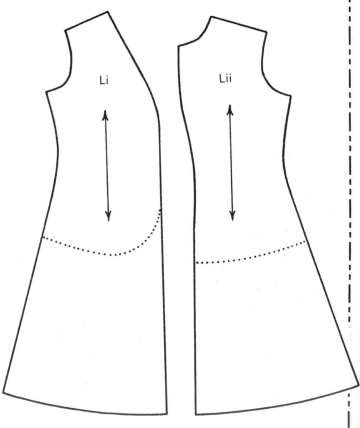

Fig 47 Lengthening the jacket pattern

a

b

c

d

Fig 48 Jackets and coats using the front-opening pattern pieces front *Ei* and back *Eii* adapted to A-line

View a This 'sailor' blouse or jacket with the front neckline cut in a V shape (see Fig 17) has a sailor collar (pattern piece *R*), shirt sleeves (pattern piece *Kiii*) gathered into cuffs, and button and buttonhole fastenings. Suitable for light- or medium-weight fabrics, eg cotton or fine wool, with the collar in a matching or contrasting fabric and trimmed with contrasting ribbon or braid. Worn over a sleeveless blouse (pattern pieces *Di* and *Dii*) with the band collar trimmed to match the sailor collar, and cuffs and a pleated skirt made in matching or contrasting fabrics. Eg a black or navy blue fine-wool blouse, skirt, jacket and collar all trimmed with scarlet ribbon or braid; or a cream blouse, jacket and collar trimmed with navy, and a navy skirt. (Shown in colour on page 127.) Suitable for antique dolls circa 1890–1910.

View b Simple jacket with plain long sleeves (pattern piece *I*), a round neckline and optional buttons and buttonholes. Suitable for any medium-weight fabric, eg wool, velveteen or needlecord. The jacket is worn with matching trousers (pattern piece *M*) and shirt (pattern pieces *Ki, Kii, Kiii* and *Kiv*) in a lightweight fabric. Eg a jacket and trousers in dark-green velvet with a white silk shirt, or a jacket and trousers in brown wool with a cream Viyella shirt. (Shown in colour on page 86.)

View c 'Buster Brown' suit The jacket has a square collar (pattern piece *Q*), shirt sleeves (pattern piece *Kiii*) with cuffs, and button and buttonhole fastenings. The jacket is cut long and has a self-fabric belt at the waist. The trousers (pattern piece *M*) are cut to knee length and made in matching fabric. Suitable for medium-weight fabrics, eg wool, heavy cotton or tweed, in plain subtle colours; the collar can be in contrasting cotton fabric. Eg a brown heavy-cotton suit with a white collar; or a beige wool suit with a black cotton collar. Suitable for antique boy dolls circa 1910–25.

View d This coat cut to meet edge-to-edge at the centre front has long plain sleeves (pattern piece *I*), frog fastenings and optional patch pockets. The pockets and sleeve ends are top-stitched to simulate cuffs. Suitable for medium-weight fabrics, best in plain strong colours, eg a red velvet coat with black frog fastenings, or a brown wool coat with brown frog fastenings. Also suitable for fur fabrics with buttons and loops as alternative fastenings. (Shown in colour on page 86.)

e   f

Fig 48 Jackets and coats using the front-opening pattern pieces front *Ei* and back *Eii* adapted to A-line

View e Jacket with long plain sleeves (pattern piece *I*), button and buttonhole fastenings and patch pockets. Suitable for medium-weight fabrics, eg wool, velveteen or felt, in plain colours trimmed with top-stitching in a matching or contrasting colour. Eg a jacket in red felt with red top-stitching; or a jacket in navy blue with white top-stitching. (Shown in colour on page 143.)

View f This 'Norfolk' jacket with the front neckline cut to V shape has a shawl collar (pattern piece *S*) and long plain sleeves (pattern piece *I*). The front has one large box pleat on each side and fastens with buttons and buttonholes. The buttoned belt is in self-fabric. Worn with matching knickerbockers (pattern piece *M*) cut to knee length and gathered into bands. The jacket, collar and knickerbockers are suitable for medium-weight materials, eg wool, needlecord or tweed in plain subtle colours, eg brown tweed or olive-green needlecord. Suitable for antique boy dolls circa 1890–1920.

Fig 49 Dresses and suits for lady dolls with peplums or overskirts

View a This dress using pintucked bodice pattern pieces front *Di* and back *Dii* adapted to a square neckline has elbow-length full sleeves (pattern piece *J*) gathered to frills and an overskirt stitched to the bodice waistline and looped up over a matching separate skirt. Both skirts have self-fabric frills. The dress and underskirt are trimmed with a narrow lace edging, ribbon and ribbon bows. The dress and underskirt are suitable for lightweight fabrics, eg lawn or silk, in plain pastel colours or small prints to match or tone. Eg a dress and underskirt in cream silk with cream lace and pale-blue ribbon and bows; or a dress in a pastel print lawn with a toning plain lawn underskirt, and ribbon and bows to match the underskirt.

View b This jacket using bodice pattern pieces front *Ei* and back *Eii* adapted to a V neckline with a shawl collar (pattern piece *S*) with squared ends has elbow-length straight sleeves (pattern piece *I*) with self-fabric and lace frills and a peplum with squared front edges. Worn with a separate long, gathered skirt with a frill at the hem in a matching fabric. The bodice, collar, sleeves and skirt are trimmed with narrow ribbon and/or lace edging and a self-fabric sash ties at the back. The jacket fastens edge-to-edge with hooks and eyes. Suitable for light- or medium-weight fabrics in plain strong or pastel colours or prints, eg a pastel print cotton jacket and skirt trimmed with cream lace, or a plain fine-wool jacket and skirt in dark green or crimson trimmed with narrow velvet ribbon or braid. Made in lightweight fabrics, the skirt might have a looped overskirt. Suitable for antique dolls circa 1875. (Shown in colour on page 107.)

View c This jacket, using bodice pattern pieces front *Ei* and back *Eii*, has a plain round neckline, long straight sleeves (pattern piece *I*) and a flared peplum. Worn with a long flared skirt in a matching fabric, the jacket fastens edge-to-edge with loops and buttons. Suitable for medium-weight fabrics, eg velveteen or needlecord, in plain strong colours or tiny prints, trimmed with narrow velvet ribbon or braid. Eg a suit in black and beige printed needlecord trimmed with black velvet ribbon; or a suit in crimson velvet trimmed with crimson braid. Suitable for antique dolls circa 1890–1900. (Shown in colour on page 135.)

Hooded cloak

The hooded cloak is made from a square of fabric, lined or unlined, and is suitable for medium-weight fabrics including felt.

Measure the doll from the top of the head to the heel, and cut a square of fabric this size. Round off one corner (see Fig 50) to make the hood, and round off the diagonally opposite corner in a shallow curve to make the hem. Cut this piece in fabric and in lining. With right sides facing, stitch the fabric to the lining all the way around, leaving a small gap to turn through. Trim the corners, turn through, slipstitch the opening closed and press. (For an unlined cloak, simply hem all the way around.) Following Fig 50, stitch casings through both layers of fabric, one-third of the length down the cloak in a curve following the hem, and around the edge of the hood, 1–2in (2.5–5cm) from the edge. Thread ribbon through the neck casing and pull up. Thread ribbon through the hood casing, pull up to fit around the face and stitch the ends securely. Tie the neck ribbon in a bow. On unlined cloaks, the casings may be made with tape or, for very small sizes, simply gather with strong thread.

a

b

c

casing

casing

Fig 50 Hooded cloak

139

8 KNITTING AND CROCHET PATTERNS

Abbreviations P–purl; K–knit; tog–together; st(s)–stitch(es); sl–slip; psso–pass slipped stitch over; st st–stocking stitch (1 row Knit, 1 row Purl); inc–increase; tr–treble; ss–slip stitch; dc–double crochet; ch–chain; sp–space.

Knitted booties
(*in small, medium and large sizes, shown in colour on page 183*)

Small (10–11in/25.5–28cm dolls) use size 14 (2mm) needles and 2 ply yarn
Medium (14–15in/35.5–38cm dolls) use size 12 (2¾mm) needles and 3 ply yarn
Large (16–18in/40.5–45.5cm dolls) use size 11 (3mm) needles and 4 ply yarn
20g knitting yarn (all sizes)
narrow ribbon (optional)

To make each bootie cast on 43 sts. Work 10 rows of st st. With right side facing, K19, sl 1, K1, psso, K1, K2tog, Knit to end. **Next row** Purl. **Next row** K18, sl 1, K1, psso, K1, K2tog, Knit to end. Repeat the last 2 rows once more so that you have decreased 6 sts altogether. Continue in st st for ⅜in (1cm). Work ⅜in (1cm) in garter stitch (every row knit), cast off. Press, fold in half and sew back and underfoot seams.

If required – thread narrow ribbon through the knitting around the ankle and tie in bows.

12in square crochet shawl
(*shown in colour on pages 39 and 183*)

size 12 (2.50mm) crochet hook
50g 2 ply knitting yarn

Make 85 chain. **1st row** Into the 5th ch from hook work 1 tr, 1 ch and 1 tr (called tr gp), * miss 2 ch, 1 tr gp into next ch, repeat from * until 2 ch remain, miss 1 ch. 1 tr into last ch to form edge st, turn. **2nd row** 3 ch to form edge st, * 4 tr into 1 ch sp of tr gp of previous row, repeat from * 26 times more, 1 tr into ch sp at edge to form edge st, turn. **3rd row** 3 ch to form edge st, * in-between 2nd and 3rd tr of 4 tr block of previous row, work 1 tr gp, repeat from * 26 times more. 1 tr into 3 ch sp at beginning of previous row, turn. Repeat 2nd and 3rd rows until work is square.

Complete by making a border of 3 rows of dc. Pin out and press according to instructions on knitting yarn band.

18in (45cm) square crochet shawl with fringe
(*shown in colour on page 183*)

size 10 (3.00mm) and size 5 (5.50mm) crochet hooks
50g 4 ply baby yarn

Using size 10 (3.00mm) hook, make 6 chain and join with ss. **Next row** (3 tr 1 ch) 4 times in centre. **Next** row * (3 tr 1 ch) in first gap, (3 tr 1 ch) in next gap. Repeat from * to form a square. Continue with (3 tr 1 ch) on sides of square and (3 tr 1 ch, 3 tr 1 ch) in the corners until work measures 18in square (or larger if required).

Edging Using size 5 (5.50mm) hook. **Next row** (5 tr, 3 ch) (1 dc, 3 ch) (5 tr, 3 ch) (1 dc, 3 ch) all around the edge using every other stitch of the previous row. **Next row** 1 dc in side of shell, 3 ch, 1 dc in top of shell, 3 ch, 1 dc in side of shell, 3 ch, 1 dc in centre dc. Continue all around the edge, fasten off. Knot fringe with 3 strands of yarn around the square.

Knitted tights, angel top and bonnet

(for 10–11in (25.5–28cm) baby dolls, shown in colour on page 39)

size 10 (3¼mm) and size 12 (2¾mm) knitting needles
50g 4 ply knitting yarn
2 small buttons, narrow ribbon, elastic

Tights

Knit two pieces on size 10 (3¼mm) needles. Cast on 24 sts. K1 P1 rib for 2 rows. **3rd row** K1, (wool forward K2 tog) to last stitch, K1. This makes the waist-casing holes. Rib 3 more rows (24 sts).

Change to st st and work 16 rows. Cast off 2 sts at beginning of next 2 rows. K2tog at beginning of next 2 rows (18 sts). Work 24 rows in st st. Cast off.

To make up Join leg seams from 2 cast-off sts to foot. Fold so that seam is inside leg and stitch foot from toe to heel. Join centre seams from front to back. Thread ribbon or elastic through waist casing holes.

Angel top

This is knitted in five pieces and joined onto a yoke.

Front Using size 10 (3¼mm) needles cast on 50 sts. St st 4 rows. **5th row** K1 (wool forward K2 tog) to last stitch, K1. **Next row** Purl. Knit 20 rows in st st ending on P row. **Next row** K2tog along whole row (25 sts). Cut off wool leaving about 6in (15cm) and slip stitches onto spare needle.

Back This is knitted in two pieces but in the same way as the front. Cast on 26 sts and follow pattern as for front. (13 sts left on each piece.) Cut wool 6in (15cm) long and slip stitches onto spare needle.

Sleeves Knit as for the two backs, but cast on 20 sts. Cut off wool leaving 6in (15cm) and slip sts onto spare needle.

Yoke Change to size 12 (2¾mm) needles and work in garter stitch (every row Knit). With right side of work facing pick up st sts first back, first sleeve, front, second sleeve, second back. Knit 3 rows.

To shape top: 1st row (K4, K2tog) across row. **2nd and alternate rows** Knit. **3rd row** (K3, K2tog) across row. **5th row** (K2, K2tog) across row. **7th row** (K1, K2tog) across row. Cast off.

To make up Using the 6in (15cm) lengths of wool, join edges of back and sleeves and front and sleeves for ½in (1.2cm). Fasten off. Turn garment inside out and sew together sleeves and side seams. Sew back seam from bottom to about 2in (5cm) below yoke. Turn up hems on bottom edge and cuffs to make picot edging and stitch loosely. Stitch buttons and button loops on back of yoke.

Bonnet

Using size 10 (3¼mm) needles, cast on 40 sts. Knit first 6 rows as for front (see above). St st 18 rows ending on a P row.

To shape back: 1st row K4, K2tog across row. **2nd and alternate rows** Purl. **3rd row** K3, K2tog across row. **5th row** K2, K2tog across row. **7th row** K1, K2tog across row. **9th row** K2tog across row. Do not cast off but cut off 6in (15cm) of wool and thread onto a darning needle. Pick up the sts left with the darning needle and pull up. Pull out knitting needle and sew together the edges of the bonnet to where the shaping begins – about 1in (2.5cm). Turn up bonnet hem to make picot edging and stitch loosely. Thread ribbon through hem casing leaving long ends to tie under the doll's chin.

Crochet matinee jacket and bonnet

(for 14–15in (35.5–38cm) baby dolls; shown in colour on page 143)

size 8 (4mm) crochet hook
50g 4 ply baby yarn
small buttons, ribbon

Matinee jacket

Back yoke Make 24 chain. 1 dc into 3rd chain, dc to end. Dc for 5 rows. **Next row** sl st over 4 sts, dc to last 4 sts, turn. Dc for 5 rows on these sts. **Next row** 4 dc, sl st over remaining sts but 4 dc at end.

Front yoke Make 12 chain. 1 dc into 3rd chain, dc to end. Dc for 5 rows. 6 dc on next row, turn. Work 5 rows. Make second yoke, reversing all shaping.

Skirt Join bodice. 2 dc into each st along bottom of yoke. **Next row** 3 ch, 5 tr, 1 ch, 1 dc, 1 ch into every other st to end of row. **Next row** 3 ch, 5 tr into top of shell, 1 ch, 1 dc into top of dc, 1 ch. Repeat this row to end for 7 rows. Fasten off.

Sleeves Make 25 chain. 1 dc into 3rd chain, dc to end. Dc for 4½in (11.5cm). **Next row** 1 dc into every other stitch. Fasten off. Sew in sleeves. **Next row** 1 dc up front, around neck and down front. **Next row** 1dc up front, around neck and down front.

Make loop buttonholes and sew on buttons as required.

Bonnet

Cast on 30 chain. 1 dc into 3rd ch, dc to end. Pattern as for skirt or matinee jacket for 7 rows. Fasten off.

Back Cast on 15 ch, dc for 8 rows. Fasten off. Sew back into bonnet stretching slightly to ensure good fit. **Next row** crochet 24 dc evenly along bottom edge. **Next row** 3 ch * 2 tr 1 ch **. Repeat from * to ** along edge. **Next row** Dc to end.

Thread ribbon through the holes to tie under the doll's chin.

Knitted leggings, matinee coat and bonnet

(for 14–15in (35.5–38cm) and 16–18in (40.5–45.5cm) baby dolls (shown in colour on page 39)

Pattern instructions are written for 16–18in (40.5–45.5cm) size.
size 16–18in (40.5–45.5cm) use size 10 (3¼mm) and size 12 (2¾mm) needles.
size 14–15in (35.5–38cm) use size 12 (2¾mm) and size 14 (2mm) needles.

For leggings, matinee coat and bonnet (either size):
80g 4 ply knitting yarn
small buttons, ribbon, elastic

Leggings

Using size 12 (2¾mm) needles cast on 40 sts, rib 2 rows. **Next row** make holes, K1, wool forward K2tog, wool forward K2tog to end, K1. Rib 3 more rows. Change to size 10 (3¼mm) needles and work in st st. Knit 4 rows. **Next row** K20, turn, Purl back. Repeat these 6 rows 3 times. Continue knitting in st st until there are 30 rows down front edge (short side).

To shape leg: Cast off 2 sts at beginning of next 2 rows. K2tog at beginning and end of next row (34 sts). Work 30 rows, 1 row plain 1 row purl.

To shape foot: Change to all plain knitting. K16 turn. K10 and work 9 rows on these 10 stitches. Pick up 4 stitches down the side of the 10 rows and Knit to end. **Next row** Knit back picking up 4 sts from other side of foot shaping, Knit to end of row. Knit 6 rows.

To shape bottom of foot: (Ensure that right side of

Plate 12
Kloth Kinder's 18in (45.5cm) boy doll wears a round-neck, long-sleeved sweater knitted in oatmeal-coloured wool.

GP Ceramic's 16in (40.5cm) 'Hilda' wears an unlined, buttoned jacket made in red felt. Her striped knitted scarf has fringed ends and the knitted hat has a pompom.

Ridings Craft's 'Emily' wears a brown V-neck cardigan knitted in brown wool with a checked skirt and matching scarf. Her beret is crocheted in oatmeal-coloured wool.

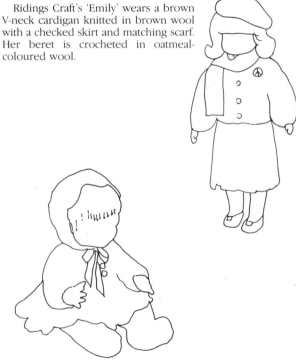

The 16in (40.5cm) vinyl baby doll wears a crocheted bonnet and matinee coat and knitted leggings in white wool.

work is facing you.) K8, K2tog, K2tog, K8, K2tog, K2tog, K10, K2tog, K2tog, K4. **Next row** Knit back. **Next row** K7, K2tog, K2tog, K6, K2tog, K2tog, K6, K2tog, K2tog, K8, K2tog, K2tog, K3. **Next row** K2, K2tog, K2tog, K7, K2tog, K2tog, K4, K2tog, K2tog, K5.
Cast off.

Other leg – make in reverse. After 6 rows of rib for waistband start with a Purl row then continue as pattern.

To make up Stitch two fronts, then two backs together. Stitch leg seams to inside of leg. Sew foot down centre, keeping leg seam to centre of inside foot. Thread elastic or ribbon through casing holes at waist.

Matinee coat

Back Using size 10 (3¼mm) needles cast on 57 sts and knit 7 rows in moss stitch. Change to st st and work 4 rows. **Next row** K2tog at beginning and end of row. Knit 3 rows. Repeat these 4 rows until there are 41 sts left. Purl 1 row.

To shape armholes: Cast off 2 at beginning of next 2 rows. **Next row** K2tog at beginning and 2tog at end of row. **Next row** Purl. Repeat these 2 rows until there are 11 sts left and slip these onto a safety pin.

Right front Cast on 39 sts and moss stitch 7 rows. **Next row** Moss stitch 20 sts, Knit to end of row. **Next row** Purl to last 20, moss stitch to end of row. Keeping the border of 20 moss sts at front edge, P2tog at beginning of every fourth row until there are 32 sts left, finishing at armhole edge.

To shape armhole: **1st row** Cast off 2 sts. Knit to end of row. **2nd row** Knit back. **3rd row** K2tog. Knit to end. **4th row** Knit back. Repeat 3rd and 4th rows until there are 18 moss sts left.

To shape neck: **1st row** Cast off 10 sts at neck edge. Knit to end. **2nd row** K2tog. Moss stitch to end. **3rd row** K2tog. **4th row** K2tog. Continue 3rd and 4th rows until last st. Fasten off.

Left front Work as for right front but reverse shaping. After knitting the 7 moss stitch border rows start as follows – plain 19 sts, moss stitch 20. Continue as for right front.

Sleeves Using size 12 (2¾mm) needles, cast on 21 sts and knit 7 rows in moss stitch. Change to size 10 (3¼mm) needles and st st. Increase at each end of next row and every fourth row until there are 35 sts (30 rows).

To shape armhole: Cast off 2 at beginning of next 2 rows. K2tog at beginning of every row until there are 5 sts left. Slip these onto a safety pin.

Collar Pick up 8 sts from right front, 5 from sleeve, 11 from back, 5 from second sleeve and 8 sts down left front (37 sts). Moss stitch 12 rows. Cast off loosely in moss stitch.

To make up Stitch sleeves to front and back on both sides. Join side seams and sleeve seams. Put the coat onto the doll, overlap moss stitch borders and mark button and buttonhole positions (double breasted). Sew on buttons. Make buttonholes by easing holes in knitting and oversewing.

Bonnet

Using size 10 (3¼mm) needles cast on 65 sts. Moss stitch 18 rows. Change to st st and work 30 rows.

To shape back of head: K5, K3tog, K5, K3tog, K5, K3tog, K5, K3tog, K1 * K3tog, ** K5, repeat from * to ** to end of row. Knit 3 rows. Continue decreasing as before on the next row and the following fourth row, working 2 sts less between the decreases on each repeat row (17 sts left). Knit 3 rows. Thread a length of wool through the 17 sts, pull up and fasten off. Stitch centre-back seam to fit doll's head.

Stitch ribbon ties to each side of bonnet, folding back the moss stitch border around the face.

Simple knitted pull-on hat and scarf

(*for 16, 18, and 20in (40.5, 45.5 and 51cm) dolls; shown in colour on page 143*)

Pattern instructions are given for 16in (40.5cm) size. Larger sizes given in brackets, ie (18in/45.5cm, 20in/51cm)
size 10 (3¼mm) and size 8 (4mm) needles
20g double knitting yarn (main colour)
small amounts of other colours

Hat

Using size 10 (3¼mm) needles cast on 60 (66, 72) sts. Rib for 2in (5cm) ending on wrong side. Change to size 8 (4mm) needles. **Next row** Knit. **Next row** Purl. **Next row** (K6, K2tog) repeat to end. **Next row** Purl. **Next row** (K5, K2tog) repeat to end. **Next row** Purl. **Next row** (K4, K2tog) repeat to end. **Next row** Purl. **Next row** (K3, K2tog) repeat to end. **Next row** Purl. **Next row** (K1, K2tog) repeat to end. **Next row** Purl. **Next row** (K2tog) to end. **Next row** Purl. **Next row** (K2tog) to end. Incorporate coloured stripes as required. Slip wool through these sts and sew seam closed. Make pompom and stitch in place.

Scarf

Using size 10 (3¼mm) needles cast on 12 sts. Knit until work is about 18in (45cm) long, changing colour to make stripes as required. Cast off. Run in ends. Make fringe at both ends.

Simple knitted sweater

(for 16, 18, and 20in (40.5, 45.5 and 51cm) dolls; shown in colour on page 143)

Pattern instructions are written for 16in (40.5cm) size, larger sizes are given in brackets, ie (18in/45.5cm, 20in/51cm)
size 10 (3¼mm) and size 8 (4mm) needle
50g double knitting yarn
2 small buttons

Back Using size 10 (3¼mm) needles, * cast on 34 (40, 46) sts. K1, P1 for 6 rows. On size 8 (4mm) needles, st st until work measures 4¼in/10.5cm (5¼in/13.5cm, 6¼/16cm) ending with P row. ** Knit 20 sts, turn. St st 7 rows. **Next row** Cast off 4 (5, 6) sts. Knit to end. **Next row** Purl. **Next row** Cast off 4 (5, 6) sts. Knit to end. **Next row** Purl. **Next row** Cast off. Rejoin wool on remaining sts. St st 6 rows. **Next row** Cast off 4 (5, 6) sts. Purl to end. **Next row** Knit. **Next row** Cast off.

Front Make as back from * to **. **Next row** Knit 12 (15, 18) sts. Turn, P2tog, Purl to end. **Next row** Knit. **Next row** P2tog, Purl to end. **Next row** Cast off 4 (5, 6) sts. Knit to end. **Next row** P2tog, Purl to end. Cast off. Slip 10 sts onto holder. Rejoin yarn, Knit 1 row. **Next row** Purl to last 2 sts, P2tog. **Next row** Knit. **Next row** Purl to last 2 sts, P2tog. **Next row** Cast off 4 (5, 6) sts. **Next row** Purl to last 2 sts, P2tog. **Next row** Knit. **Next row** Cast off in Purl.

Sleeves Knit two. Using size 10 (3¼mm) needles, cast on 20 sts. 4 rows K1, P1 rib. **Next row** Increase 1 st in every st (40 sts). Using size 8 (4mm) needles, st st until work measures 4in (4½, 5) 10cm (11.5, 12.5). Cast off. Sew in all ends. Sew up side seams and sew in sleeves. Join shoulder seams.

Neckband Using size 10 (3¼mm) needles, with left back facing, pick up 10 sts along back, 5 along left side of neck, (K2tog) 5 times on sts on holder, 5 sts along right side of neck and 10 sts along right back (35 sts) K1, P1 rib 6 rows. Cast off in rib.
    Make loop buttonholes and sew on small buttons.

Simple knitted V-neck cardigan

(for 16, 18 and 20in (40.5, 45.5 and 51cm) dolls; shown in colour on page 143)

Pattern instructions are written for 16in (40.5cm) size, larger sizes are given in brackets, ie (18in/45.5cm, 20in/51cm)
size 10 (3¼mm) and size 8 (4mm) needles
50g double knitting yarn
3 or 4 small buttons

Back and sleeves Make as simple sweater.

Fronts Using size 10 (3¼mm) needles, cast on 17 (20, 23) sts, K1, P1 rib for 6 rows. Using size 8 (4mm) needles, st st till work measures 3½in (4½, 5½) 9cm (11.5, 14) ending on P row. Decrease 1 st at right edge until 7 (10, 13) sts remain. Cast off.
    Make second front reversing all shaping. Make up cardigan as sweater.

Front band Using size 10 (3¼mm) needles, cast on 5 sts. K1, P1 rib until work fits both fronts and around the back neck when slightly stretched, incorporating 3 or 4 buttonholes where required. To make buttonholes: K2, yarn round needle, K2tog, Knit to end. **Next row** Purl to end. Stitch band to cardigan and sew on buttons to match buttonholes.

Crochet beret

(medium size shown in colour on page 143)

size 8 (4mm) crochet hook
20g double knitting yarn.

Make 4 ch, join with ss. Make 3 tr (1st tr) and continue making trebles in a spiral motion until the edge of the beret measures 1in (2.5cm) larger than the doll's head. **Next row** 1 decrease in every other tr. Cast off. Make pompom and sew in place if required.

waist edge

centre front

centre back

A
KNICKERS

fold of fabric

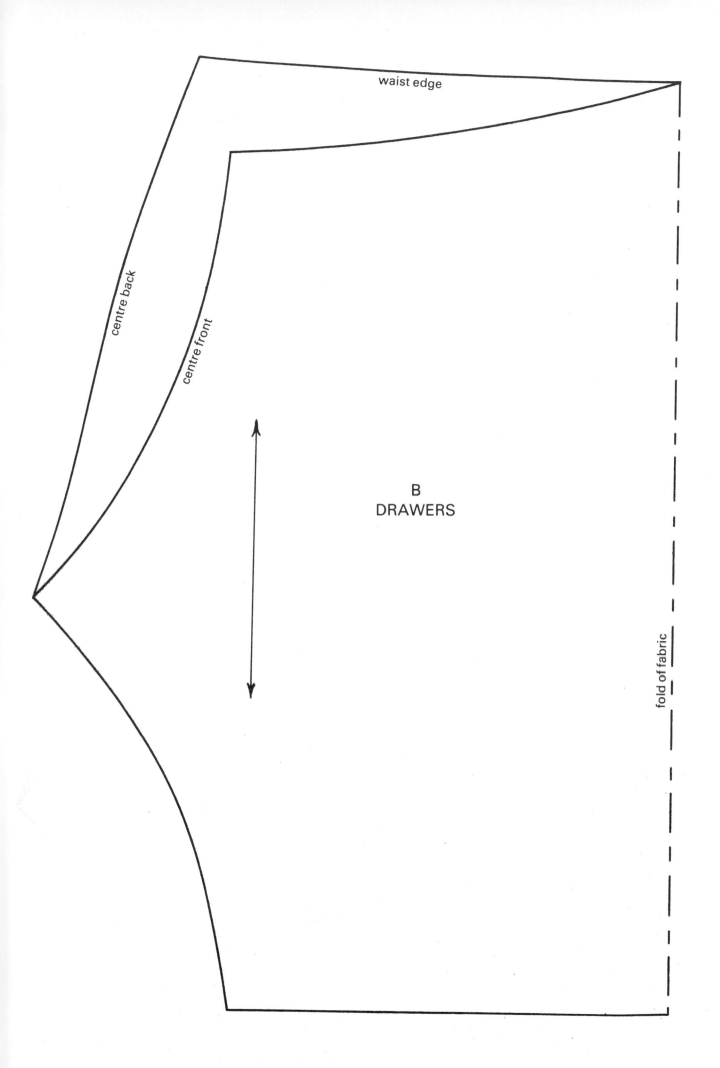

waist edge

centre back

centre front

B
DRAWERS

fold of fabric

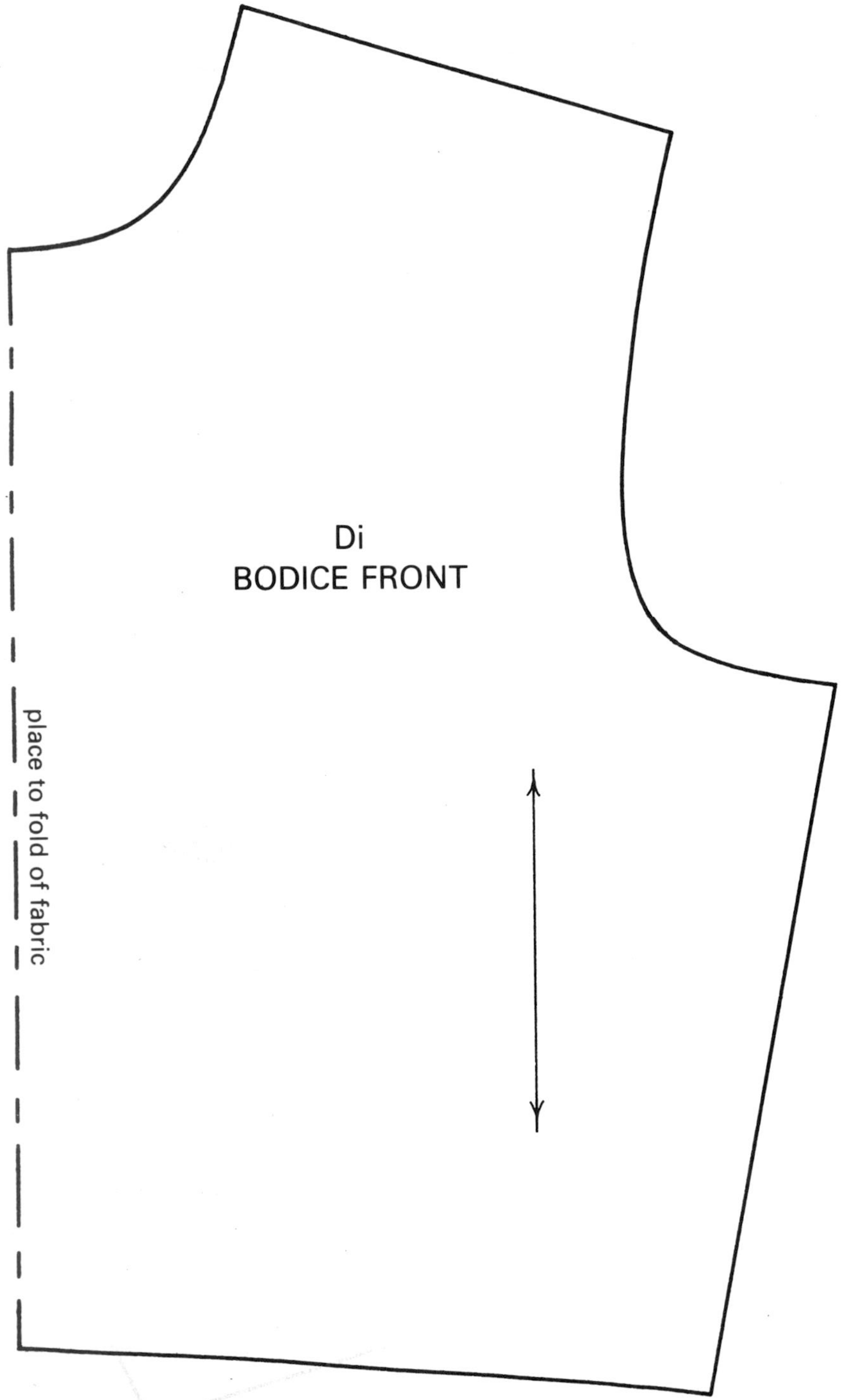

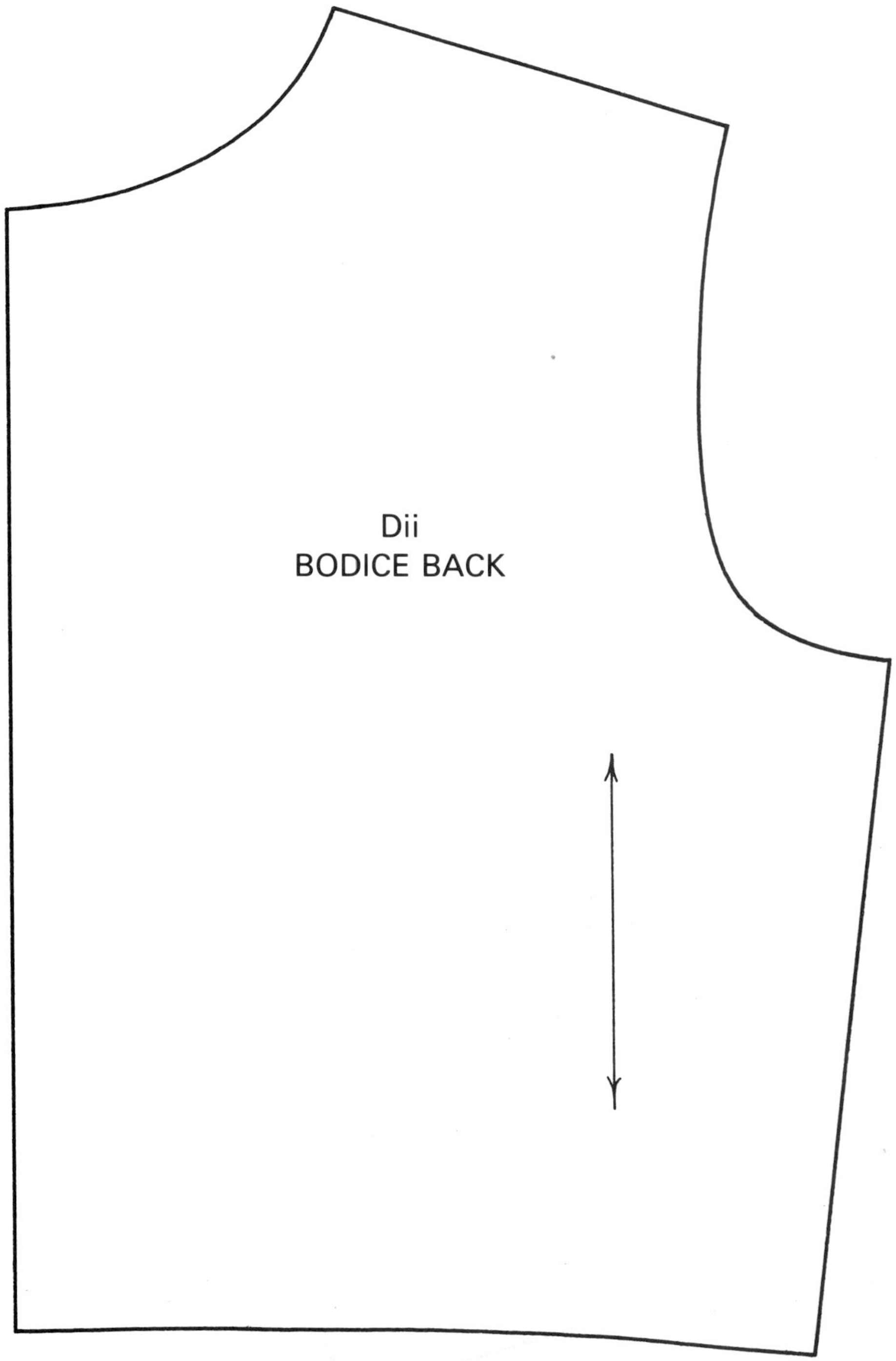

Dii
BODICE BACK

Di
BODICE FRONT

place to fold of fabric

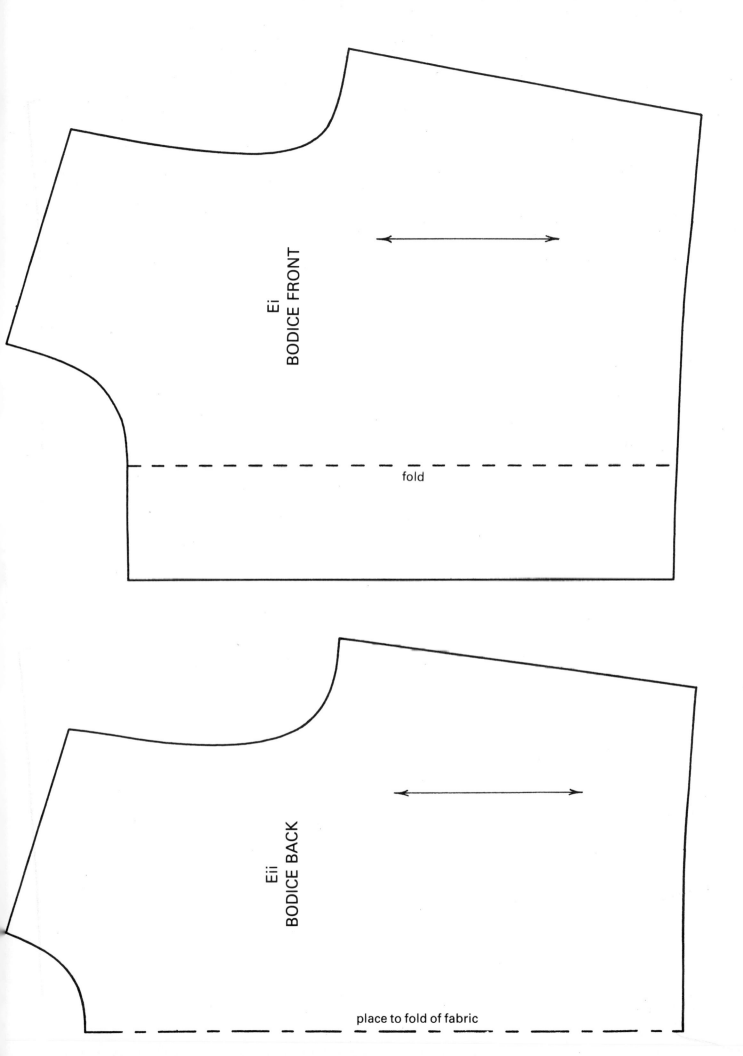

Ei
BODICE FRONT

fold

Eii
BODICE BACK

place to fold of fabric

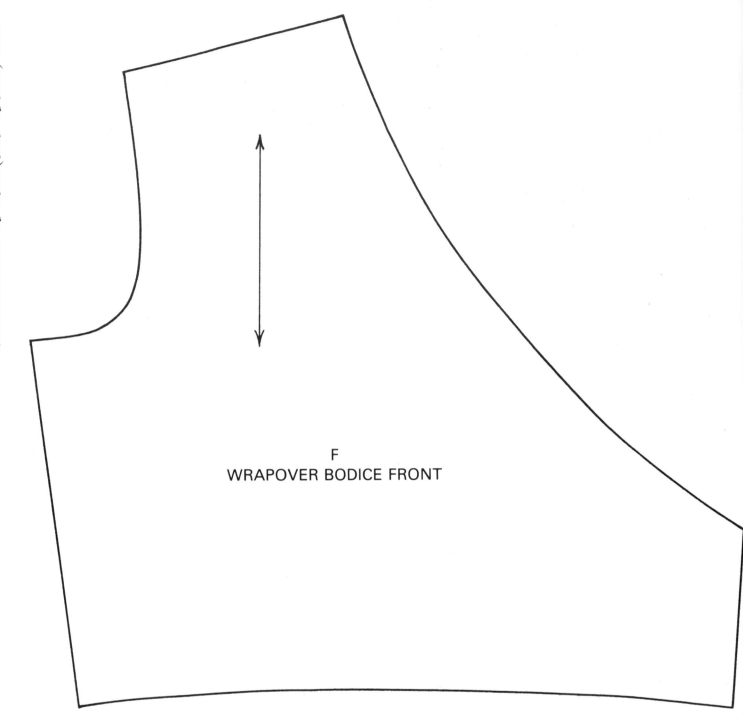

F
WRAPOVER BODICE FRONT

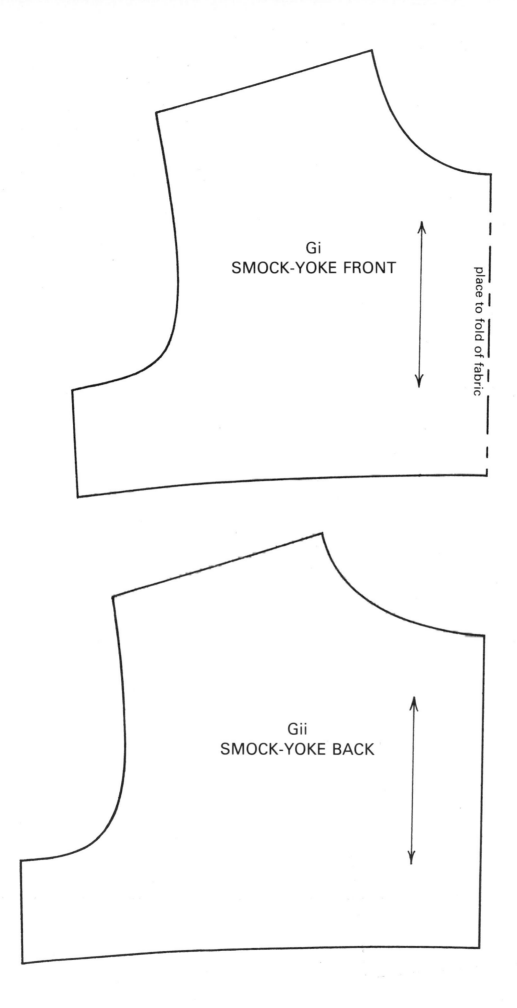

Gi
SMOCK-YOKE FRONT

place to fold of fabric

Gii
SMOCK-YOKE BACK

ease

gather

I
STRAIGHT SLEEVE

J
FULL SLEEVE

place to fold of fabric

place to fold of fabric

R
SAILOR COLLAR

place to fold of fabric

Q
SQUARE COLLAR

O
PETER PAN
COLLAR

place to fold of fabric

S
SHAWL COLLAR

Hi
ROUND-YOKE FRONT

Hii
ROUND-YOKE BACK

centre back

place to fold of fabric

gather

Hiii
ROUND-YOKE SLEEVE

A

Ni
FRENCH DRESS FRONT

Nii
FRENCH DRESS BACK

B

lengthen as required

place to fold of fabric

Niii
FRENCH DRESS PLASTRON

P
ROUND COLLAR

gather

A

B

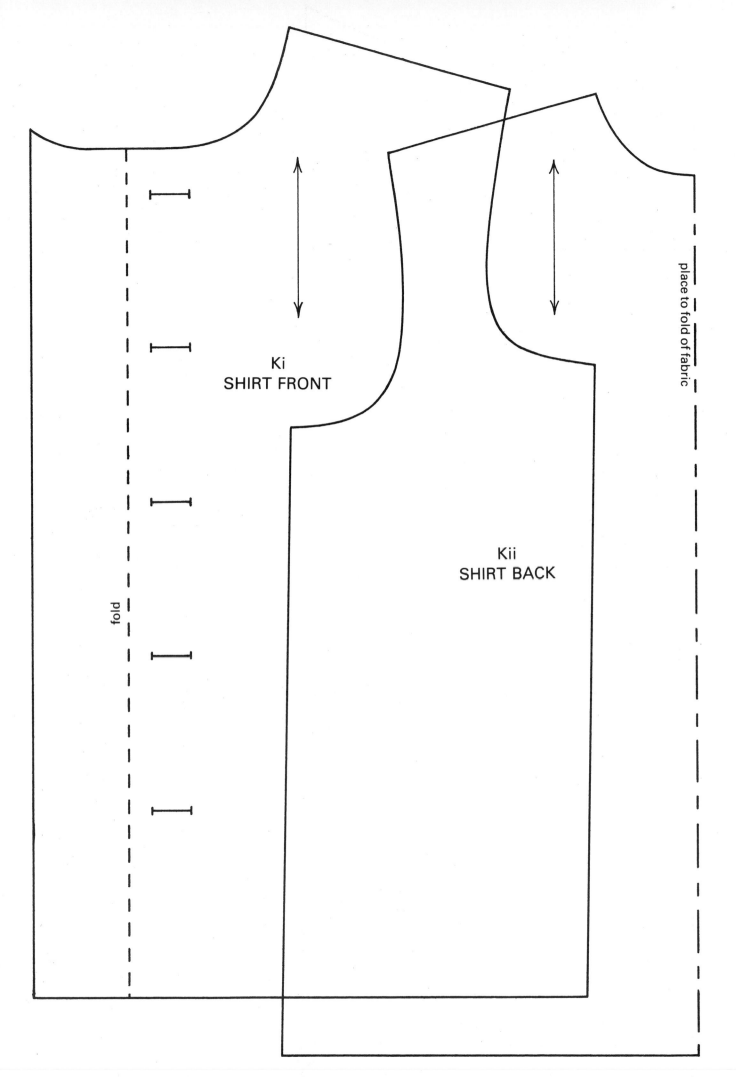

place to fold of fabric

Ki
SHIRT FRONT

Kii
SHIRT BACK

fold

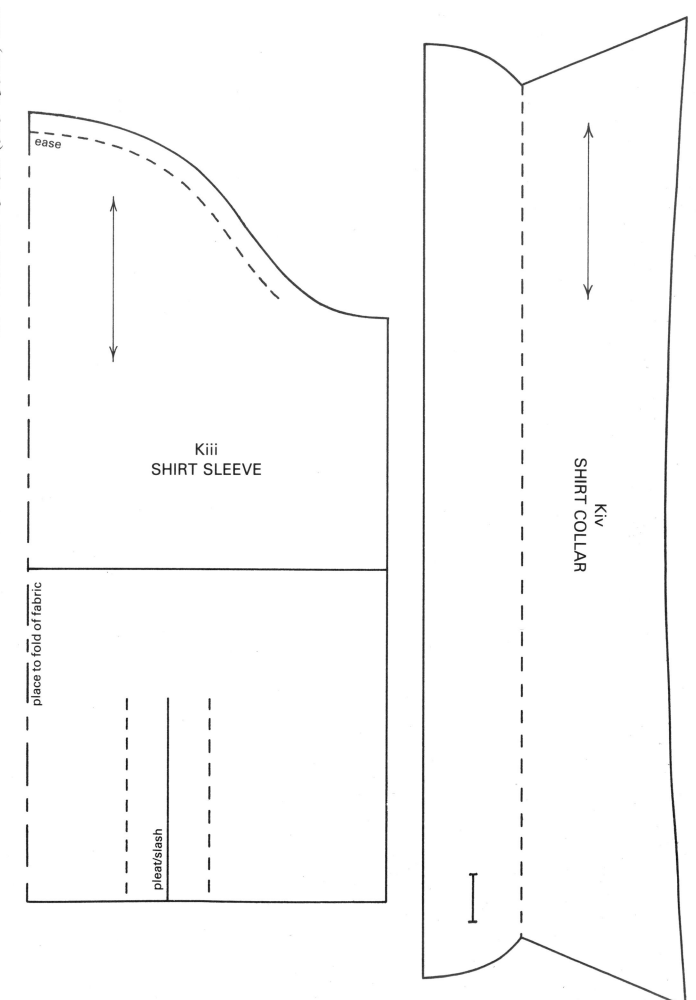

ease

Kiii
SHIRT SLEEVE

place to fold of fabric

pleat/slash

Kiv
SHIRT COLLAR

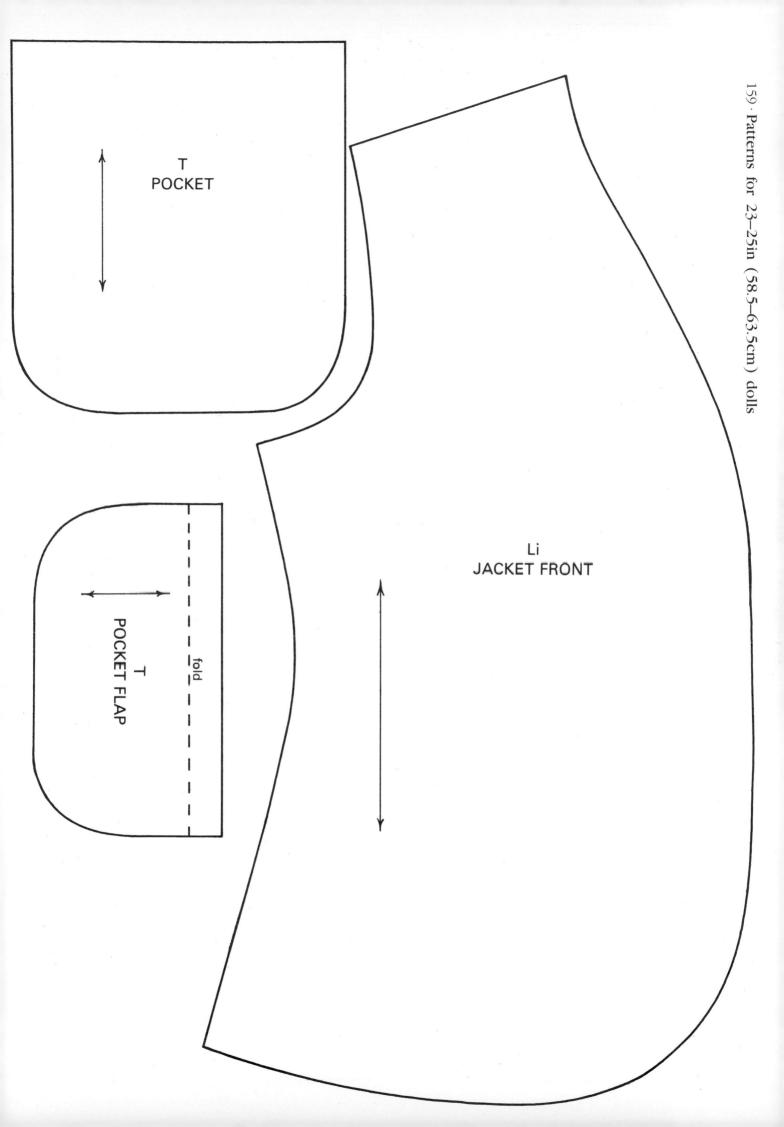

T
POCKET

T
POCKET FLAP

fold

Li
JACKET FRONT

T
POCKET

Kii
JACKET BACK

U
CUFF

wrist edge

waist edge

centre front and back

M
TROUSERS

place to fold of fabric

lengthen as required

9 HATS AND BONNETS

Baby bonnets

A variety of baby bonnets may be made in one or two pieces, by measuring the doll's head.

One-piece bonnet
(Fig 51a)

Measure over the top of the doll's head from below one ear to below the other ear. Measure from the forehead to the centre back of the head. Cut a rectangle of fabric this size plus seam allowances. Fold the piece in half and stitch the centre-back seam to make a pointed cap. Stitch across the point and trim. Hem and trim the front edge as required. Hem the lower edge to form a casing, thread ribbon through the casing and pull up to fit.

This very simple bonnet can be made in wide lace or broderie anglaise trimming (omit the front hem), either unlined or lined with coloured silk to match the ribbons.

Two-piece bonnet

A two-piece bonnet is made with a brim and a crown. Fig 51b has a narrow brim, made by measuring over the doll's head from under the ears and from the forehead to the top of the head, and a full round crown cut as a circle (use a dinner plate or similar as a guide). The brim is made in two pieces, stitched together right sides facing around the outside edge, rounding-off the corners. The crown has a casing made around the lower edge – about one-third of the circle – and gathers around the remainder, pulled up and stitched to the back edge of the brim. Elastic is threaded through the casing to fit the back of the doll's head, and ribbon ties are stitched to the brim at either side.

Plate 13
The 18in (45.5cm) doll at the centre of the picture is a reproduction SFBJ 252, made from a kit from Reflect Reproduction Dolls. She wears a round-yoke dress in yellow silk with full elbow-length sleeves. The yoke and cuffs are in ivory lace over silk and a deep ivory lace frill outlines the yoke. The matching shirred silk hat, lined with lace, is worn as a bonnet with ribbon ties under the chin and trimmed with artificial flowers.

The 18in (45.5cm) doll on the left is a reproduction Jumeau, made from a kit from Reflect Reproduction Dolls. She wears a French dress with a bodice and sleeves in dark-green velvet, turn-back cuffs, a gathered plastron and a pleated skirt in eau-de-Nil silk crêpe. The dress is trimmed with old lace and has silk crêpe sashes which tie at the back. The dark-green velvet picture hat is lined with gathered silk crêpe, has a wired brim and is trimmed with a silk crêpe band and bow and a feather. She holds a 4½in (11.5cm) jointed doll, fully dressed from Sunday Dolls complete with her own tiny doll.

The 20in (51cm) reproduction A. Marque from GP Ceramics on the right of the picture wears a dark-green silk dress with a pouched-front dropped waistline, gathered frilled skirt and full elbow-length sleeves. The dress bodice, sleeves and skirt are trimmed with old lace over the silk and the neckline has a lace band collar. Dark-pink ribbon bows trim the shoulders and match the wide ribbon sash. Tiny brooches made from life-size earrings trim the neckline and sash. The straw hat is from Mrs E. Harvey, Dolls' Milliner, and is trimmed with a bow of the dress fabric.

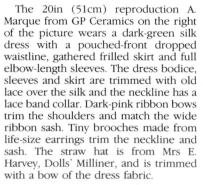

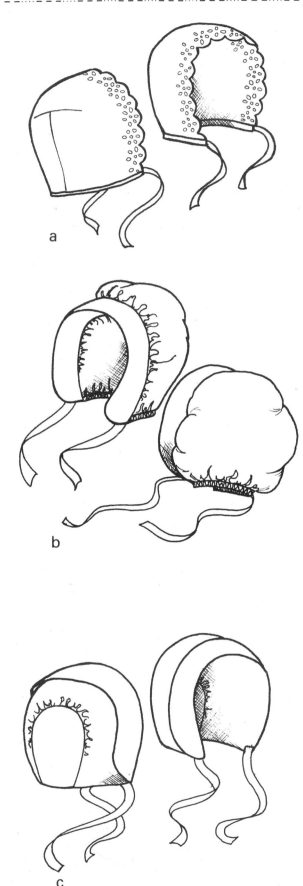

a

b

c

Fig 51 Baby bonnets

Fig 51c has a brim turned back around the face, and a back edge gathered into a small back crown. Measure the doll's head from under the ears, across the head; and for the other dimension of the main piece measure from the forehead to the centre-back of the head and double this measurement. Cut two main pieces. Cut a small shaped piece to cover the back of the head in fabric and in lining. Stitch the two main pieces together, right sides facing, around the outside edge, rounding-off the corners. Gather the back edge. Stitch the fabric back crown to the lining across the straight bottom edge. Pull up the gathers on the back edge of the brim to fit the back crown and stitch. Hem the lining over the seam. Put the bonnet on the doll to turn back the brim, and stitch ribbons to either side.

Both two-piece bonnets may be made in lace or broderie anglaise, pintucked fabric (for the brims) and trimmed with lace or broderie anglaise frills, ribbon bows or rosettes, or flower motifs.

Mob caps

A mob cap is made from a circle of fabric (use a plate, LP record etc as a guide) cut to fit closely or full as you prefer. In fine fabrics, the mob cap may be lined in matching or toning fabric – for this method, cut two pieces. With right sides facing, stitch the fabric to the lining all the way around leaving a small gap to turn through. Trim the seam, turn through, slipstitch the opening closed and press. A gathered lace frill may be sandwiched between the two pieces as they are stitched together. Stitch two rows ¼in (6mm) apart – through both layers – to make a casing 1–2in (2.5–5cm) from the edge. Thread elastic through the casing to fit the doll's head.

An unlined mob cap is made by cutting one piece. Hem the edge – or face with bias-cut fabric – wide enough for the frill and casing. Stitch bias binding to the inside to make a casing (or stitch a channel through the faced edge) 1–2in (2.5–5cm) from the edge. Thread elastic to fit the doll's head. Lace trimming may be whipped to the hemmed edge, or gathered lace frill sandwiched between the two pieces, as the facing is sewn on.

The mob cap is best made in lightweight silk or cotton fabric. Consider also cotton fabric with broderie anglaise or lace frill.

Berets and caps

The unlined beret (Fig 52b) is made from a circle of felt or fabric, gathered around the edge to a band cut to fit the doll's head. It can be trimmed with a pompom or a rolled felt 'stalk' stitched to the centre. Cut a wide band and a semi-circular peak, cut in two pieces stiffened with iron-on Vilene. Stitch together right sides facing around the curved edge, trim and turn through. Stitch the peak to the lower edge of the

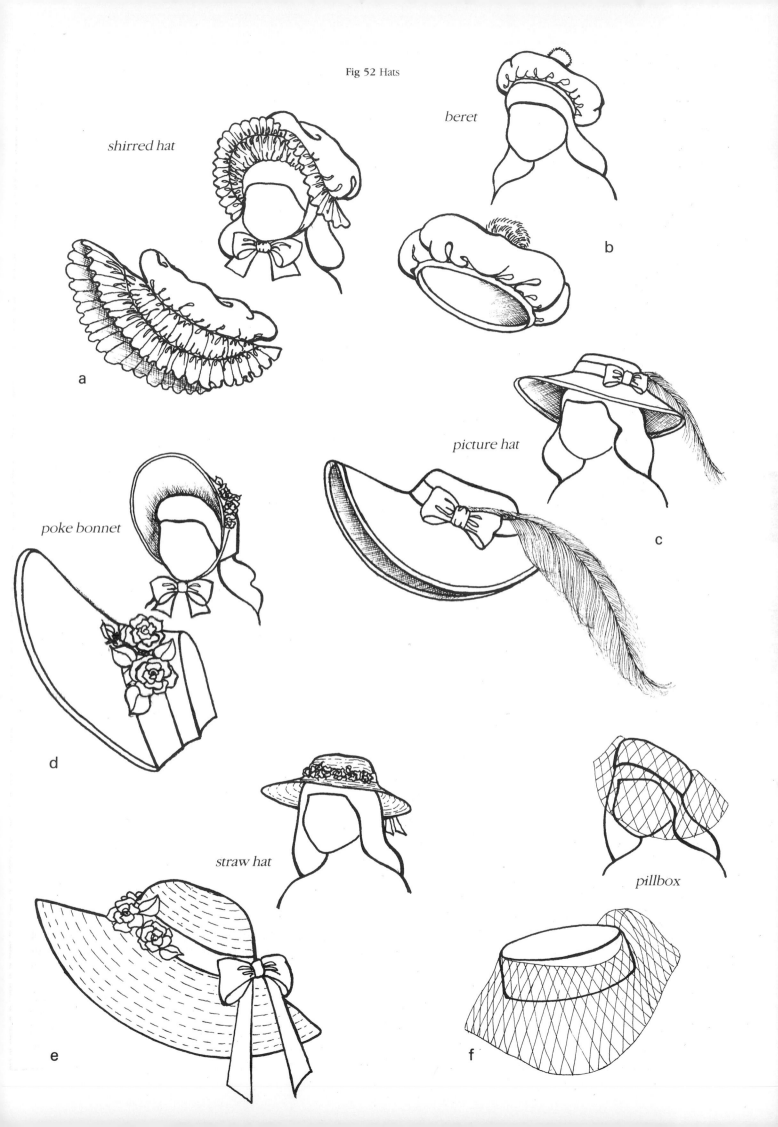

Fig 52 Hats

shirred hat

beret

picture hat

a

b

poke bonnet

c

straw hat

pillbox

d

e

f

band to make the beret into a 'baker boy' cap. Felt is particularly suitable for both of these styles, or the cap might be made in tweed and trimmed with a tassel for an antique boy doll.

The pillbox cap (Fig 52f) is made from a wide band, cut to fit the doll's head, and a crown circle cut to fit the band. With a peak (see above), the pillbox will make a boy's cap. It might be made in velvet or satin and trimmed with flowers, feathers or a veil for lady dolls, in fur fabric to match a coat, or in felt or tweed for boy dolls – and should be lined with lightweight fabric cut from the same patterns. To make the pillbox, cut the band and crown in fabric and lining. Make up hat and lining separately. Stitch the back seam in the band. Stitch the crown to one edge of the band. Turn up the lower edge of the band and press. Put the lining inside the cap and slipstitch to the lower edge. (For a peaked cap – stitch peak to the lower edge of the band before sewing in lining.)

Picture hat
(Fig 52c) (*pattern pieces Y*)

The pattern is given in small, medium and large sizes. Measure the doll's head circumference and compare with the hat side piece to gauge size. The hat is made in hat felt (unlined), or in fabric with a lining and a wired brim.

To make the hat in hat felt, cut one brim, one side and one crown. Trim the seam allowance from the back edges of the brim and side pieces, and join the seams with whipping stitches. Join the seam in the brim at the centre back. Join the seam in the side at the centre back. Stitch the crown into the side at the top edge. Stitch the lower edge of the side to the brim – turn the hat right side out.

To make the hat in fabric, use medium-weight fabric (eg velvet) for the hat and lightweight fabric (eg silk) for the lining. (Note: The brim may be lined with stiffened self-fabric, or with plain or shirred silk lining.) Cut the brim, side and crown in fabric and lining. Stitch the back seams on the brim and side fabric pieces and stitch the crown into the side (top edge). Stitch the back seam in the side lining piece and stitch the crown into the side (top edge).

Make up the shirred lining (if required) from a strip of fabric 1½ times as long as the brim outer-edge circumference. The fabric strip should be the same width as the brim centre-front in the middle of the piece, tapering at both ends to match the back brim-width. Stitch the centre-back seam, then gather both edges and pull up to fit the brim *wrong sides* facing. Tack the lining to the brim on both edges.

If using a self-fabric brim lining, stitch the brims together right sides facing, around the outside edge, turn through and press. Stitch the brim to the lower edge of the side. Put the crown/side lining inside the hat and hem over the seam.

If using a silk (plain or shirred) lining, stitch the brim to the lining wrong sides facing around the

Plate 14
The 25in (63.5cm) doll on the left is a reproduction AT14 from Reflect Reproduction Dolls. She is wearing an ivory brocade jacket with a shawl collar, cuffs and pocket flaps. The jacket is trimmed with pink taffeta binding, cream lace edging and flower braid and has pearl buttons on the jacket front, cuffs and pocket flaps. The sleeveless dropped-waist dress in pink taffeta has a box-pleated skirt and gathered lace over the bodice. A shaped belt in ivory brocade edged with pink taffeta binding fastens at the back. The straw bonnet from GP Ceramics is lined with gathered pink taffeta and trimmed with flower braid, a large taffeta bow and a feather. The pendant is a life-size earring. The beige leather buttoned boots are from Recollect.

The 25in (63.5cm) antique doll on the right wears a white dotted-swiss dress with a bound neckline, full sleeves with lace cuffs and a gathered skirt with a frilled hem. The bodice and skirt are trimmed with inset lace. The sash is pink satin ribbon, and the bodice is trimmed with tiny pearl bead 'buttons'. The brooch is a life-size earring. The doll carries an 8in (20.5cm) mohair teddy bear from Hugglets.

outside edge and the inside edge. Stitch the brim to the lower edge of the side. Put the crown/side lining inside the hat and hem over the seam. Trim the raw outside edge of the brim and bind with bias-cut lining fabric, leaving a small opening at the back. Thread millinery wire through the binding. Tape the wire ends together and close the opening.

The hat can be trimmed with a ribbon or fabric band, bows, feathers or flowers. It can be secured to the doll's head with hat elastic under the back hair, or a hat pin.

Millinery wire can be found in haberdashery departments (or at Ridings Craft); small flowers can be bought from hat shops, department stores and cake-decorating shops. Marabou feathers in a wide range of colours are available from Ridings Craft. Hat pins can be bought in most hat shops or department stores or, for small dolls, use glass-headed pins or beads glued onto needles.

Warning Never use millinery wire, artificial flowers, feathers or hat pins on a doll for a young child.

Shirred hat
(Fig 52a)

The shirred hat is designed for fine, lightweight fabrics, eg lawn or silk. The crown may be lined; fabric and lining are worked as one piece.

To make the shirred hat, measure the doll's head circumference. Cut a piece of fabric 3 times this length and twice as wide as you want the brim plus seam allowances. Cut a large circle of fabric (and lining) for the crown.

Seam the short edges of the brim piece, fold in half along the length and press. The folded edge becomes the outside edge of the brim. Stitch a casing along the length of the brim piece 1–2in (2.5–5cm) from the folded edge. Gather the back edge of the brim, pull up the gathers to fit the doll's head and fasten off. Gather around the outside edge of the crown (circle) piece and pull up to fit the brim. Stitch the brim to the crown and neaten this seam with bias binding. Thread millinery wire through the brim casing (making the brim larger or smaller as you wish by using a longer or shorter length of millinery wire) through a small opening in the back seam. Bind the wire ends and close the opening. Trim the hat as required.

To make the shirred hat into a bonnet, simply stitch ribbon ties to either side of the back brim – when tied, this pulls the brim to the required shape.

Poke bonnet
(Fig 52d) (*pattern pieces Z*)

The pattern is given in three sizes – small, medium and large. Measure over the doll's head from below the ears and compare with the side piece to gauge the size. Sew by hand – oversewing all seams together to reduce bulk. The bonnet is designed for medium-weight fabrics including felt. All pieces should be backed with iron-on Vilene to stiffen and prevent fraying. Line with lightweight fabric.

To make the bonnet, cut two brims, one side and one crown in stiffened fabric and one side and one crown in lining. Stitch the back edge of the side piece to the back on both fabric and lining. With right sides facing, stitch the fabric to the lining across the lower edges of the back and sides, turn through and press. With right sides facing, stitch the brims together around the outside edge. Turn through and press. Stitch the brim to the front edge of the side, and hem the lining over the seam. Stitch ribbon ties to both sides and trim as required. A gathered lace frill may be stitched inside the bonnet brim.

Straw hats
(Fig 52e)

Inexpensive straw hats in natural colour in a range of sizes are available from many of the specialist suppliers, including Hello Dolly, Recollect and Ridings Craft. Fine English straw hats and poke bonnets in a range of colours and sizes are available from GP Ceramics.

If you prefer to make straw hats, use natural or artificial raffia (available from garden or art shops). Artificial raffia is available in a range of colours in matt or shiny finishes. Plait long lengths of raffia, knotting the lengths at both ends. Starting at the centre, coil the raffia and oversew each coil to the next one (using thread for small hats, raffia for larger ones) (see Fig 56). Keep coiling and sewing – using more lengths as required – until you have a shallow saucer-shaped hat of the required size. Cut off and secure the end on the underside. Steam the hat over a kettle – or immerse it in hot water – to make it pliable, then mould it to the required shape using the doll's head (covered in a polythene bag) or a bowl, jam jar or basin. As it dries, reshape occasionally. Flat brims are shaped by ironing with a steam iron. Rolled or curved brims can be held with pegs or elastic bands as they dry out. Leave the hat until it is completely dry, then trim as required. (Commercial straw hats can also be reshaped by this method; eg a dome-shaped crown can be steamed and flattened under a weight over a jam jar, or a flat brim can be steamed and curved to make a bonnet.)

Straw hats can be trimmed with ribbon bands and bows, feathers or artificial flowers. It is usually easier and neater to glue these trimmings in place when the hat is on the doll's head to gauge the best effect. (I recommend UHU for this.) Hats can be secured with hat pins or hat elastic under the back hair.

Warning Do not use these trimmings on hats for dolls intended for small children.

Shirred linings can be made for straw hats and bonnets in the same way as for the picture hat (page 166).

A velvet hat or bonnet which has become crushed by handling during making-up will benefit from being steamed over a kettle to raise the pile.

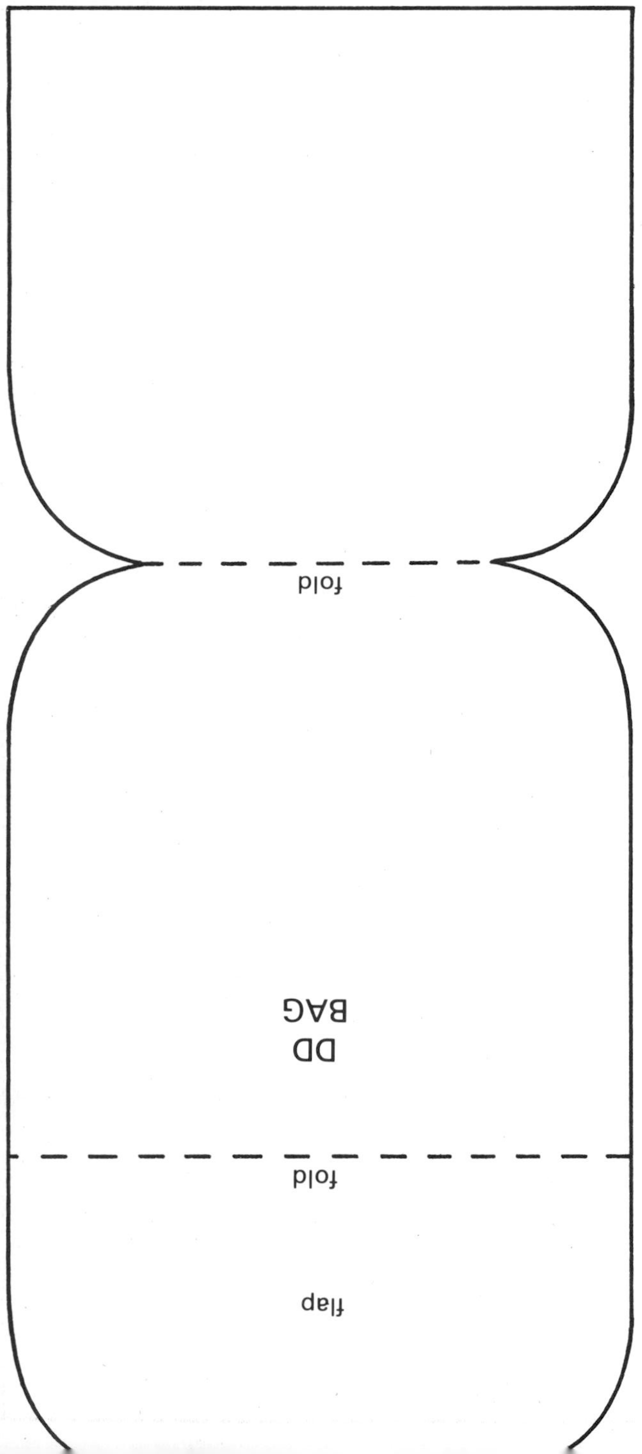

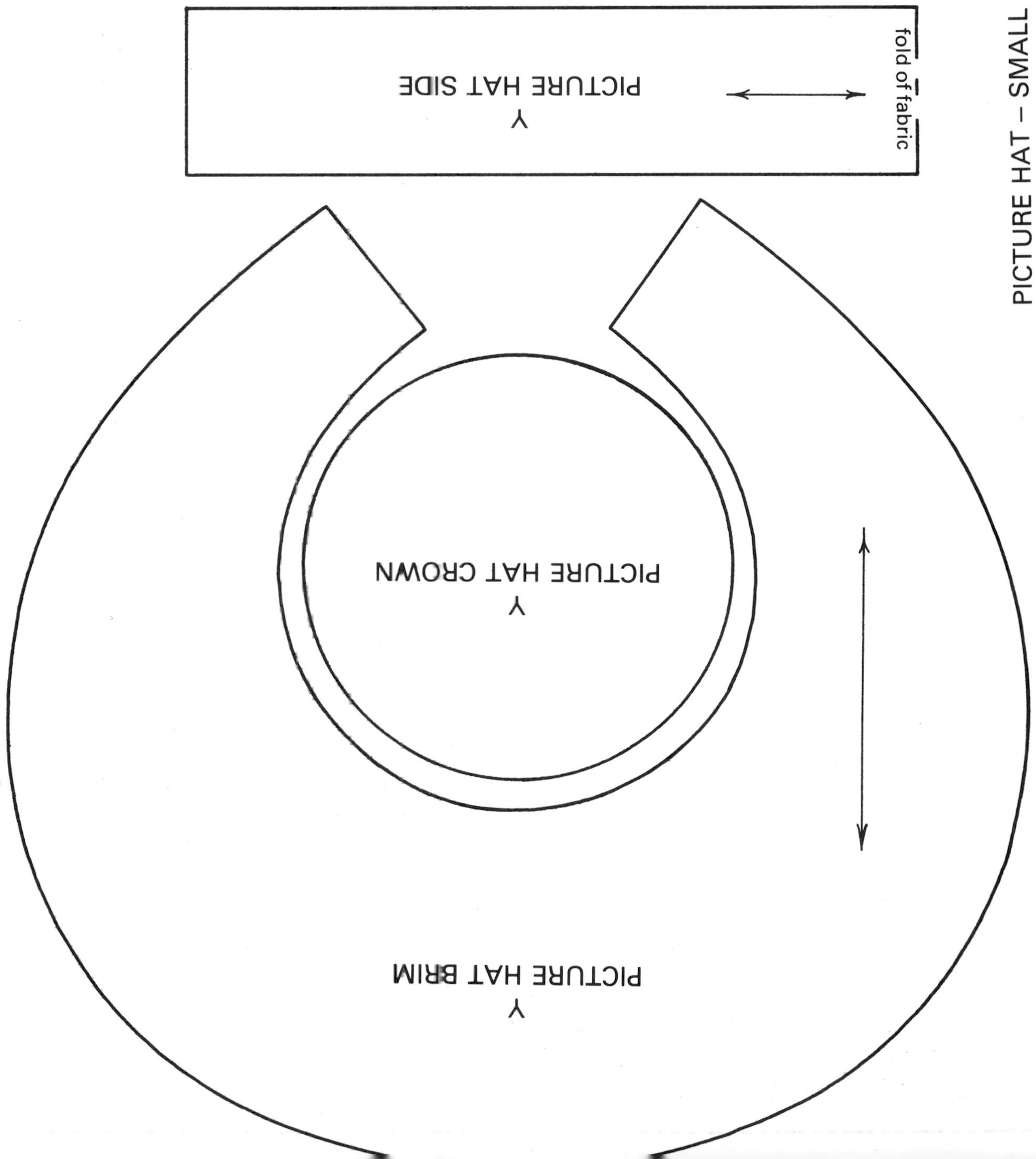

flap

fold

DD
BAG

fold

fold of fabric

Y
PICTURE HAT BRIM

Y
PICTURE HAT CROWN

Y
PICTURE HAT SIDE

fold of fabric

PICTURE HAT – SMALL

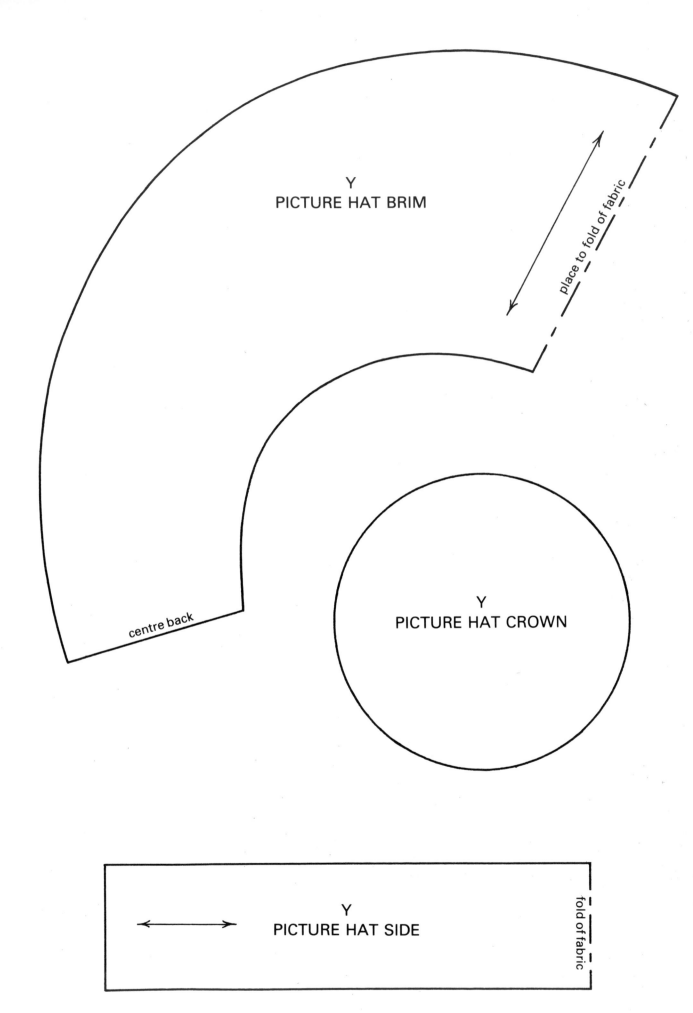

Y
PICTURE HAT BRIM

place to fold of fabric

centre back

Y
PICTURE HAT CROWN

Y
PICTURE HAT SIDE

fold of fabric

PICTURE HAT – MEDIUM

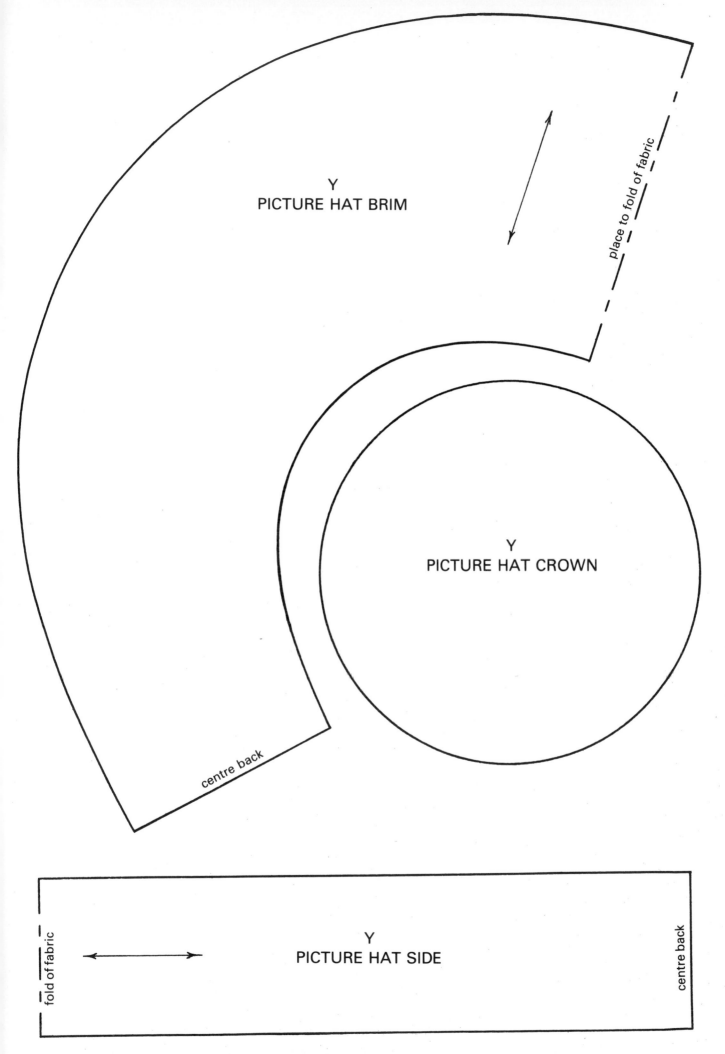

Y
PICTURE HAT BRIM

place to fold of fabric

Y
PICTURE HAT CROWN

centre back

Y
PICTURE HAT SIDE

fold of fabric

centre back

PICTURE HAT – LARGE

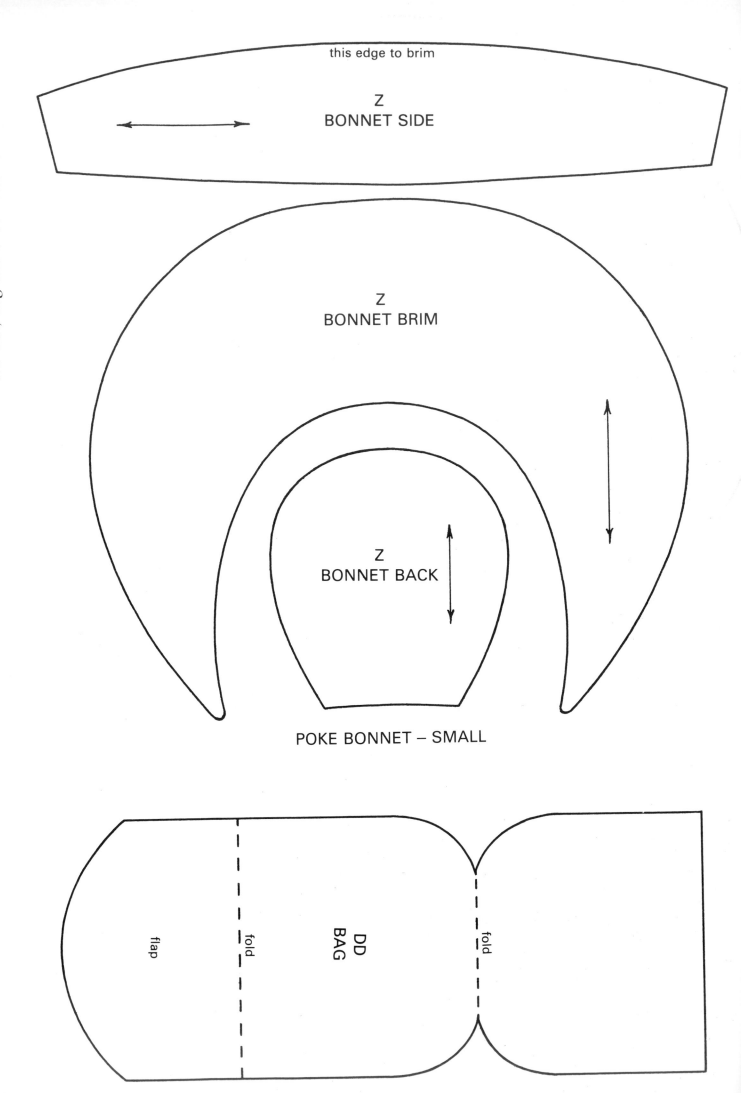

this edge to brim

Z
BONNET SIDE

Z
BONNET BRIM

Z
BONNET BACK

POKE BONNET – SMALL

flap

fold

DD
BAG

fold

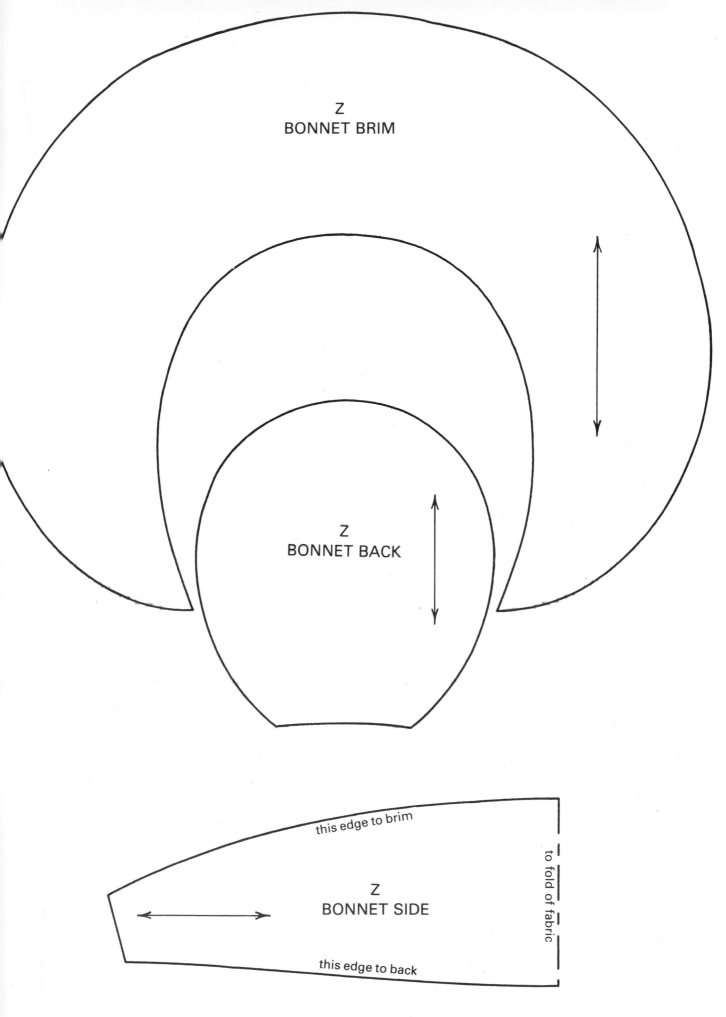

Z
BONNET BRIM

Z
BONNET BACK

this edge to brim

Z
BONNET SIDE

to fold of fabric

this edge to back

POKE BONNET – MEDIUM

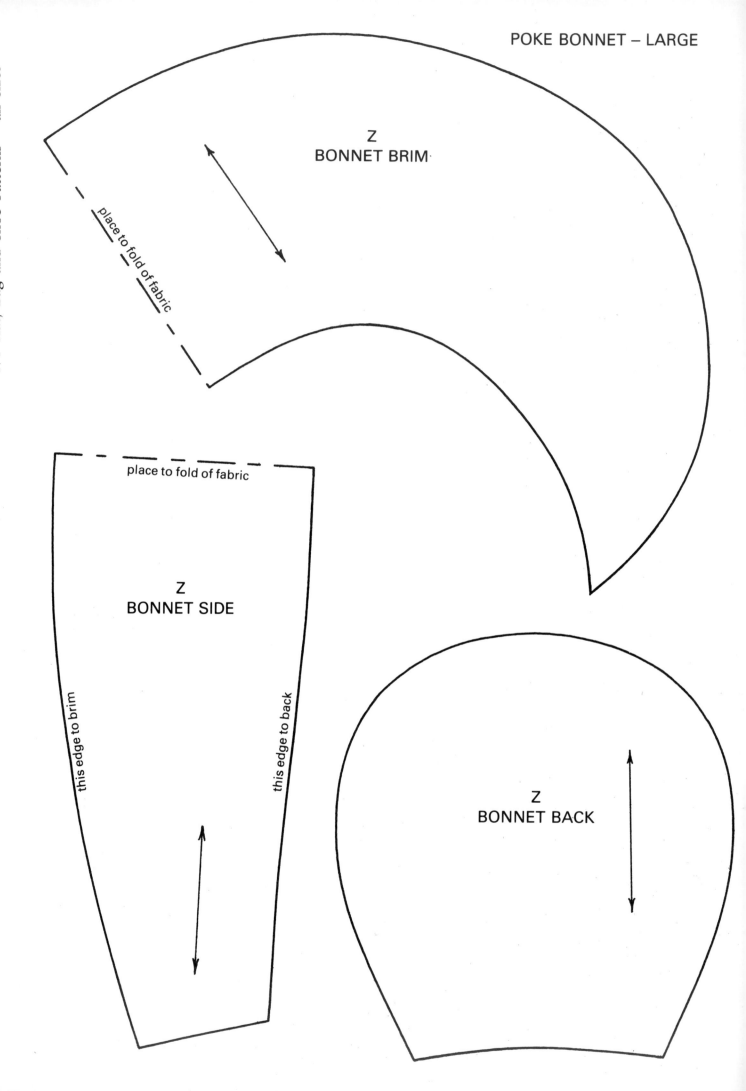

174 · Hat, Bag and Shoe Patterns – all sizes

Z
BONNET BRIM

place to fold of fabric

place to fold of fabric

Z
BONNET SIDE

this edge to brim

this edge to back

Z
BONNET BACK

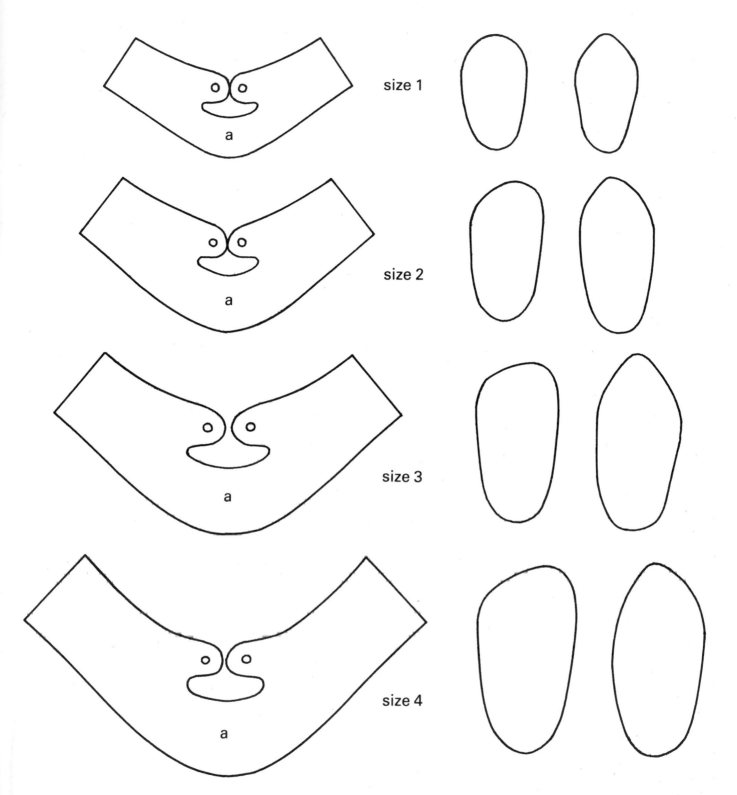

size 1

a

size 2

a

size 3

a

size 4

a

SHOE PATTERNS SIZES 1–4

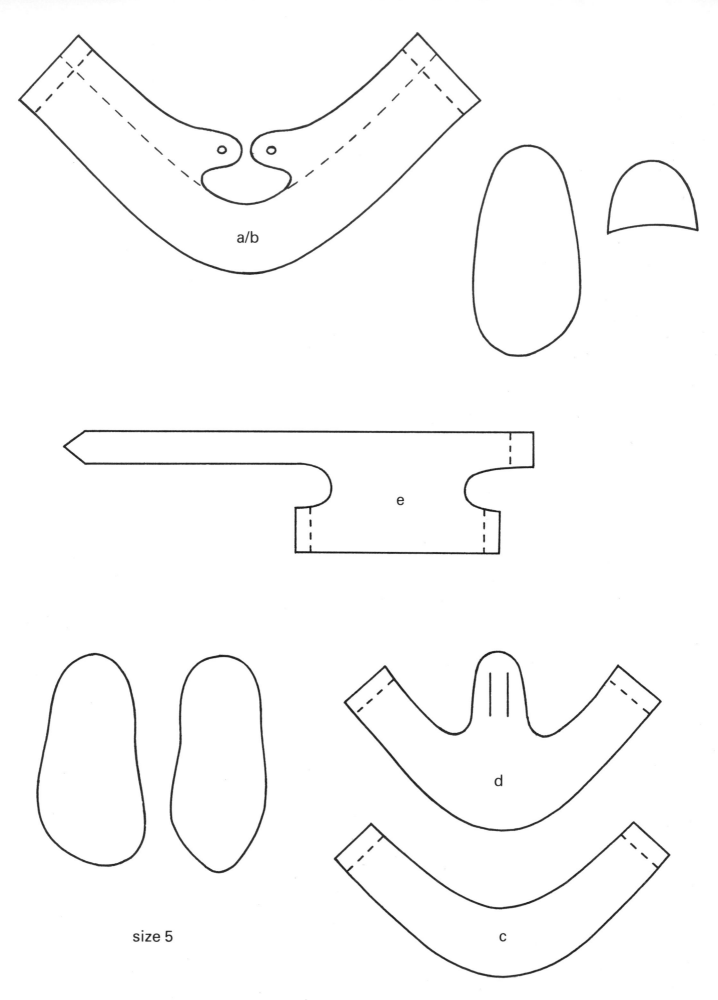

a/b

e

size 5

d

c

SHOE PATTERNS SIZE 5

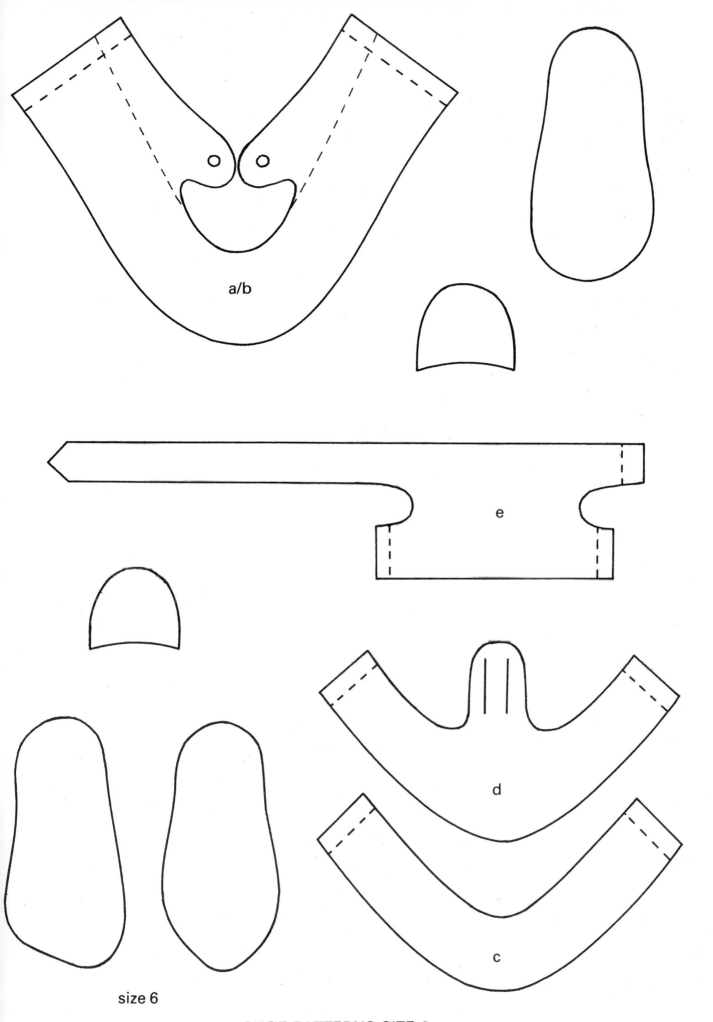

a/b

e

d

c

size 6

SHOE PATTERNS SIZE 6

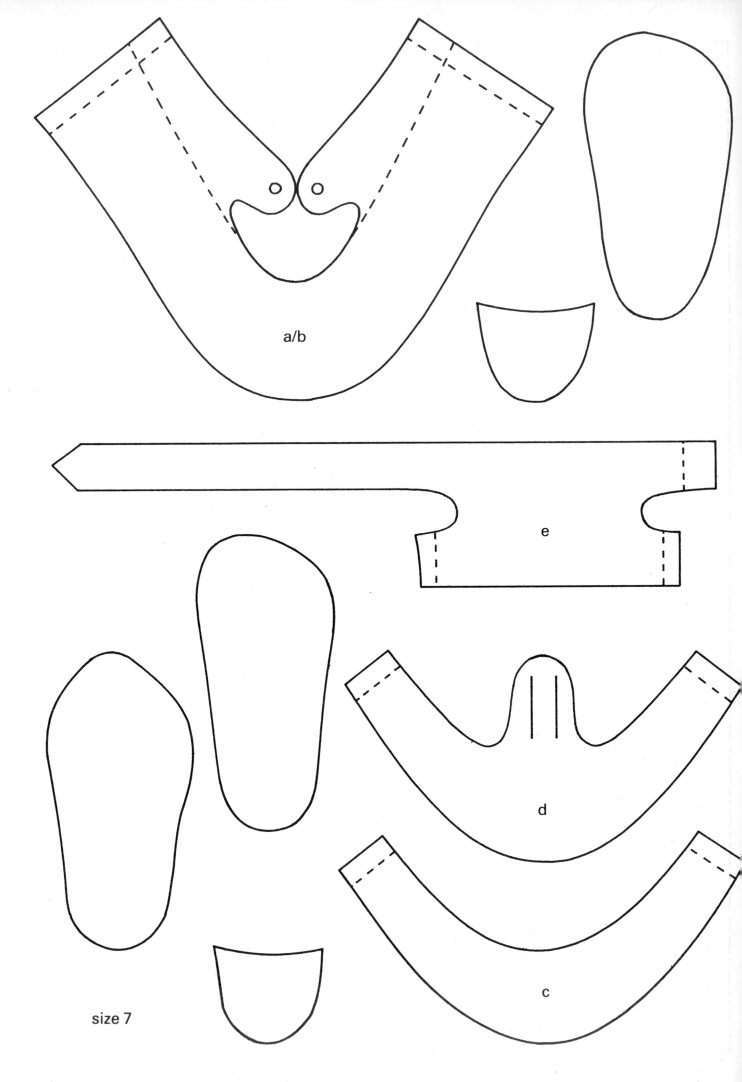

a/b

e

size 7

d

c

SHOE PATTERNS SIZE 7

The shoe patterns are given in three sizes for each style and in four smaller sizes for tie shoes. For dolls with hard bodies they are made on the doll's foot. (For soft dolls, use another doll with the same size feet as a 'last'.) To gauge the size, draw around the doll's foot and measure against the sole patterns.

The shoes are designed for leather (or imitation leather) which may be cut from old handbags, purses or leather clothing provided it is not too thick. Leather pieces can be bought from Pittards (see 'Stockists') in bags of assorted colours. Fine (glove) leather should be backed with lightweight iron-on Vilene before cutting to prevent it stretching. (Check that the Vilene is thoroughly bonded before cutting.) The shoes look more realistic if the soles (and heels) are made in a thicker brown leather. UHU glue is recommended for gluing the shoe parts together. Lay the doll on its back, with bare feet and legs in the air, while you work on the shoes. Secure the card soles to the feet with little

pieces of Blu-Tack to prevent them slipping while you work. The card inner soles should be cut from firm cardboard – the type used on the back of writing pads is ideal; cereal packets are too flimsy. Any of the sole patterns may be used with any of the upper patterns; the pointed sole is recommended for antique French dolls, and the wide round toe for antique German dolls.

Tie shoe
(*style a*)

Cut two uppers in coloured leather. Cut a pair of soles (and heels) in brown leather and another pair in cardboard. Secure the card soles to the doll's feet. Stitch the centre-back seams in the uppers. Open the seams, flatten them and tape over them with surgical tape (from chemists) to stiffen the shoe back. Slip the

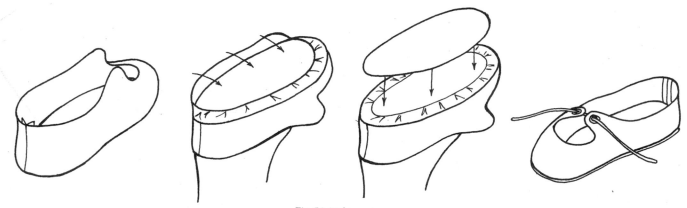

Fig 53 Making shoes

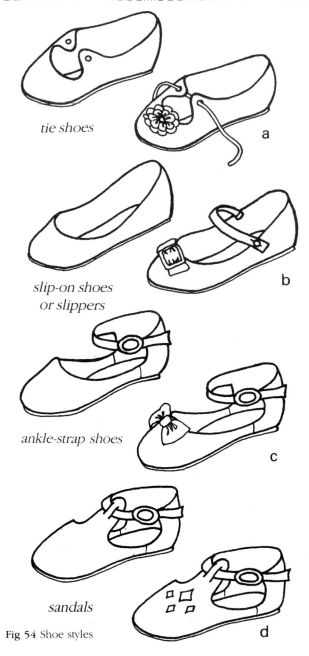

tie shoes

a

slip-on shoes or slippers

b

ankle-strap shoes

c

sandals

d

Fig 54 Shoe styles

upper (upside down) over the doll's foot, and pull the lower edge over the card sole. (See Fig 53.) Smear glue around the card sole, and press the leather in place as smoothly as possible. It may be necessary to make small snips in the leather to make it lie flat. Cover the inner side of the leather sole in glue and press into place. Leave the glue to dry thoroughly. Glue the heel in place on the sole – lining up the edges – and leave to dry. Remove the shoe from the foot and punch holes on either side of the upper for ribbon ties. For a professional finish tiny eyelets (from Sunday Dolls) may be punched into the holes.

Slip-on shoe
(*style b*)

The same patterns are used, but the upper pattern is trimmed along the line shown on the pattern. Make up the shoes as above. This style might have a strap over

the instep, stitched or glued to the inner side, and fastened with a buckle sewn to the outer side. Or it might have ribbon ties stitched or glued to each side – to tie in bows over the instep or cross and tie around the ankle (like ballet shoes).

Style b may also be used to make dolls' slippers in felt or fabric. Bond the felt or fabric to iron-on Vilene before cutting out, and bind the top edge with narrow bias strip or ribbon. Stitch the back seam and make up as before. Trim the front of the slippers with ribbon bows or pompoms.

Ankle-strap shoe
(*style c*)

The upper is cut in two pieces, the back e and front c. Stitch the back to the front at both sides. Open and tape the seams. Make up the shoes as described above. Slip a small buckle onto the ankle strap on the outer side, and glue the strap end under. Remember to cut a *pair* (reverse pattern) of back uppers; the buckle is on the outside of each shoe.

Sandal
(*style d*)

The sandals use the same back-upper pattern (e) and the front (d). Before making up, patterns may be punched into the fronts with a leather punch – or snipped with small sharp scissors. Cut slits in the vamps for the straps. Make up the shoes and fit buckles as for style c, and thread the straps through the vamps.

Trimmings

Shoes may be trimmed with tiny buckles with leather tabs or ribbon bows through them, a ribbon rosette or bow, or flower motifs.

To make the ribbon rosette, cut a length of ribbon in the appropriate width, eg, for small shoes, 1½in (3.7cm) of ¼in (6mm) ribbon; for larger shoes, 3in (7.5cm) of ½in (1.2cm) ribbon. Blanket stitch the short ends together. Gather with tiny stitches along one edge, pull up tightly and fasten off. Stitch a small bead to the centre of the rosette. Glue the trimmings (UHU is excellent for the purpose) to the shoe fronts – with the shoes on the doll to gauge the best position.

Tiny buckles and narrow ribbons for shoelaces are available from Sunday Dolls (see 'Stockists').

The leather buttoned boots worn by some dolls in the photographs are available in a range of colours and sizes from Recollect (see 'Stockists').

Fitting notes If your doll's feet fall between two sizes, use the larger size patterns. Forcing the feet into shoes which are too small may tear them, but overlarge shoes can have a little cotton wool pushed into the toes to fill them out.

11 ACCESSORIES

Bustle pad and bust improver

Lady dolls whose figures need a little help to make their costumes 'sit' properly might wear bust improvers or bustle pads under their dresses (see Fig 55). The bust improver is made in fine lawn or silk fabrics, in white or pastel colours, and consists of two little round bags, stuffed with soft stuffing. The bags are stitched to a shaped backing of the same fabric which is pinned to the doll's underwear. The bustle pad is made in similar fabrics, as a semi-circular bag, lightly stuffed, with tapes stitched to either end. The bustle is tied around the doll's waist – under the dress

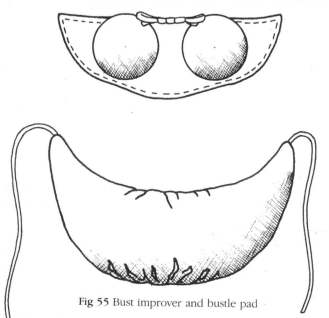

Fig 55 Bust improver and bustle pad

– and makes the back skirt stand out. The bustle is particularly appropriate with the looped skirts of the 1870s, and with Edwardian costumes. Worn with a petticoat with a padded hem (see Chapter 2, 'Underwear') it will make the correct shape to support a crinoline skirt.

Bags and baskets

Dolls' baskets in a variety of sizes and shapes are available from GP Ceramics and make charming accessories. They can be fixed to the doll's hand with a little Blu-Tack, and filled with artificial or dried flowers or miniature 'shopping'.

To make baskets, use natural or artificial raffia, plaited into long lengths knotted at both ends. Start at the centre of the base of the basket, coil the plaited raffia and oversew (with raffia) one coil to the next working outwards to the required size, then work upwards to make the sides of the basket. Oversew around the top edge to strengthen, then stitch a length of plaited raffia to each side to form the handle (Fig 56).

Life-size coin purses, found in department stores, can often be used as handbags for larger dolls, perhaps with a ribbon, cord or jewellery chain handle. Smaller dolls need bags specially made for them, as these purses are too large.

The pattern *DD* is for a flap-over shoulder-bag. It is given in two sizes and can be made in leather or fabric – lined or unlined. To make an unlined leather bag, use fairly thick leather (perhaps from an old purse or handbag). Fold the bag and topstitch all around the outside and the flap.

To make a lined bag, use soft leather (glove leather is ideal) or fabric, and a lightweight fabric lining. Cut both pieces from the pattern (the finished bag will be a little smaller than the pattern). With right sides facing, stitch the two pieces together around the outside, leaving the straight edge open. Trim, turn through and press. Slipstitch the straight edges together. Fold the bag in such a way that right sides are facing and oversew the side seams; turn through. Alternatively, the bag can have bound edges: stitch the two pieces together (sandwiching a layer of wadding if required) with *wrong* sides facing, all the way around the outside edge; fold the bag, and bind the outside edges – including the flap – with bias strip. The bag may be fastened with a loop and button or press-stud. Use ribbon, cord or leather strip for the strap, gauging the length over the doll's shoulder and stitching the ends inside the fold of the flap.

Fig 56 Plaited raffia basket and hat

Plate 15 – Accessories
At the top of the picture is a shirred hat made in yellow silk and a straw hat from Recollect trimmed with ribbon and artificial flowers. Below them are two poke bonnets, one in blue felt, one in crimson velvet, both trimmed with ribbons, flowers and feathers. To the right is a green velvet picture hat, lined and trimmed with eau-de-Nil silk crêpe, and below that fur-fabric hats and a fur-fabric muff. On the left of the picture is a straw hat made from plaited raffia and two flap-over bags, one in quilted cotton with bound edges, one in brown leather. In the centre of the picture are two crocheted shawls, a lace parasol and a walking stick. The tiny doll is from Sunday Dolls, the books and baskets from GP Ceramics.

The shoes are all made from patterns in the book and instructions are also given for the bags, handkerchiefs, baby's bib, jewellery and teddy bear. The striped belt is a watch strap, the miniature knitting is worked on cocktail sticks, and patterns are given for the knitted booties.

The same pattern may be used to make a handbag, by cutting off the flap. Cut one piece in fabric, one in lining. Stitch the side seams on both pieces and turn in and tack the top edges. Put the lining inside the bag and slipstitch the two pieces together at the top edge.

The two bags shown in colour on page 183 have fancy clasps made from square metal plaques taken from an old belt. The plaques have been bent diagonally across the middle and hammered flat over the top of the bag. The handles are lengths of jewellery chain stitched to either side.

Bags of this sort can be made in velvet, leather or small pieces of embroidered fabric and trimmed with silky lampshade fringe or tassels. The bag might contain a tiny coin purse, a miniature perfume bottle (made from glass beads?), a handkerchief, or a tiny notebook and pencil.

A larger bag, made in brown leather, would serve as a school satchel – a small one, made in a pretty fabric makes a delightful accessory for a lady doll.

Handkerchiefs

Dolls' handkerchiefs should be made in fine cotton lawn, white or coloured as you prefer. Cut a square, perfectly on the straight grain of the fabric. Make the smallest possible hem, and whip on lace trimming, mitring the corners. Add an embroidered flower or initials if you wish, and tuck the handkerchief into a pocket or sleeve.

Scarves and shawls

Patterns for knitted and crocheted scarves and shawls are given in Chapter 8. The baby's shawl patterns may also be used for lady dolls, in colours to suit the doll's costume.

Fabric scarves and shawls can be made in a variety of ways, as squares, rectangles or triangles of fabric with hemmed, sealed or fringed edges.

A simple cotton scarf can be made to match the dress, by cutting and hemming a triangle of fabric large enough to tie over the doll's head or around her shoulders. Woollen scarves can be rectangular, with the long edges sealed with Fray Check (or hemmed) and the short edges fringed. A shawl in woollen fabric might be a square, with all the sides fringed, or a triangle with the long edge sealed with Fray Check and the shorter edges fringed. To make the fringes, the fabric must be cut squarely on the straight grain; then the threads are pulled out, one at a time, from the edges. If necessary, a fine line of Fray Check will prevent further fraying. Fringed shawls may also be made by stitching lampshade fringe to the edges of a fabric piece – this method is particularly attractive for patterned or embroidered silk shawls. A self-fabric frill on a triangular scarf makes a fichu.

Consider also using life-size handkerchiefs as dolls' scarves and life-size scarves as dolls' shawls. A paisley-patterned headscarf looks very authentic as a doll's paisley shawl, and fine white mohair headscarves made beautiful baby dolls' shawls.

Bibs

The baby's bib pattern *BB* is given in two sizes, and might be made in any suitable fabric. Cut one bib in fabric and one in lining. With right sides facing, stitch the two pieces together around the outside (sandwiching a gathered lace or fabric frill if required), leaving the top edge open. Trim, turn through and press. Cut a length of matching ½in (1.2cm) wide bias binding long enough to bind the top edge and form ties, and press the binding folded in half. Stitch the edges of the binding together along the length, sandwiching the top edges of the bib in the centre. The bib might have whipped-on lace trimming or an embroidered or appliqué motif.

Parasols and walking sticks

The walking stick and parasol handle shown in the photographs are made from dowelling, with the handles whittled to shape with a craft knife. A simpler alternative would be to use fine dowelling, with a suitable large bead for the handle – glue the dowelling into the bead. Shape the tapered end of the stick with sandpaper. Alternatively, an artist's paintbrush handle can be used to make the stick for the parasol. Check that the stick is the correct length for the doll. The parasol cover could be made in fabric, perhaps to

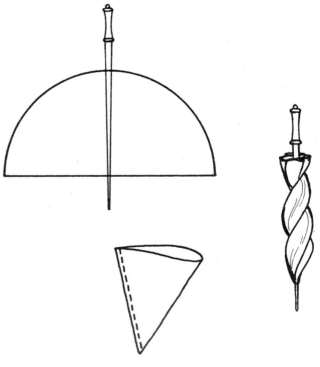

Fig 57 Making the parasol cover

match the dress, or in lace with a coloured silk lining. To make the cover, measure the length of the stick from below the handle to above the end, and cut a semi-circle of fabric and lining. With right sides facing, stitch the fabric to the lining – leaving a small gap on the straight edge to turn through. Turn through and press. Whip on the gathered lace, trimming around the curved edge. Fold the piece, and seam the straight edges to make a cone. Push the end of the stick through the point of the cone and secure with a little glue. Furl the cover around the stick and tie with ribbon (Fig 57).

Consider trimming the walking stick or parasol with a ribbon bow tied below the handle, or with small tassels or flowers. It may be fixed to the doll's hand with a little Blu-Tack, or tied to the wrist with narrow ribbon. Either accessory looks charming on a lady doll in walking costume, especially if she can be posed to 'hold' the stick.

Muff

The muff shown in the colour plates is made of fur fabric, but velvet would be equally suitable. It makes an attractive accessory for girl and lady dolls dressed in outdoor costumes especially when made to match a fur hat or a velvet coat.

To make the muff, cut a rectangle of both fabric and lining to the required size. Seam the short edges on both pieces to form tubes, and turn in the long edges. Put the lining inside the muff and slipstitch the edges together. Cut a length of cord or ribbon to fit the doll, and stitch the ends inside the muff. Trim if required with a ribbon bow or artificial flower. Check that the muff hangs below the doll's waist level, so that the hands can rest comfortably inside it.

Jewellery

Tiny pearl and coloured beads are available from several of the specialist suppliers (see 'Stockists') and may be strung to make dolls' necklaces and bracelets. If they are strung on fine silk ribbon (from Sunday Dolls) rather than thread, the ends may be left long, and tied at the back of the doll's neck, so that the necklace can be taken off.

Small cameo brooches, lockets, necklaces and earrings are available from GP Ceramics in a range of designs suitable for antique and modern dolls.

To make dolls' jewellery, beads, buttons and life-size jewellery provide the materials.

Life-size earrings make good brooches for dolls – either glued in place, or with the metal shank pushed through the dress fabric and secured on the inside. Some life-size earrings are small enough to use for dolls with pierced ears, or earrings may be made from small beads and fuse wire (see Fig 58). For dolls without pierced ears, glue small beads to their

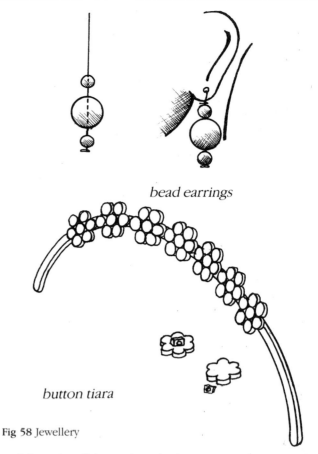

bead earrings

button tiara

Fig 58 Jewellery

earlobes. Small brooches, lockets or pendants can be used on larger dolls, perhaps with the chain shortened, and pretty buttons also make good brooches. Fine gilt or silver jewellery chain makes good necklaces for small dolls or bracelets for larger ones.

The tiara shown in colour on pages 183 and 187 is made from diamanté buttons, with the shanks cut off, and the backs sanded flat. The buttons are glued to the curved metal bone from an underwired bra which fits the shape of the doll's head perfectly. (Larger bra sizes will fit larger dolls' heads – smaller bras for smaller dolls.) Use the same method to make a tiara from an old diamanté necklace. Cut out the centre part of the necklace (usually the metal is soft enough to do this with scissors) and glue it to the metal underwire. As these 'bones' have flat sides, the buttons or stones are held firmly upright, and the ends of the bone are pushed into the doll's wig, so the tiara is held securely in place. An epoxy resin glue is recommended for this work, as it allows sufficient time before drying to place the buttons just where you want them.

As an alternative to 'jewels' try gluing artificial flowers to the underwire for a bride or bridesmaid's head-dress. Flower wreaths may also be made by covering a pipecleaner circlet with narrow ribbon and stitching or gluing artificial or dried flowers around it.

Ribbon chokers look attractive on lady dolls with low necklines, either soft silk ribbon, tied in a bow to one side or at the back, or velvet ribbon with a hook-and-eye fastening at the back. The velvet choker might have a flower to one side or a 'jewel' at the centre front.

Toys

Child dolls might have small toys of their own, perhaps a small car for a boy or a doll for a girl. These can often be found in toyshops or gift shops. Some of the specialist suppliers also sell miniature toys which make beautiful accessories for larger dolls. Shown in colour on pages 2 and 183 are miniature books from GP Ceramics from a range which includes sets of school books and a white bible which would be perfect for a bride doll. The exquisite miniature dolls are 4½in (11.5cm) tall jointed porcelain collectors' dolls each with her own 1in (2.5cm) jointed porcelain doll; they are available ·made-up and dressed from Sunday Dolls. The teddy bear shown in the plate on page 39 is the smallest in a range of real mohair teddies from Hugglets. (See 'Stockists'.)

Other toys can be made, for example a peg doll, or the fishing net (made from dowelling, wire and net) and small jar, or the miniature piece of knitting worked on cocktail sticks.

The little teddy in Fig 59 is made in felt or velveteen. Draw the pattern onto a double thickness of fabric and stitch around the outline leaving a small gap under one arm. Turn through, stuff, and close the gap. Mark the features with a black felt-tipped pen and tie a ribbon bow around the neck.

The doll may carry a posy of artificial flowers or a real lollipop. Most accessories can be secured with a little Blu-Tack or a safety pin – but do be careful with these small items on dolls for children.

Fig 59 Teddy bear

Plate 16
The 24in (61cm) reproduction AT11 from GP Ceramics in the centre of the picture wears a collarless jacket in black velvet, bound with black satin, with cut-back fronts to show mock waistcoat fronts stitched inside the jacket. The waistcoat fronts and cuffs are made in cream brocade bound with black satin, and fasten with hooks and eyes and mock buttons. The neckline and sleeve ends are trimmed with cream lace. The sleeveless, dropped-waist dress in cream brocade has a box-pleated skirt overlaid with old black lace. The costume is trimmed with small glass buttons, a black silk frog fastening, cream silk tassels and a crimson artificial flower. The picture hat is made in black velvet and trimmed with a black ribbon bow and cream feathers.

The 22in (56cm) reproduction Bru from Reflect Reproduction Dolls on the left wears a ball gown of cream lace over silk with a scooped neckline, puffed elbow-length sleeves, a gathered skirt and a looped lace overskirt. The bodice, with a V-shaped waistline, and the skirt are made separately. The neckline, sleeves and overskirt are trimmed with silk-ribbon roses and bows. Artificial flowers and silk-ribbon bows are worn in the hair.

The 22in (56cm) reproduction Bru from Creations Past on the right of the picture wears a black net, satin and sequined ball gown made from an old evening dress. The gown has a scooped neckline, elbow-length sleeves and a long flared skirt trimmed with narrow lace edging and ribbon bows on the shoulders. The matching detachable train hooks onto the gown at the back waistline. The doll wears a 'diamond' tiara made from buttons and a bra underwire, as well as black feathers in her hair and a black velvet-ribbon choker, and carries a black velvet handbag.

HOW TO PUT IT RIGHT!

Let us assume that you have followed the instructions, that you have cut the patterns and fitted the garments on the doll – but somewhere along the way something has gone wrong and it doesn't fit properly. This does happen from time to time – even to Dior I expect! The golden rule is *don't panic*! Very often it can be saved. Have a cup of coffee, calm down, even leave it till tomorrow – then read on . . .

The neckline is too big

Try moving the top back-fastening over a little, *or* whip a narrow gathered-lace trimming around the neckline, *or* make a collar and sew it in (see Chapter 4, 'Collars'), *or* run a line of small gathering stitches around the inside of the neckline and pull up slightly, *or* make a bias-cut band collar and whip it to the neckline on the inside, *or* make an applied yoke with band collar (see Chapter 3, 'Making Dresses').

The neckline is too small

This calls for drastic measures – be brave! Cut off the neckline and bind or face the raw edge with bias strip. If the dress has a collar, salvage the collar and stitch it into the new neckline. (Try moving the top back-fastening first!)

The bodice is too big

Try putting a liberty bodice (see Chapter 2, 'Underwear') or a knitted vest on the doll to fatten her up a bit, *or* try a piece of Terylene wadding, cut to shape, under the bodice (make a wadding 'vest' if necessary), *or* try moving the fastenings over (a front opening might become double breasted, an edge-to-edge fastening might become an overlap fastening), *or* take in the side seams, *or* make darts in the front and back bodice.

The bodice is too small

Try moving the fastenings – an overlap fastening can become edge-to-edge, fastened with hooks and eyes or loops and buttons. If still not enough, bind the edges with matching fabric (light- or medium-weight fabrics only), press flat and make new fastenings, *or* stitch a placket of matching fabric inside one edge and fasten the other edge to the placket with hooks and eyes. (Extend the placket through the waistline into the skirt.)

Armholes are too big (sleeveless bodice)

For petticoats, whip on lace edging. For dresses, bind with matching fabric or consider setting in sleeves.

Armholes are too small (sleeveless bodice)

Cut off the armhole and bind or face the raw edge with bias strip.

Armholes are too small (bodice with sleeves)

No simple solution. Carefully cut out the sleeve around the armhole on the bodice. Take the top edge of the sleeve apart and put in new gathering threads. Set the sleeve into the new armhole and neaten.

Sleeves are too tight (short sleeve)

No simple solution. Carefully cut the sleeve out of the armhole. Discard the old sleeves; make up new sleeves and set them into the new armholes.

Sleeves are too tight (long sleeve)

If only the bottom part is too tight, cut it off and hem the raw edge to make short sleeves, *or* proceed as for when short sleeves are too tight.

Skirt is too short (gathered skirt or flared skirt)

Let down the hem, and face the raw edge with matching fabric or bias binding to make a new hem, *or* consider adding a frill (see Chapter 3, 'Making Dresses') in matching fabric, *or* stitch slightly gathered lace – longer than the hem – inside the hem to look like a petticoat frill. If you have this problem on a tucked skirt or petticoat, let out one or two tucks, and press to remove the fold and stitching lines.

Skirt is too long (gathered skirt or flared skirt)

Let down the hem. Cut off the amount required and make a new hem.

Skirt is too short (pleated skirt)

If the skirt has a hem, let it down and face the raw edge with wide bias binding or lightweight fabric (the best match possible) to make a new hem; re-press the pleats. *Or* try the 'petticoat frill' as above.

If the skirt is made with a folded edge, try the 'petticoat frill' as above, *or* (drastic measure) cut through the underside layer of fabric and make a hem on the outer layer. Neaten the raw edge on the under layer and re-press the pleats.

Skirt is too long (pleated skirt)

If the skirt has a folded edge, hem the folded edge to the inside and re-press the pleats. If the skirt has a hem, let it down, cut off the surplus and make a new hem. Re-press the pleats.

Jacket fronts are too small

Leave it open, *or* fasten with a frog fastening or loops and buttons, *or* make up false waistcoat fronts and stitch inside the jacket fronts – fasten the waistcoat fronts.

Jacket fronts are too big

Move the fastenings – edge-to-edge can be made to overlap, overlap can become double breasted.

Coat fronts – as for jacket fronts.

Drawers/petticoat are too long

Make tucks – two or three small ones, or one large one, will reduce the length by 1–2in (2.5–5cm).

If all else fails – take it off and put it away, it will fit another doll one day!

SEWING TIPS

✂ To make threading the needle easier, cut the end of the thread at an angle.

✂ Thread the needle as the thread comes from the reel, knot the end you cut off. This helps prevent the thread snarling.

✂ To make an almost invisible hem, use threads pulled from the fabric to sew with. This works especially well on silk fabrics.

✂ Prevent seams on tiny garments from fraying by painting glue along them with a small paint brush. (Fray check is the modern alternative).

✂ Paint glue (or Fray check) on the cut edges of buttonholes before they are stitched to prevent fraying and make the sewing easier.

✂ If cotton fabrics are limp, starch them (spray starch is useful) before cutting out the garment. A light spray starch will make crisp hems and pintucks on cotton fabrics.

✂ Always press fabrics before cutting the garment. Always check that the pattern is squarely on the grain of the fabric.

✂ Press seams as you sew them. A sleeve board makes a very useful miniature ironing board.

✂ Always use two threads to make gathering. Stitch between them and pull out the lower thread.

✂ Make gathers small, neat and even by stroking them gently with a pin or needle. 'Set' them by pulling firmly at the lower edge of the piece – holding the gathered edge in the other hand.

✂ Pin up the hem of a garment on the doll to judge the most attractive length and to ensure that the hem hangs straight.

✂ Use blanket stitch on the wrong side to join the cut ends of lace or ribbon. This makes a strong, neat seam and prevents fraying.

✂ When making fabric sashes, cut the fabric on the bias grain. The sash will fold and drape better.

✂ Many knitting patterns for babies can be used to make doll's clothes by using finer yarn and smaller needles.

✂ Renew your sewing machine needle often. They get blunt and cause the thread to ravel. Always use a new (fine) needle for sewing with silk fabrics.

✂ When using hooks and loops to fasten an edge-to-edge back closure, alternate hooks and loops down each side to make a more secure fastening.

✂ Always measure button placements with a ruler so that buttons are evenly spaced.

✂ Elastic bands will make simple 'garters' to hold up a doll's stockings.

✂ To personalise your doll's clothes, sew in your own label. Cash's name tapes are the right size and inexpensive – they can be ordered from the childrens' clothes department in most stores.

✂ Many dry cleaners will clean doll's clothes for free – they seem to find it amusing!

LIST OF STOCKISTS

All the stockists listed here provide a mail order service. They all make a charge for their catalogues, so please contact by telephone or write enclosing a sae for catalogue prices.

Sunday Dolls 7 Park Drive, London SW14 8RB (01-876 5634) A very wide range of dolls' haberdashery including fine laces, silk ribbons, buckles and beads. Tools for making ribbon bows, rosettes and roses, glue guns and pleaters. Also exquisite miniature porcelain dolls and doll kits.

Recollect Studio The Old School, London Road, Sayers Common, W Sussex BN6 9HX (0273 833314) A wide range of reproduction porcelain dolls with composition bodies or as kits. Also straw hats, shoes, boots and doll stands.

Hello Dolly Honeysuckle Studios, Paul, Penzance, Cornwall TR19 6UA (0736 68002) Budget and medium-priced porcelain doll kits. Also a good range of socks, stockings, tights, straw hats and shoes. Small-scale trimmings, buttons and flowers.

Ridings Craft 749 Bradford Road, Batley, W Yorkshire WF17 8HZ (0924 440702) Budget-priced porcelain doll kits. Also a good range of trimmings, fabrics, flowers, feathers, beads and buttons. Dolls' straw hats, tubular stocking material and doll stands.

Reflect Reproduction Dolls 334 Chester Road, Boldmere, Sutton Coldfield, W Midlands B73 5BY (021-350 2092) A wide range of reproduction porcelain dolls as kits.

GP Ceramics Unit 6, Albert Road Industrial Estate, Luton, Bedfordshire LU1 3QF (0582 411001) A wide range of reproduction porcelain dolls and kits. Also laces and trimmings, fine straw hats and bonnets, dolls' jewellery and accessories.

Creations Past The Dolls House, Stone Hall Common, nr Worcester WR5 3QQ (0905 820792) Fine-quality reproduction porcelain dolls and kits.

Village Fabrics 30 Goldsmiths Lane, Wallingford, Oxfordshire OX10 0DN (0491 36178) Superb range of cotton fabrics in tiny prints and plain colours. Sample pack containing swatches of all fabrics available.

Pittards Sherborne Road, Yeovil, Somerset (0935 74321) Bags of leather pieces in assorted colours.

Mrs E. Harvey – Dolls' Milliner Please phone (01-904 6001) Fine-quality dolls' hats in straw and silk.

Kloth Kinder 14 Poplar Avenue, Runcorn, Cheshire, WA7 5HT (09285 64538) Cloth dolls with moulded heads and stockinette bodies available as kits.

Hugglets The Old School, London Road, Sayers Common, W Sussex BN6 9HX (0273 697974) Fine-quality traditional jointed mohair teddy bears with leather pads in a range of sizes.

Ray Cornford St Lawrence, Camel Street, Marston Magna, Yeovil, Somerset (0935 850 646) Dolls' spectacles made to order.

Sasha Dolls Sadly, the company that made Sasha Dolls has ceased trading, but stocks are still available from ABCeta Playthings Ltd, 45 St Petersgate, Stockport, Cheshire SK1 1DH (061-480 4480).

BIBLIOGRAPHY

Arnold, Janet. *Patterns of Fashion 1660–1860* and *1860–1940* (Wace, 1966)

Coleman, Dorothy etc. *The Collectors Book of Dolls' Clothes* (Robert Hale, 1978)

Dodge, Venus A. *Making Old Fashioned Dolls* (David & Charles, 1985)

Ewing, Elizabeth. *History of Children's Costume* (Batsford, 1977)

Victoria and Albert Museum. *Four Hundred Years Of Fashion* (V&A and Collins, 1984)

Tozer, Jane and Levitt, Sarah. *Fabric of Society* (Laura Ashley, 1983)

Willet, C. and Cunnington, Phyllis. *The History of Underclothes* (Faber, 1981)

Yarwood, Doreen. *English Costume from the 2nd Century BC to the Present Day* (Batsford, 1979)